UPRISING

*The manuscript of this book was the
recipient of the 2018 Writers' Award from
Copyright Licensing New Zealand*

*The author and publisher acknowledge
the support of the Federated Mountain Clubs'
Mountain and Forest Trust in the
production of this book*

Nic Low is a writer of Ngāi Tahu and European descent who divides his time between Melbourne and Christchurch. His writing on wilderness, technology and race has been widely published and anthologised on both sides of the Tasman. His first book was *Arms Race*, a collection of speculative fictions shortlisted for the Readings and Steele Rudd prizes, and named a New Zealand *Listener* and *Australian Book Review* book of the year. He is co-director of the WORD Christchurch festival.

dislocated.org

UPRISING

NIC LOW

Walking
the
Southern
Alps
of
New
Zealand

TEXT PUBLISHING MELBOURNE AUSTRALIA

textpublishing.com.au

The Text Publishing Company
Swann House, 22 William Street, Melbourne Victoria 3000, Australia

Published by The Text Publishing Company, 2021

Cover design by Chong W.H.
Cover title type by Morgan Mathews-Hale, Kaitiaki Studios
Cover photo by Nic Low
Author photo by Jon Terry
Page design by Jessica Horrocks
Typeset by J&M Typesetting
Route maps by Simon Barnard
Colour map by Isobel Joy Te Aho-White
Plate photos by Nic Low

Printed and bound in Australia by Griffin Press, part of Ovato, an accredited ISO/NZS 14001:2004 Environmental Management System printer.

ISBN: 9781925355284 (paperback)
ISBN: 9781922253873 (ebook)

A catalogue record for this book is available from the National Library of Australia.

For Ahi

Contents

5. Nōti Hinetamatea (Copland Pass)

6. Sealy Pass

7. Tioripātea (Haast Pass)

8. Aoraki

9. Te Rua–o–te–moko Ki Murihiku (Fiordland to Southland)

Uprising

Note to the international reader

Throughout this book, I refer to my iwi (tribe), Ngāi Tahu, as 'we' or 'us'. I don't speak for the tribe; this is just the Māori way of doing things. At times I also refer to my Pākehā (European New Zealander) ancestors as 'we' or 'us'. I'm not Pākehā, but Pākehā society formed me too—it's common for anyone who's Māori to hold overlapping identities, and walk in both worlds.

That said, it's also the Māori way to claim that your ancestors were the best-looking and most intelligent, and liked to jump over mountains or travel on the backs of whales. Our histories are multiple and parochial. There are sources listed in the endnotes, but there's no hard line between history and myth. And if this book seems biased towards Ngāi Tahu, that's because it is—but only because we're so good-looking and smart, and our ancestors...

I've used Māori place names wherever possible, with a preference for spellings recorded in *Kā Huru Manu*, the Ngāi Tahu atlas. More than geographical markers, these names carry our history and mana whenua (authority over the land), and our identity: when we stand to speak, our most basic form of introduction is

✶ relating to parish/church

to name our ancestral mountains, rivers, lakes and coasts. Māori names are initially followed by the English ones in brackets.

I've also used Māori for key concepts not easily explained in English, or where a Māori word is in common usage in New Zealand English, initially with a summary translation. You'll find a glossary of sorts at the back.

Aside from the tribe's official name, Ngāi Tahu, I've also preferred our southern Kāi Tahu dialect, which replaces the 'Ng' with 'K'. A macron over a vowel makes the sound longer. Here's a pronunciation guide:

Vowels
A as in car
E as in egg
I as in see
O as in or
U as in loo

Select consonants
Ng as in sing
Wh as in far out
R like the Spanish 'r', lightly rolled so as to be close to a 'd'

Examples (start slow, then speed up)
Ngāi Tahu: **Nigh Taa**-hoo
Whakapapa: **far**-car-pa-pa
Karakia: ca-rah-**key**-ah
Tapu: **tup**-poo
Te-Mawheranui-o-kā-kūhā-o-Tū-te-raki-whānoa: just kidding.

To the Mountains

How then are we Ngāi Tahu going to walk through
this ancient landscape in the new century—this
landscape scarred by memory? How will the
coming generations of our tribe see this land and
this coast? Will they sing to it? Will they sing the
old songs or will they sing their own?

—Tā Tipene O'Regan, 1999

There were mountains outside my window: a range of peaks lifting
cold and fierce into the blue. Looking up from my desk, I felt the
rush of joy that mountain lovers feel in the presence of the real
thing. I felt at home. There was Aoraki, the highest in Aotearoa
New Zealand, cloaked in snow. There were his brothers, with
their stone faces tattooed by glacial ice. But I was in Australia,
where the hills are stumps like old men's teeth. I looked again. The
peaks grew before my eyes, boiling up into the sky, and I had to
laugh. For a moment, I'd erased the dusty plains of south-eastern

Australia and turned a bank of storm clouds into Kā Tiritiri-o-te-moana, New Zealand's Southern Alps.

From the outset, Kā Tiritiri-o-te-moana have been seen as a mirage. When the explorer Māui first sighted a distant white gleam on the horizon, he thought they were clouds. As his waka (canoe), Mahaanui, approached, the clouds resolved into icy summits. He named them Kā Tiritiri-o-te-moana after his mistake. I'd make his mistake in reverse. *conversations w/ ancestors*

Through the open window the peaks disintegrated, and I felt the first gust of an approaching storm wind. I'd spent a decade away from home, and that wind was home calling. They say it happens to everyone who's Māori, sooner or later.

I was born on a narrow, mountainous island to a Ngāi Tahu mother and a Pākehā father. The jagged line of the Southern Alps marked the horizon of my childhood in Christchurch, on the east-coast plains of the South Island. We often spent school holidays in the mountains. I was nine when Dad took my two brothers and me on our first overnight tramp, in the Arthur's Pass National Park.

When we reached the Anti Crow Hut, looking across the Waimakariri River valley to the gleaming glacier spilling from the southern flank of Kaimatau (Mt Rolleston), we heard for the first time how our great-uncles Geoff Harrow and Deryck Morse had arrived at that same hut late one night to find it packed with young trampers. Every bunk was occupied. No one offered to make room.

The two men, both in their seventies, sat down to prepare dinner. While they waited for their billy to boil, they fell to reminiscing.

'You remember carrying the cement up here, Horse?' Geoff

said, maybe a little louder than necessary.

'I do. It was damned heavy. Worth it, though. Look how well the place has held up.'

The others in the room fell quiet. Deryck hid his smile. Without a word, two of the youngsters moved their stuff onto the floor.

•

On my Pākehā side our family is full of mountain people. Our European heritage is primarily English, Irish and Scottish, but it's in the Southern Alps we feel most at home. In 1902 a party of twenty Lows travelled in horse-drawn wagons from their South Canterbury farms to visit Aoraki (Mt Cook), an eighteen-day round trip. Family legend says at that time they were the biggest party ever to visit, and people mistook them for a travelling circus. A generation on, my great-uncles were both presidents of the Canterbury Mountaineering Club in their day. Geoff made the first ascent of the Nepalese giant Baruntse on an expedition led by Sir Edmund Hillary, and once led a club trip that put eighteen people on Aoraki's summit in one day. Their generation handed down respect for the mountains to my dad and his generation, who in turn gifted it to ours.

Walking has taught me to treasure time spent among forces older and slower than anything I can download from the internet. I love the South Island's river valleys and ranges backed by glaciated peaks. I love the names like spells: Ōtehake and Waitāwhiri, D'Archiac and Crow. I love the stillness of river flats at dusk, and the steady *chink chink* of crampons and axes at dawn. Most of all, I've learned that a good trip is one where you don't meet anyone else.

Years ago, high in the Nelson Lakes National Park, my brother

Tim and I came across a wiry man standing motionless beside Blue Lake. He was gazing into the indigo waters with such intensity that we crept past without a word. When we came back six hours later he was still there, watching the surface as if some mythical beast was about to burst from the lake. This time we stopped to chat, and it turned out to be the renowned landscape photographer Craig Potton. He told us that he'd been coming to photograph Blue Lake every year for thirty years. With a rueful smile he said the best shot he'd ever taken was the first.

I remembered that famous photo. It contained no people. Few of New Zealand's iconic landscape images do. We all grew up surrounded by books and calendars and billboards depicting virgin forests and untouched peaks. We followed the ethos of no-trace camping, passing through the mountains like ghosts. We longed for postcard views so pristine they could be from before, or maybe after, civilisation itself. What we craved was a landscape without history, untrodden by humans.

There's a name for that: *terra nullius*. The legal fiction of unoccupied, unclaimed land. A name that hides what's underneath.

•

On my mother's side we are Ngāi Tahu, Kāti Māmoe and Waitaha, the indigenous peoples of the vast majority of Te Waipounamu (the South Island). Known collectively today as Ngāi Tahu, our tribal territory covers more than half of New Zealand's land mass, and every southern National Park. We understand the landscape through whakapapa: complex genealogies that connect us to each other, and to the land, and to the atua (Māori gods). Whakapapa begins here on earth with our oldest terrestrial ancestor, Aoraki, son of the Sky Father, Raki. Aoraki came down from the heavens with his brothers to meet Raki's new wife, the Earth Mother, Papa-tūānuku. After a long voyage across endless ocean, they gave up their search and prepared to return home. Aoraki made a mistake in the ritual karakia (incantation) needed to lift the canoe back to the heavens, and the vessel was wrecked. The brothers climbed onto the overturned hull and waited for rescue. Their hair grew white, and in the blast of southerly storms they froze, and turned to stone. The South Island is Aoraki's canoe, and he and his brothers are the Southern Alps.

In the old days people didn't discover places. They created, became, are, the land.

According to our oral traditions, around eight centuries ago the first of our human ancestors came to Te Waipounamu. The Waitaha people made landfall at Whakatū, at the top of the island, in the waka Uruao. Their leader and captain, Rākaihautū, took half the crew and marched down the eastern side of the Alps, giving names to rivers, valleys and peaks that are still in use today. With his kō (staff used for digging), Tūwhakaroria, Rakaihautū carved out the inland glacier lakes. Some say he used his kō as a walking stick, and discovered rather than dug the lakes, but who's going to keep such a pedestrian story alive for close on a thousand years?

These Waitaha ancestors were Eastern Polynesian seafarers when they arrived, but their mountainous new home made them Māori. They hunted the abundant birdlife, built networks of vil-lages and camps and quarries, and transplanted Pacific traditions into this new landscape. Next came the tribal groupings of Kāti Māmoe and then Ngāi Tahu, who migrated internally from the North Island over the next few hundred years. The modern iwi known as Ngāi Tahu formed in the way the braided east-coast rivers form, with many tributaries blending and taking on a common name. Through intermarriage, warfare and alliance in the face of external threats, we became one, unified by descent from the ancestor Tahupōtiki.

Ngāi Tahu were among the first and most intensively colonised tribes, with European and American sealers and whalers in our territory from the late eighteenth century. Most New Zealanders have some knowledge of the North Island's Land Wars, which saw tribes dispossessed at gunpoint. Few know how Ngāi Tahu lost half of New Zealand's landmass, including all of the inland high country and Alps, without a shot being fired. Most of our chiefs welcomed settlement, and sold land on the condition that a tenth of the area would be reserved for the tribe's use, and that the Crown would build hospitals and schools. The land passed into European ownership, but the millions of acres that should have been reserved never materialised. The hospitals and schools were never built. The solemn contracts of sale were ignored. Over time, travel into the high country and mountains became trespass. Without an economic base for the tribe, poverty, and loss of language and culture, became widespread.

After seven generations of tribal activism, the Crown finally acknowledged serious wrongs. Ngāi Tahu reached a settlement in 1997. Redress included land, the renaming of key places, the return of pounamu (greenstone, a prized type of jade), some share in environmental management, a formal apology from the New Zealand prime minister representing the Crown, and NZ$170 million in cash. Our highest peak was renamed Aoraki / Mt Cook. Though meagre compared to what was owed, this redress, along with legal recognition of Ngāi Tahu as a people, allowed the tribe to rebuild.

Ngāi Tahu now has assets worth NZ$1.5 billion. Income is spent on language, cultural, business and wellbeing programmes that were inconceivable a generation ago.

Today the tribe has 68,000 registered members. But when Mum was growing up, people hid their Māori heritage. With her olive skin and long, dark, wavy hair, she was constantly asked about her ancestry. Whenever she asked her father, Percy, he would shout at her: 'You're Tahitian!' or 'American Indian, of course!' or 'Spanish!' Sometimes he'd dismiss the question with an angry wave of his hand. As a child he'd been sent away to be raised by his Pākehā grandparents, who wouldn't have anything or anyone Māori in the house. Percy's mother, Emerald-Anne, a flamboyant, hard-drinking jazz singer who spoke fluent Māori, was barred from visiting. Percy went to the same school as his siblings, but was actively discouraged from playing with them because they were being 'raised Māori'. So he grew up estranged. He has spent decades of his life in the United States, and is an ardent lover of American architecture and jazz; he has never openly acknowledged being Māori. Mum once showed him a photo of a group of Māori women posed on the wide porch and steps of a smart villa.

'Do you know who these people are?' she asked.

'Wouldn't have a clue. Looks like a bunch of horis to me,' he replied.

The horis—a racist slur—were his grandmother and his great-aunts.

But at the dinner table, he was forever railing against the injustices Ngāi Tahu suffered over land sales. He could eat three dozen oysters without pause. Cheques arrived, payments for logging on family Māori land, which he handed to my grandmother Noeline without comment. He simply accepted, again without comment, that his mother was a matakite (able to foresee events). And when Mum turned twenty-one, he gave her a very old hand-carved taoka pounamu (greenstone pendant), and a huge framed portrait of a striking Māori woman in a woven cloak. She holds a mere pounamu, the carved greenstone blade that was the weapon of chiefs, and stares the viewer down. She looks untouchable, and faintly amused.

'Who *is* she?' Mum had asked.

'Wouldn't have a clue,' Percy said—his usual response when asked about anything Māori—and turned and left the room.

Though we never knew who she was, throughout my childhood she watched over us from the top of the stairs.

Then, when Mum was working as a teacher, Percy summoned her to a small meeting of Ngāi Tahu people convened by Ngāi Tahu MP Whetu Tirikatene-Sullivan. She talked about the desperate need for Ngāi Tahu people to study law, given the loss of land.

'That's what you should do,' Percy directed. Mum changed careers—she had no choice—but she loved it from her first lecture.

Years later, my parents woke in the night to loud crashing. They thought someone was breaking in. They threw open the bedroom door, shouting: 'Who's there?'

They found the portrait of the Māori woman propped against the wall on the ground floor, upright, staring out at them with her tattooed face and mysterious smile. The hanging cord on the heavy wooden frame had snapped, and she'd tumbled end-over-end down two flights of stairs, only to come to rest with the glass intact.

A local kaumātua (elder), Katarina Daniels, didn't bat an eyelid. 'Of course she didn't want to be stuck up there!' she said.

'She wants to be part of the family.'

Mum took it as a tohu, a sign. She started putting out feelers to the tribe, asking questions, finding kin. Doors opened fast, until the Ngāi Tahu world became one of the focal points of our lives.

So my brothers and I were raised as middle-class Pākehā (music lessons, Lego, protesting against nuclear armageddon), but also as Māori, in an urban, political sense. Mum's clients were all Māori. She made trips to the United Nations in Geneva as part of the Māori delegation working on the Declaration on the Rights of Indigenous Peoples. Talk of colonisation and the Treaty of Waitangi was standard dinner-table fare. We got dragged around various marae (the ceremonial courtyard and complex of build- ings, including the meeting house, where tribal business takes place), and learned conversational Māori at high school. My first real job, at eighteen, was as a designer with the Ngāi Tahu Devel- opment Corporation, making history and language resources. And before bailing out of law school to pursue literature, I cut my teeth arguing land rights with Pākehā farmers' kids.

But I knew little about the deeper history of Ngāi Tahu, or how our ancestors really saw the land. I wasn't the only one. Most Ngāi Tahu are now urban, and more than half live outside our tribal boundaries. Our elders won protections, built an enduring eco- nomic base, and were investing in people, culture and language. But, as Tā Tipene O'Regan, senior leader, academic, company director and the tribe's chief negotiator with the Crown, observed:

> It will all be residue with no meaning, laws without sub- stance, hollow things, husks of an older generation's history—if we have failed to ensure [our people] have

the capacity to walk the coast and the mountains of our
island...and to know, and care, that that is the womb
from which we spring as a people, that this is the source
of who and what we are.

I'd never associated Māori with the mountains. We were a coastal
people, as far as I knew. I'd only heard stories of mountain exploration from Dad's side. But when I saw the Southern Alps through
my window in Australia, I thought: there have to be other stories.

•

The thought stayed with me for years, until finally it was time to
board a plane home, maybe for a few years, maybe for good. I'd
quit my job to write, ended a long-term relationship, and wanted
to spend time with my parents while they were alive and well.
I sent out a barrage of emails arranging interviews and walks.
I packed my tramping gear, mountaineering boots, and axes
and rope. Then, at the last minute, I threw in a printout of my
great-great-grandfather's memoirs, which I'd been putting off
reading for years.

In seven handwritten notebooks, Captain John Hunter
detailed his life growing up as a white gentleman among the dusky
southern Ngāi Tahu.

'You have to read it,' Mum had told me on the phone almost a
decade earlier. Fascination and dismay mingled in her voice. 'He
rides round on a thoroughbred horse meeting the natives, and his
father owns a sailing ship and the finest estate in the country.'

'And?'

'I think it's fiction. Read it. You'll see why.'

She emailed a copy but I never opened it, knowing that once I read my ancestor's memoir I'd be obsessed. Heading home meant I would finally make the time. But most of all, I was hungry to find traces of Māori history in the Alps.

In Christchurch, I paid a visit to Takerei Norton, the head of Ngāi Tahu's archives department. A well-built, quietly confident man in his early forties, Takerei welcomed me into Ngāi Tahu's gleaming headquarters with a hand clasp and hongi. At his desk, he pulled up a satellite image of the South Island on his screen. From the long white feather of the Southern Alps to the sweep of the east and west coasts, the image was deeply familiar. But not a single place name was in English. I sat forward in my chair. Incredible: here was southern New Zealand before Europeans came. The land shimmered with names like stars.

Built over decades from oral histories, maps, books and manuscripts, the Cultural Mapping Project has over six thousand original names so far. What it shows is the opposite of wilderness. From major peaks to minor streams the landscape was named, known, owned. More than a map of place, it's a map of history. In an oral society the land is the book, and the place names are the writing. Reading is moving through the landscape, recalling the stories as you go.

'For Māori, and Kāi Tahu in particular...the names are more than just signposts in the landscape,' says Tā Tipene. '[They] carry heritage and history; they're what people call mnemonics; the name triggers a whole lot of associated memory.'

Takerei clicked on a box, and thousands more points filled the map: archaeological sites showing early Māori occupation, ancient designs drawn on limestone caves, fragments of double-hulled ocean-going canoes, a woven backpack stashed in a cleft of rock four or five hundred years ago. I stared at the spot on the map where the backpack was found, at Flock Hill in the Waimakariri Basin. I'd been there. I'd been to dozens of these places without realising the stories they could tell. The inland plains and high country held many hundreds of camping spots, food harvesting sites and permanent settlements. Every place name was a key to unlocking history. More than a dozen trails led through the Southern Alps.

I thought: if we navigated today's mountains using this ancient memory-map, where would we end up? If I talked to the right people and read the right books, could I wander back into the past? How hard could it be?

After we'd finished looking at the maps, Takerei took me to meet Trevor Howse, one of the key kaumātua and researchers behind the project. I was so excited that I talked at him for half an hour—trails! walks! a book!—like a namunamu (sandfly) buzzing around the head of a chief. Trevor is a former truck driver not known for suffering fools. He sat and listened with a faint smile, and answered my questions with questions of his own. When I finally shut up, he said, not unkindly: 'You know, our tīpuna [ancestors] worked on this for generations. I've been working on it for forty years. And no one does it because they get thanks or recognition.'

He looked at me directly for the first time. 'They do it because it's the right thing to do. So, you've got to be committed, and you've got to be serious.'

I bit my lip and nodded. *If you're still interested in a few years*, he was saying, *come back. Then we'll talk.*

•

Over the next five years I dived into the archives, read the work of *storytelling*

Ngāi Tahu historians, spoke with elders and leaders, and devoured every scrap of knowledge about the mountains I could find. I attended the tribe's wānaka pūrākau (traditional history workshops), sitting with a small group of historians, educators, storytellers and whakapapa experts to dive deep into the past. I also ran up hard against my limitations with the Māori language, and pursued some knowledgeable people who never returned my calls. Doors remained closed—as they should. Like all iwi, we're ultimately a collection of hapū (sub-tribes) and whānau (families), and many keep their stories to be told by their own. Others shared things that I'd never record—burial-cave locations, for example. But what I could share, I loaded into my pack and took for a long walk.

This book is about walking as a form of knowing. Armed with Takerei's maps, I crossed the Main Divide of the Southern Alps more than a dozen times, trying to understand how our forebears saw that land. What did it mean to define your identity by sacred mountains, or actually to see them as our ancestors, turned to stone? Whether traversing foothills or climbing ice, my travelling companions and I looked for traces of the greenstone trails, the wars with the rival tribe Ngāti Toa, the creation stories, the loss of land and the fight to get it back. When you search for the past, you inevitably find the present as well. I met some of the people leading Ngāi Tahu's reconnection to high and wild places along the way.

Nō reira, nau mai, haere mai ki kā ara tipuna o Kā Tiritiri-o-te-moana: come with me on a journey on the old trails across the Southern Alps. I'm a student rather than a teacher, and what's in here barely scratches the surface of Ngāi Tahu knowledge. But it does, I hope, show that rather than wilderness, the mountains are full of history—everywhere you look.

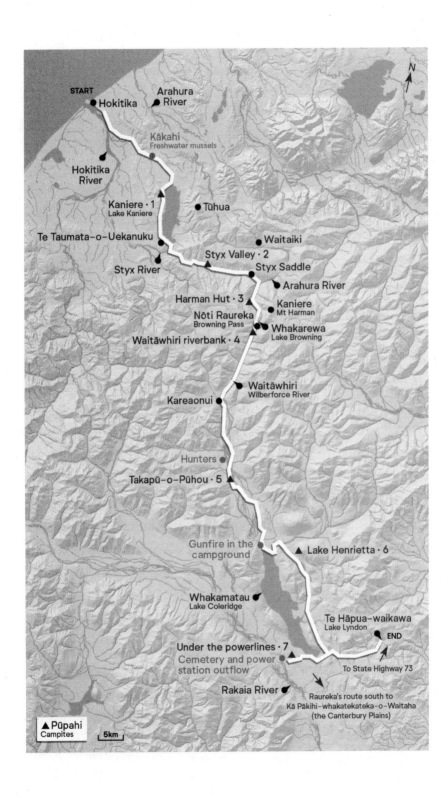

START
Hokitika

Arahura
River

Kākahi
Freshwater mussels

Hokitika
River

Kaniere · 1
Lake Kaniere

Tūhua

Te Taumata-o-Uekanuku

Waitaiki

Styx Valley · 2

Styx River

Styx Saddle

Arahura River

Harman Hut · 3

Kaniere
Mt Harman

Nōti Raureka
Browning Pass

Whakarewa
Lake Browning

Waitāwhiri riverbank · 4

Waitāwhiri
Wilberforce River

Kareaonui

Hunters

Takapū-o-Pūhou · 5

Gunfire in the
campground

Lake Henrietta · 6

Whakamatau
Lake Coleridge

Te Hāpua-waikawa
Lake Lyndon

END

Under the powerlines · 7
Cemetery and power
station outflow

To State Highway 73

Rakaia River

Raureka's route south to
Kā Pākihi-whakatekateka-o-Waitaha
(the Canterbury Plains)

▲ Pūpahi
Campsites

5km

N

1

Nōti Raureka

On a beach close to the main street of the small town of Hokitika, I wove through a crowd of tourists and down to the water's edge. At my back, the Alps walled in the coast with five hundred kilometres of sharks' teeth. To my left, the Hokitika River's glittering silver mouth opened onto Te Tai-o-Rehua, the Tasman Sea. Small children darted around me like fish. Their laughter turned to static each time a breaker boomed ashore. In my hand I held two small pipi shells chalky with age. I'd picked them up next to an old village site on the opposite coast, near where I grew up: a little something from Te Moananui-a-Kiwa, the Pacific Ocean. Perhaps the remnant of some old feast.

The only Māori blessings I knew by heart were translations of Christian prayers. Plenty of families still know older rituals for starting journeys, but in mine, you had to go back to my great-great-grandparents to find that lore. But it seemed important to mark the start of this journey, even in a half-arsed, improvised way. I wanted to acknowledge Takaroa, atua (god) of the sea. On an island, all journeys ultimately begin and end at the coast.

I crouched and placed the shells on the dark sand, then retreated up the beach. I didn't dare take my eyes off the monster surf. The koha (offering) lay glinting in the sun; then a wave roared in and sucked back out, taking the shells on its tongue.

I smiled. A lot of Māori stories are about the disastrous consequences of improvising rituals, or impersonating priests, or getting your karakia wrong. Oh well. I hefted my pack onto my back, and started up the beach towards the distant blue peaks.

Since the early nineteenth century, this rugged coastline has been the domain of Kāti Waewae, a hapū (sub-tribe) of Ngāi Tahu. The story of how they came to possess this prized territory starts with a woman named Raureka, who set off into the mountains from near here, in around 1700.

In those days there were separate peoples on either side of the Alps. My Ngāi Tahu ancestors were settling the east. Kāti Wairaki had lived in the west for a long time, and it was said that they held deep knowledge of the land. (Soon after Ngāi Tahu arrived, we sent delegations over to learn from their priests, but trouble started when our men were more interested in flirting with Kāti Wairaki women than learning esoteric lore.) The two tribes were distantly related, but the mountains formed a barrier between our domains.

The story goes that Raureka was a rakatira (chief; of high rank) from Kāti Wairaki who left her home on the coast and headed into the mountains. From the Main Divide of the Alps, ridges extend like fingers towards the coast at Hokitika, with thickly timbered valleys and swampland in between. Lake Kaniere lies in one of these valleys. On reaching the head of the lake, Raureka walked up the Styx River, crossed over into the Arahura River and continued south until she stumbled across a pass to the east. The lake at the top is called Whakarewa (Europeans called it Browning), and the pass in Māori is Nōti Raureka. Legend has it that she was the first person to cross the Alps.

Raureka emerged from the mountains starving and at her wits' end. According to kaumātua James Russell from Arahura, she wandered down the Rakaia River to the area around Te Umukaha (Temuka) on the plains, where she encountered a group of Ngāi Tahu men hewing a canoe. They took her in, fed her and warmed her by the fire. In return she laughed at their inferior tools. She unwrapped a brilliantly sharp toki pounamu (greenstone adze) and demonstrated the keenness of the blade.

It's not hard to imagine the men passing the tool from hand to hand, each testing the edge with his thumb. It's sometimes said that this axe was the first pounamu Ngāi Tahu had seen.

Pounamu ranges in colour from near black to vibrant green to a pearly green-grey, is as hard as steel, and, more importantly, is incredibly tough. Carving a single piece using traditional methods can take years, but the results are beautiful and lethal. Pounamu adzes, weapons and jewellery were as prized in Raureka's time as they are today. Each piece has its own mauri (life-force) and wairua (spirit); the most celebrated have their own whakapapa and name. The history of the West Coast is inseparable from the desire to possess the stone. And here was Raureka arriving on Ngāi Tahu's doorstep with knowledge of a route through the mountains to the source.

Raureka married in the east, and guided an expedition back over the pass, opening a passage between the two coasts. It became a corridor for traders and war parties, and a century of intermittent fighting followed. Finally, Ngāi Tahu conquered and absorbed Kāti Wairaki, and took possession of the West Coast.

Over the next ten days I was going to retrace Raureka's route over the pass and through to the eastern plains, along what is now a remote tramping track. Crammed in with my food and fuel were a dozen versions of her story, from early published sources to oral history from the present day. As with so many old tales, its truth is hard to pin down. Some say she went wandering, others that she was visiting relations. Historians say Ngāi Tahu had encountered pounamu long before Raureka arrived—yet it's the only story we tell about seeing the stone for the first time. Most accounts agree she was a historical ancestor—except for one, which claimed she never existed at all. My plan was to read the stories in the landscape, and to study the mountains for clues. I'd try to walk where she walked, camp where she camped, and do my best to get inside her head.

There was one problem, though. Most of the divergent accounts tended to agree on one thing: that Raureka was pōrangi. Mad.

·

At the top of the beach, my travelling companion for the first day stood waiting, a woman I barely knew. Leigh was a Pākehā West Coaster, born and raised in the bush, a writer with a dreamy air that seemed at odds with the camouflage cap pulled down over her wild blond hair, and the full-sleeve tattoo. She lived in Melbourne, but had returned to the Coast (as the West Coast is often called) to finish a memoir. We'd met two days earlier at the pub, after an introduction from a mutual friend.

Clambering up the breakwater of jagged rock towards her, I tried not to feel disappointed. Before leaving Australia I'd invited a number of key Ngāi Tahu figures to come on walks. The response had been great. But once we got down to the details, plans evaporated. The real tohuka (experts) were too busy to go ten days carrying a pack. Many were older, some in poor health. I naively asked a pounamu carver I knew if I could tag along on a journey into the hills to gather the sacred stone, and he stopped returning my calls. People knew my family, but no one had seen my face in fifteen years. So here I was, walking with a complete random. She'd expressed interest in joining me when we'd chatted at the Kumara pub. A couple of beers in, I thought: why not?

Now, I squinted up at her, and tried to conceal my second thoughts behind a smile. Leigh knew nothing about Māori history. I just hoped she wouldn't slow me down.

'So why did Raureka leave home?' she asked as we paced through Hokitika's wide colonial streets.

'She had a fight with her family,' I said. 'But no one says why. She just wandered off.'

'Must have been a big fight.'

'We've got plenty of stories about women leaving their husbands, or taking off with another man,' I said. 'Maybe she had a Ngāi Tahu lover on the other side.'

Leigh scoffed. 'That's a long way to go to see your boyfriend.'

'You know what they say about Ngāi Tahu men.'

'What, that they live a long way away?'

Heading south-east through an industrial area, we scanned the sheer faces of the Alps where they climbed into cloud. Rising from sea level to two-thousand-metre peaks not far inland from the town, they offered no gap to suggest a pass. And for every pass, there were a thousand dead ends. You would have to be a little mad to wander up there without some kind of plan.

At least for the first twenty kilometres to Kaniere (Lake Kaniere), Raureka must have known where she was going. The lake was a major mahika kai (a place where food and resources are gathered and grown), with a village on its shores. Leigh and I followed the old track along the modern highway, pressing back to avoid trucks belligerent with logs. We finished our water, and the tarmac shimmered like water ahead. We descended to the Kaniere River, and I knelt to drink.

'Wait!' Leigh said.

The boulder beside me in the shallows had soft brown eyes and velvet ears, and trailed tendrils of blood: a deer's severed head.

Still thirsty, just past the turnoff to Kaniere, we finally headed up into the cool darkness of the bush. On the ridge above the river, a silver gleam caught my eye. I instinctively felt that it was something valuable, like spotting a wallet dropped in the street. It was a black and bronze mussel shell. Several more lay in the leaf litter. What were mussel shells doing this far from the coast?

Even if Raureka had stormed off, surely she would have grabbed something to eat. I could see her with a woven flax kete of mussels bumping on her hip. If she'd stopped here to eat and tossed the shells down the bank, how long would they lie untouched?

'Hey, look at these!' Leigh called.

A water race whispered beside the track. Beneath the slow-moving current lay hundreds of freshwater mussels.

'Kākahi,' I said. 'They were a staple for inland travellers.'

'Are they any good?'

'No idea. They're pretty rare.'

We climbed down the bank and slipped our hands into the cool water. The shellfish were strangely heavy, dense with life. Leigh passed hers to me one at a time, and they weighed in my hands like gold.

Camped on the shingly western shore of Kaniere, we lit a fire and boiled a dozen kākahi in their shells. They slowly opened, and when I shucked one and put it in my mouth with Leigh looking on, I had to avert my eyes. The flesh tasted obscurely sexual: a muddy succulence on the tongue.

'That good, huh?' Leigh said.

'Silty,' I said. 'But not bad.'

Leigh prised apart the lips of another kākahi and slipped the meat into her mouth. She screwed up her nose.

'In the old days,' I said, 'they used the shells to cut the umbilical of newborns. Then they'd bury the placenta. The word for placenta and land is the same: whenua.'

'Huh. Interesting,' she said, eyes bright, and I wished fleetingly that I was with someone who could teach me, and then felt mean.

It was a hot, humid night, and after dinner we swam naked in the oily dark to wash away the grime of the road. Though I hadn't been aware of the tension of the last few months, now I felt it release. I'd been packing up my life in Melbourne, wondering if I'd be back. I'd had a bitter falling-out with a dear friend. And after a couple of lonely years spent single, I'd fallen in love with another close friend. When I'd broached the subject, she responded with fury, that I'd read the signals wrong. Whatever Raureka's reason for leaving home, I understood her desire to bail: to put one foot in front of the other and head for the hills. Now, I was out of signal range, floating weightless in this immense body of water, tingling from the first thirty kilometres on the road.

Leigh turned for shore, leaving me alone. The air was profoundly still. Three small fires burned across the far side. People had been living on these shores for centuries, and some say this was actually Raureka's home. Stars pricked the water around me. Canoes lay like fallen trees pulled up on the sand. The fires opposite winked out. I pictured Raureka with her travelling cape pulled up under her chin, watching the night. A place looks different when you know you're leaving it behind.

I thought: I want to be changed by these journeys, these hills.

·

By daylight Kaniere lay in a long velvety expanse, eight kilometres long and two wide, coloured a deep green by the heavily timbered hills all around. The higher inland peaks waited at the head of the lake, brooding under drizzly cloud. In the end, Leigh had been good company, but I was ready to cover ground and immerse myself in Raureka's story. After breakfast Leigh bade me farewell. We hugged, and breathed in and slowly out.

'You know, Rae's brother is somewhere up on Styx Saddle,' she said, stepping back. Rae was her stepmother. 'He was killed in a plane crash. They never found the body.'

I nodded, not sure how to respond. 'I'll pay my respects when I get there,' I finally said. 'I guess I'll see you next time I'm back on the Coast. Good luck with the writing.'

Her eyes flicked up to meet mine. 'You too.' She held my gaze for a moment, then turned away with a faint smile. 'Bye.'

She disappeared into the bush, headed home to work on her own book. I jacked my pack onto my back and went on around the lake's edge in a buoyant mood.

·

By mid-morning, the day was breathless and fiercely hot. Sweat dripped down my face and plastered my shirt to my back. I'd decided that out here, anything could be a clue; as I walked, I studied the landscape in a way I'd never done on a normal tramping trip. An hour on, I noticed a cloudy green stone the size of a fantail egg embedded in the dirt.

With a flicker of excitement I prised it free. It looked a little like pounamu. I spat on the stone and gave it a quick polish. It glowed green, then quickly faded as it dried. Damn. Serpentine—'serp', as some call it—looks exactly like pounamu when wet, but it's a fool's gold. By contrast, raw pounamu is usually covered with a whitish rind, and looks almost indistinguishable from ordinary river stones.

Even if I found pounamu here, I had no right to take it. All pounamu belongs to Te Rūnunga o Ngāi Tahu. You need permission, or specific local rights determined by whakapapa (lines of ancestral descent).

In Raureka's day, her Kāti Wairaki people controlled pounamu on the Coast. As a high-born woman of the tribe, her whakapapa would have secured her claim. I had no direct bloodlines to Kāti Waewae, who are kaitiaki (guardians) of pounamu in this area today.

Still, I was tempted to pocket my pebble. I wasn't enough
of a novice to mistake it for the real thing, but serpentine has a
beauty of its own. It seemed fitting because I wasn't exactly the real
thing, either, with my tall, skinny frame, pale skin and blue eyes.
I dropped the stone into my pocket, added a handful of rough
polishing pebbles and pushed on. The stones clicked and rasped
with each step.

·

The further I got from the coast, the more I saw Ngāi Tahu in
the landscape. A recent storm had toppled dozens of trees, and
through a gap in the canopy I glimpsed Tūhua pushing up into
steely cloud on the other side of the lake. Tūhua was Kāti Waewae's
sacred mountain, presiding over the greenstone rivers, and their
touchstone when introducing themselves. The minute someone
said 'Ko Tūhua te mauka' (Tūhua is my mountain) you knew
where they were from. Senior leader Lisa Tumahai, chair of the
tribe's overall governing body, and the elected representative for
Kāti Waewae, later told me, 'I've got whānau who've walked to the
top of Tūhua. It's an easy climb in the scheme of things, but being
up there, there's this absolute sense of knowing who you are.'

Further on, I paused on a sandfly-infested beach to study the
rumpled green hill at the head of the lake. Its English name is
Mt Upright, but the old name, Te Taumata-o-Uekanuku, dates
back to Raureka's time. When she shared knowledge of her pass
with Ngāi Tahu, they sent fighting expeditions back across the
mountains almost immediately. One of the earliest was led by my
ancestor Te Rakitāmau. Here at this lake he and his party encountered a Kāti Wairaki force led by the famous chief Uekanuku. In
the ensuing battle Uekanuku was killed. The summit above me

commemorated his life and death: taumata can mean summit or height, and also resting place.

From the head of Kaniere I dropped down to the Styx River, thinking about the choice Raureka had to make. Left went up the Styx River valley; right, to the flats where the Toharoa, Kokatahi and Hokitika rivers flowed out of the hills. Rivers are the pathway into the high mountains, but none of these suggested an easy route. I stood under the weight of an overloaded pack, wishing I'd left the fresh fruit and books behind, thinking: which way would you go? If you were travelling solo, with limited supplies? If you were wandering mad? Raureka went east, up the Styx, and so did I.

That afternoon and the following morning, after a night camped beside the track, I climbed steadily, wading in and out of the river where landslides had devoured the track. Past Grassy Flat Hut on the way up towards Styx Saddle, I heard a rising, shrieking whistle, then an excited twittering. Four or five birds.

I threw down my pack and shouldered off the track into a dense thicket of mānuka. I could hear the birds just ahead of me, but each time I moved they seemed to move as well. Soon I was surrounded, the twittering coming from all sides. I crept forward, hoping to catch a glimpse. Could it be?

Crack. A stick broke underfoot, and I saw orange and green shapes flash overhead, chattering madly. Yes—kākā! In Raureka's time the native parrots flocked in their thousands, but now they're rare in the wild. I worked my way back to the track, feeling lucky. Then I noticed the bone embedded in the earth beside my pack.

It looked like a tibia, long and graceful, green with age, and snapped in half. There was a small hole in one end that looked like it'd been drilled clean through. Distinctive gouges like teeth marks on the other end. Strange: it had to be from a deer, but to me it looked human.

Whatever the animal, the rest of its skeleton had to be close. I searched the track, then extended my search into the surrounding bush. I found myself in a forest of gnarled fuchsia trees that had been weirdly miniaturised by the sub-alpine conditions. I felt like a giant with my head brushing against the canopy. The light was soft and dappled; all was silent. A spider waited in its web. I held my breath. Luminous green on all sides. How quickly the path is lost.

A war party disappeared in this stretch of the valley. The chief Pūhou, who was perhaps the man Raureka married, led an expedition back west. On Styx Saddle, five hundred metres from where I was, his party split in two. He took one group of warriors down the Arahura, while his son's party came this way down the Styx. They never reached Kaniere. Hypothermia, avalanche, ambush— no one knows. They simply vanished.

Crouched in the undergrowth, I could hear individual leaves fall. One, then another, then a billion more, turning to earth, covering everything inch by inch. There were ancestors buried all over this country. The word for bone and the word for tribe are the same: iwi. Your whakapapa joins you to your ancestors, and your ancestors are the places you spring from. Perhaps it would be the same for our Pākehā descendants, too. I thought about Leigh's stepmother's brother, killed when his plane went down: he and his friends were somewhere up here, too.

Toitū te whenua, you often hear—translated as 'leave the land undisturbed'. How could you, when you were going to be part of the land yourself? The better sentiment is 'cleave to the land'. I dug into the loam, looking for bones, gathering history in dirty half-moons beneath my nails.

·

On the swampy saddle between the Styx and the Arahura, the man coming towards me looked like a young Hunter S. Thompson. He wore a floppy hat and psychedelic Hawaiian shirt, and carried a large gun.

'Hey,' I said. 'Seen many deer?'

'Not yet,' said Hunter, slinging his rifle over one shoulder. 'You? Any sign?'

'I saw a severed head back by the highway, but nothing since.'

A short guy with the barrel chest of Hunter S. Thompson's Samoan attorney brought up the rear. Hunter was a journalist named Patrick; his sidekick, a plumber called Nick. They'd just crossed the Divide using Raureka's route. I told them about her journey.

'You mean Māori used this route?' Patrick asked.

'Raureka discovered it. And lots of expeditions came this way, until an avalanche—'

'Hang on,' Patrick said, intrigued. 'But she wouldn't have had *shoes*. Or shelter. She'd have been wet and cold most of the time!'

I pondered that after we said goodbye. Raureka would have had tough woven flax sandals, padded gaiters to protect her shins, a waterproof thatched cape, perhaps even a warm dog-skin cloak. In the bush, she'd have lived on fern root, eels and birds, and slept in a quick shelter built from saplings, bark and branches. But she was heading into the alpine zone, where there was nothing to eat and nowhere to hide from storms. Why would she have kept going south?

At the edge of Styx Saddle I got my first glimpse of the Ara-hura, far below. The river ran north through a green-and-gold valley, in two slate-blue braids. I'd known I'd reach the Arahura, but now, looking down at the sacred river from the spot where Raureka might have stood, an idea suddenly put down roots: per-haps she knew where she was going.

I looked up the riverbed towards the Main Divide: shattered mountaintops and reefs of intimidating cloud; nothing to suggest a pass. Yet Raureka was meant to have wandered up that way and accidentally discovered the only viable route in the area. Faced with the landscape itself, the story made little sense.

But the Arahura—that was a sacred landscape down there, the most famous source of pounamu in the country. Kāti Waewae are guardians of the river today, and their people know every inch of its banks. In Raureka's day her Kāti Wairaki people would have been the same. It only took the first Polynesian explorers a few decades to track down all the sources of useful stone in the entire country, including some well above the bush line. They found traces in riverbeds, then followed the rivers up into the hills to find the source. In the search for pounamu, surely Raureka's peo-ple would have explored the Arahura to its headwaters. If you followed the river through its bends, hour by hour, where did you end up? At Raureka's pass to the east coast.

I was speculating, of course, but perhaps she'd seen it on a pre-vious expedition. Perhaps her iwi knew about it, but no one had crossed it before. But whatever the case, when she stormed off into the mountains, she may have had a route in mind.

I continued on in a great mood, climbing steadily above the Arahura's western bank towards Raureka's pass. The nor'west afternoon swelled at my back, and within the hour a dirty wall of cloud came sweeping up the valley behind me. I decided against an exposed campsite at Whakarewa, the lake at the pass, and stopped instead at the simple six-bunk Harman Hut.

I had the place to myself, and after dinner I slouched on the deck to watch the storm break. A final sunbeam slanted through the thunderheads to strike a massive landslide coming off an unnamed peak to the west, turning the raw stone to burnished gold. Beyond the peaks, the western horizon was one great line of fire. This was a mythical place—the Arahura valley is the setting for our creation myth of pounamu. I'd brought the tale with me, thinking it might shed light on Raureka's journey through the same landscape.

·

Back in the ancestral homeland of Hawaiki, two taniwha (giant water serpents) were locked in a long-running feud. Poutini was the guardian taniwha of pounamu, while his nemesis Whatipu guarded hōaka (grindstone, which could cut pounamu).

One day when Poutini was being chased across the ocean, he took refuge from Whatipu in a sheltered bay on Tūhua Island, off the North Island's east coast. There, he saw a beautiful woman come down to bathe. Her name was Waitaiki, and when she stripped off and dived into the sea, Poutini fell in love—or maybe lust.

Poutini swam silently across the bay and, with a faint ripple, snatched Waitaiki up and sped across the ocean to Tahanga, on the Coromandel Peninsula. By the time they arrived, she'd turned blue with cold. The great serpent lit a fire on the beach to keep her warm.

Waitaiki's husband was the powerful chief Tama-āhua. Back

on Tūhua, he found Waitaiki's discarded clothes and knew something had gone wrong. He gathered his men, and hurled his magic tekateka spear into the air. It hung quivering, pointing to Tahanga. They paddled to the mainland at speed.

They were too late. Poutini's fire had gone out, leaving cold ash. He'd taken Waitaiki south to Whangamatā, on the shores of Lake Taupō, where a new fire burned. And so a great chase began, south to Rangitoto, across Cook Strait to Whangamoa, to Onetahua at Farewell Spit, past Pāhau out the back of the Barrytown pub, and down to Takiwai in Milford Sound.

Finally, Tama-āhua's tekateka led him north again. Crossing the Arahura, he noticed its waters were warm. Through powerful karakia he knew his wife was in distress somewhere upriver. He began preparations for war.

Poutini knew he'd been discovered. He also knew that he didn't stand a chance against Tama-āhua in a fight. Being jealous and bad-tempered, he decided that if he couldn't have Waitaiki, no one would. In the upper Arahura, he transformed her into his own essence, pounamu, then laid her in the riverbed. Then he slipped past Tama-āhua and out to the coast.

On discovering Waitaiki turned to stone, Tama-āhua wept over his wife's lifeless form. He grieved, and then, when the time for mourning was over, he named a nearby mountain Tūhua, after their island home, and another after himself, so he could watch over his lost love.

The way that we tell the story today, Tama-āhua returned to Tūhua, where he eventually got onto Tinder, remarried and moved on. Poutini got the coastline renamed after him—Te Tai-o-Poutini—and he still swims up and down it, protecting Waitaiki and the people of the Coast. And in the spring floods, Waitaiki sends her children down the river for us to find.

•

I closed my e-reader and lay back on the deck, stretching out my aching shoulders as the first rain began to spot. I love the Poutini story because it's actually an oral map. Tūhua, where the chase began, is home to a prized black obsidian used for knives. At Tahanga there was a quarry where basalt was taken for adzes. Taupo had metamorphosed argillites, Pāhau flints for drilling pounamu, and so on—Poutini's tale maps key quarries across thousands of kilometres.

Conversely, the landscape here maps Poutini's story. I'd set off from Te Tai-o-Poutini, Poutini's coast. I'd passed the mountain named Tūhua near Lake Kaniere, and the mountain Tama-āhua was somewhere up on the dark skyline to the north. A few kilometres downriver, Waitaiki lay as the embodiment of the main pounamu source. And all of this was along Raureka's route.

That night I climbed into my bunk feeling strangely exhilarated. The pieces didn't quite connect, but I felt like I'd glimpsed some new logic in the landscape, like seeing a campfire flickering on a distant steep ridge where you'd never expect to find life.

•

In the morning the storm still hadn't broken, and I stepped out into a valley thick with humidity and heat. Down at the Arahura I finally greeted the famous river, crouching to splash water over my face and drink from my hands. I stood, dripping, the wind cooler on my cheeks. The rugged head of the valley was visible now, and it looked essentially the same as it would have in Raureka's time.

The wind was quarrying mist from about the peak called

Kaniere (Mt Harman). South along the ridge, the Arahura came pouring out of the clouds in a hundred-metre-high waterfall. Beyond that, glimpses of blue gave the first real sign that I was approaching the Main Divide; the weather was often sharply different on either side. I climbed steadily around the side of the cliffs, through alpine scrub then steep tussock, sweating hard. I quit the West Coast and followed Raureka up into luminous mist. The world disappeared.

Near Nōti Raureka, Raureka's pass, visibility dropped to a couple of metres. Small cairns of stacked stones guided me through the whiteout, emerging a few steps in front, disappearing a few steps behind. There was no sign of Whakarewa, the lake at the pass. Then I felt a rushing sensation all around me. The mist blew away and I was suddenly looking straight at the water, only metres in front of me.

Whakarewa was more vapour than liquid: a silver arc lifting away into smoke. Again, that hurtling sensation, and the fog closed back in. It started to rain. I removed my pack and bent over, rummaging for my jacket. When I straightened to put it on, I looked up and the world had disappeared. Entirely.

'What the *fuck*?'

One minute I'd been walking through a misty sub-alpine landscape. The next, I felt like I'd been swallowed by a black hole. Impossibly large dark curves filled my entire field of vision, shading from grey to black, surrounding me on all sides. I turned my head and the void was everywhere, seemingly inches from my face, yet stretching off to infinity. I reached out a hand like a blind man and met no resistance. There was nothing there. Vertigo shot through me. There was no sky, no earth. I blinked hard in the rain, swearing aloud.

In another heartbeat the mist burned away. The distant snow-covered peaks of Tau-a-Tamateraki snapped into focus, and I saw huge lenticular clouds immediately overhead—long, smooth UFOs, thunderous and silver-black. They were harbingers of the worst storms, and almost close enough to touch. I grabbed my camera and fumbled it to my eye. The battery died. I shook my head in disbelief.

I must have been swallowed by one of those clouds. Or maybe it had passed inches from my face, and I'd seen its underbelly reflected in the lake. Shreds of mist continued to stream past. The light flickered between dawn, noon and dusk. It felt like time was running at a different speed.

Slowly the front moved off. I flopped down on the tussock and put the billy on to gather my thoughts.

Reality is always shifting in the alpine world, from sweeping vistas to whiteout, from sunshine to storms. Normally I welcome that shift, and the feeling of being tiny and humble among the peaks. But if you lose your bearings, uplifting solitude can flip to a sense of threat.

In the back of my mind, I was thinking about another man who'd walked this trail in search of Raureka, twenty-five years earlier. Barry Brailsford was at the time a respected educator: a Pākehā man who'd written two notable books on Ngāi Tahu history, including one detailing our trails through the mountains. But on his expedition over Nōti Raureka, he'd started looking for portals to other worlds. He came to believe he was subject to an ancient prophecy, and could 'time-shift' from place to place along the trail. What had he seen up here?

I pushed the thought to one side. What about Raureka, who the stories say was mad? She'd crossed this pass hungry and alone. Even if she'd been of sound mind when she set out, could her experiences up here have left her scarred?

I'd read early colonial accounts which said that old-time Māori feared the mountains. Lightning about the peaks could be an omen of death. Walls and towers of mist, so common and so substantial in the New Zealand mountains, were considered the fortresses of the patupaiarehe, the fairy people whose distant fires left no trace. The geologist Ernst Dieffenbach, the first European to climb Tongariro in the North Island, was guided most of the way, but his guides refused to set foot in the snow. Dieffenbach wrote that, to Māori, 'the mountains are peopled with mysterious and misshapen animals; the black points, which he sees from afar in the dazzling snow, are fierce and monstrous birds; a supernatural spirit breathes on him in the evening breeze.'

Dieffenbach and others were talking about specific sacred mountains. Every iwi and hapū has at least one local peak that embodies the tribe's spirit. Those mountains stand as a living symbol of mana (prestige and spiritual power). They're where your ancestors' bones are buried, and a touchstone in speech and song. The summits represent the head, the most sacred part of the body. It's no wonder Dieffenbach's guides wouldn't set foot on top of their sacred peak.

In Te Waipounamu, Ngāi Tahu have always lived in the shadow of high mountains. Our Alps are extensive—five times the area of the European Alps—with more than two thousand peaks that rise more than two thousand metres high. Travel through the mountains was once relatively common for us, whether for trade, pounamu gathering, family occasions, warfare or the exchange of knowledge. Years after Raureka's journey, this pass was made tapu (sacred) when an avalanche wiped out members of a Ngāi Tahu war party; up until then, it likely was not—even if the mountaintops on all sides were. I doubted an alpine crossing alone would have shattered Raureka's mind.

.

By the time I'd finished a mug of gritty coffee, the front had moved off and visibility had lifted, and with it my mood. I could now see why Raureka's discovery was such a prize. The broad snowgrass saddle offered a straightforward path across the Main Divide, unlike Mt Kaniere on one side and the smashed teeth of Twin Peaks on the other. Whakarewa, the source of the Arahura, lay in the centre of the saddle like a giant silver eye. I padded round the lake's edge and peered over the far side of the pass, straight down at the Waitāwhiri, the Wilberforce River, five hundred metres below.

This was Raureka's Rubicon. A raindrop falling at her feet would flow into Ngāi Tahu territory, and on to the Pacific Ocean. A raindrop at her back would end up where she began, in Kāti Wairaki territory at the Tasman Sea. We'll never know why she chose to go on. In a way she was defecting, taking state secrets across enemy lines. Maybe she was drawn to the unknown, like so many Polynesian explorers. Her forebears had been curious about what lay over the horizon of the Pacific Ocean. Who wouldn't be curious about what lay on the other side of the Alps?

The descent was steep and fast and joyous. I plunged my boots into loose scree and charged down in moon strides. Halfway, I paused and looked across the slope to my right. In the late afternoon sun, pockets of shadow suggested caves. I dumped my pack and set off west on a rising traverse, towards where Hamer Falls plunged to the valley floor. Soon I was poking my nose into flax bushes around the base of cliffs, then scrambling up between rock ledges, climbing hand over hand towards likely-looking overhangs.

Somewhere on this southern face of the pass was a famous cave, big enough to house whole travelling parties, and the standard place to sleep on the journey west. In the 1860s, a Kaiapoi elder who'd walked the route described its location to Europeans. Early goldminers camped there, and it's possible Raureka did as well. It also featured in a story about a treasure trove of pounamu. Unfortunately, no one had seen the cave for a century. Most likely it'd been buried by rockfall, but I was still keen to find a trace.

Free of my pack, it was a pleasure to move upwards. My breathing slowed. The world narrowed to each fistful of scrub, each boot edged into the rock. The drop into the valley grew beneath my feet.

Don't mess this up, I told myself. *No mistakes.*

Finally I hauled myself up onto a ledge and found—a cave! With mossy boulders piled in one corner. Even knowing the idea was ridiculous, I allowed myself to wonder. What if...

Years after Raureka's route had become a common link between the coasts, a party of Ngāi Tahu fighting men was returning home with a fortune in pounamu. The story goes that a scout named Ngātororangi intercepted them near the pass. Like the legendary Greek soldier who ran from the Battle of Marathon to Athens to deliver news of victory (which is where the marathon comes from), Ngatororangi ran more than a hundred kilometres across the Canterbury Plains, swam the major rivers and ascended to the pass to deliver his message: Kaiapoi Pā, a Ngāi Tahu stronghold on the east coast, was under attack. The warriors hid their hoard of pounamu and sped home to join the fight. Ngatororangi collapsed, and was nursed back to health in the cave. The pounamu was never found.

Perched high up the side of the pass, I scraped moss from the nearest boulder, only to find a dull rock. Same with the next. The cave wasn't really a cave, more a dismal overhang where two people could huddle in a storm. And the pounamu story was a little fanciful—but I didn't mind. I sat back on my haunches, delighted with my absurd eyrie. Here, just on the eastern side of the Main Divide, the weather was sharply distinguished from the west. Fine-weather cloud and a few early stars feathered a crisp blue sky. The view was breathtaking. At my feet the young Waitāwhiri started its journey to the east coast.

PART II: NŌTI RAUREKA (BROWNING PASS), CANTERBURY ALPS. SUMMER.

The next morning I tracked the tumbling alpine waters of the Waitāwhiri through rapids and pools. The landscape was profoundly different here. The sky was bigger, the mountains set further back, flooding the sparse tussock and shingle valleys with light. I'd grown up on this side of the island, and it felt comforting. But to Raureka, it must have seemed another world after the tangled green bush of her home.

In the rough bouldery riverbed I maintained a hard march through the morning and afternoon. I'd been meandering until now, but today I was set on covering more than thirty kilometres. My pack swayed and chafed, and a furnace nor'-west wind harried me on. In the open valley floor I felt exposed to the sun and watching eyes. There'd been several mahika kai in this valley. I pictured Raureka scanning the horizon for cooking fires or movement among the matagouri scrub. Nothing, yet.

Just before I turned east at Kareaonui, I looked back over my shoulder, as Raureka might have done to fix her route home. The singular form of the peak known as Kaniere stood above the pass. Seen from the west, it had merely been a bump on the end of the ridge. From this side it was visible for miles. I'd wondered why Mt Kaniere and Lake Kaniere shared a name, and surely here was the answer: the mountain was an enormous signpost pointing to the greenstone lake.

Afternoon ripened into evening, yet the temperature kept climbing. As I walked the land became a giant umu, an oven of hot stones radiating heat from above and below. The midsummer sun at my back refused to set. I went on for hours, stepping on my shadow where it fell at my feet.

Finally I waded through the now-substantial river one braid at a time, and crossed the valley towards Takapū-o-Pūhou, an old mahika kai at the foot of Mt Scarcliff, and another marker of Raureka's passage: Pūhou was the Kāti Māmoe and Waitaha chief many say she married. I didn't bother filling my water bottles; there'd be water there. I felt deranged by the wind and flayed by the sun. It was time to stop.

On an old river terrace with good flat ground for my tent, I dropped my pack and took my water bottles to the nearby stream. It was dry. I stared down at the cracked mudpan like a forlorn child. A silver shimmer caught my eye back out in the valley. Without a thought in my head I turned and marched back out among the baking stones. But when I reached water it was just a scummy puddle as thin and scattered as broken glass. I went on, an automaton.

The wind brought snatches of rushing water and I followed, delirious with thirst. The river couldn't be that far away. Again and again I crested shingle-banks to find dead rivers, driftwood ribs scattered, knuckles of piled stone. I began to laugh aloud with each new defeat, as if it was Raureka herself I was hoping to find.

Almost at the opposite rim of the valley, I finally reached one small clear braid and stooped to drink. The main flow remained hidden. I filled my bottles, then stumbled back to camp. I'd spent the entire day walking beside the river, then gone an extra six kilometres to get water. I felt a little mad.

It was close to 10 p.m. by the time I'd eaten. I lay on my back and watched the sky fill with stars. It was one of those exquisite, sweltering nights you get in the Canterbury Alps, with the pale firmament soaring overhead and the dark weight of the mountains on all sides. Raureka would have seen signs of habitation here, would have started to anticipate contact. I drifted into a waking dream of the campfires of strangers not far off, the feeling of hunger, the rich, charred smell of roasting birds, voices calling—Haere ki te moe! Go to bed!—only it was my mother's voice, and I was drifting and warm, slipping away into sleep.

Crack! Crack!

Something snapped me awake.

Gunshots. Did I dream that?

I rolled onto my belly. Through a black fringe of grass I saw lights a few hundred metres up the valley. A powerful beam swept over the ridge above. Shadows fled up the slope.

Hunters.

I should shout. Flash my head torch. Or, like Raureka, stand and stumble towards them, hot wind roaring in my ears, moving into the light of their fire until I came face to face with their raised weapons and hard looks. I imagined hands at my shoulders helping me to sit. Great sucks of cool water spilling down my face. Roast weka meat pushed into my hands. Lurching away beyond the rim of their fire to eat while they watched and laughed. I'd see the men's stone adzes laid against the unfinished hull of a tremendous canoe. I'd laugh, half-chewed pulp spilling from my mouth, and mock their blunt tools. Tell them who I was, and sink my pounamu axe into their wood. Watch their tattooed faces when they saw its bright edge.

He aha tērā?

He pounamu.

Nō hea tērā wahine?

He wahine nō Poutini. Ka pōraki mai ka tae ki ruka o te mauka—

Blam!

Another round cracked off into the trees, startling me from my reverie.

I had to alert the hunters to my presence. But I was exhausted. They weren't going to shoot a tent. I army-crawled inside, and passed out.

•

Over the next two days I tracked the Waitāwhiri out towards the plains where Raureka's meeting with Ngāi Tahu occurred. I was in the rhythm of walking now, and the kilometres clicked over fast. Today was day six, and I felt like I was returning to an alien world. Signs of the modernity increased—cattle, fences, the gleam of distant 4WDs. Away to my right the braided river whispered and foamed until, at the foot of Castle Hill, a concrete canal syphoned off half the flow and piped it to the hydroelectric scheme at Whakamatau (Lake Coleridge).

I followed the canal down to where its glittering expanse ran south for fifteen kilometres between steep glaciated hills. At the canal outflow, an old man stood casting a rod. I raised a hand, and—

Crack! Crack! Crack!

Gunfire spat from the derelict campground at our back. We both flinched into a crouch, and stared into the trees. More shots rang out at close range. Probably the same hunters, doing target practice.

'Idiots, wasting ammunition,' the fisherman said angrily when the reports died away. 'Gave me a hell of a fright. Where are you off to with that pack?'

It'd been close to a week since I'd held a conversation. My tongue felt leaden. 'To the Rakaia Gorge. Just walked from Hokitika.'

His eyes widened. 'All the way from the Coast?'

I gabbled about searching for traces of a Māori woman who'd come this way, three hundred years ago.

Silence. His face took on a look of fatherly concern. We both knew these landscapes scuff out all trace of your passage in a matter of days.

'Well, okay then,' he finally said. 'Do you want a ride?'

God, it was tempting. The route ahead was another hundred kilometres of farmland and hard roads. But that's where Raureka went, and so would I. 'Thanks,' I said. 'But I'll be okay.'

'Well, I'll be coming past later, so if you change your mind, stick out your thumb.'

I kept on round the edge of the lake, heading for Lake Coleridge Village on the far side. I fell in with two young Israeli soldiers walking the Te Araroa trail, and we talked about war, and slept in a paddock, and compared with their experiences I felt sane. And then, reading in my tent after they'd turned in, I finally discovered why Raureka had gone mad.

The Pākehā writer James Cowan published a popular account of Raureka's journey in the 1930s. The idea that she was mad seems to stem from him. His source text read: 'He wahine nō Poutini a

Raureka. Ka haere taua wahine. Ka pōrangi mai ka tae ki runga o te maunga.' In a footnote by the leading Ngāi Tahu scholars Atholl Anderson and Te Maire Tau, I learned that Cowan got the translation wrong.

He had her wandering crazed into the mountains because he rendered pōrangi as mad. That's the most common meaning, but it also connotates headstrong or stubborn. And there's also another sense, when the word is used as a verb: to wander or search. The original says Raureka would 'pōrangi pounamu', search for pounamu. Given the context, the translation should be: 'Raureka was a woman from the West Coast who went *searching* in the mountains.' It wasn't hunger or hostile spirits that drove her mad, but bad scholarship. (Later, not a single kaumātua I spoke with considered her to have been mentally unwell. 'It was more like, "You want to go off into the mountains? You've got to be mad!"' said James Russell from Arahura, with a smile.)

Tomorrow I wouldn't picture her drifting along the lake's edge like Ophelia, trailing a hand in the water, singing to herself. I'd imagine her rugged up beside a fire, watching the blaze and thinking through tomorrow's route. She carried valuable pounamu, and was a chief with rights to the stone. Perhaps she was hungry and tired, and operating outside what was expected of a person of aristocratic birth. But the story looked very different if you assumed that she knew what she was doing. Whatever that was.

When Raureka reached Arowhenua, married into Ngāi Tahu, and revealed her route across the pass, that effectively spelled the end for Kāti Wairaki. Tensions came to a head when they ambushed a major Ngāi Tahu party at Lake Māhinapua, south of Kaniere. Kāti Wairaki tohuka chanted up a great storm that cut a swathe through the Ngāi Tahu canoes. Tānetiki, eldest son of Tūrakautahi, the founder of Kaiapoi Pā, was the leader of the expedition. He and numerous other senior chiefs drowned. The ancestor Hikatūtae (who's sometimes jokingly called 'the under-taker') cut off their heads and swam with them across Māhinapua, then carried them back across Nōti Raureka for burial on ancestral land. Hokitika, where I'd begun, was named for his grisly task. Hoki means to return; tika means directly, in a straight line, or just, correct, true.

After that, Ngāi Tahu assembled a huge fighting force from across the east coast, and brought its full force to bear. Te Tai-o-Poutini, the West Coast and its sacred pounamu rivers, came under our control. And you could argue that Raureka was respon-sible for it all.

•

Lake Coleridge Village wasn't at the lake, nor was it really a vil-lage. It was New Zealand's first hydro-electric power station, sur-rounded by a giant arboretum containing two-thirds of the world's species of pine. I scrambled down through dark groves of Cauca-sian firs and Mexican weeping pines, inhaling the sharp scent of alien sap. At the bottom, a brochure informed me which trees were used by Native Americans. Unbelievable, I thought, given the indigenous history right here. Underneath the village grave-yard was a fourteenth-century Māori campsite where I planned to spend the night.

Pine needles gave way to concrete. Apart from a corporate retreat with a handful of cars out front, the tiny village was deserted. Yet again parched and looking for water, I walked the two streets, past shuttered houses to the manicured village green, and the weathered concrete power station at its heart. The enormous building was strangely beautiful: an industrial cathedral where there should have been a small church. I stood with my fingers hooked through the chain-link fence out front, listening to the unsettling hum of the generators inside.

A little further on, I found the cemetery itself: a gloomy circle walled in by more pines. Seventeen prefabricated concrete rectangles served as graves. They looked like they'd been poured from the same cement as the power station. Each had a number stencilled on it; 5 and 5A were a husband and wife. Only a handful of the slabs were occupied, the rest empty and waiting: the dead not yet in the land. I was surprised to see four men moving ahead of me, but before I could speak they vanished through a gap in the pines.

I paced the perimeter, looking for traces of the campsite that had been here. I found a homemade sign—*This Macrocarpa Tree Was Hit By Lightning On Saturday 22 January 2000*—and nothing else. But in the 1950s, workers digging in the graveyard unearthed a fireplace of blackened boulders filled with immense charred bones. The campsite was old, dating from 1340 to 1420. The bones came from moa, the huge flightless birds that kept our earliest ancestors in abundance. Further bones came to light, plus charred tussock used to build the fire, and an obsidian knife. It was the knife that had drawn me here.

Tūhua, where Poutini and Waitaiki's story begins, is a volcanic island famous for its obsidian knives. The tusk of volcanic glass found here at Lake Coleridge Village came from Tūhua, a journey of more than a thousand kilometres. Contemplating the people who'd carried the knife all that way, and how they'd perhaps used Poutini's story as their oral map—again I felt the presence of some other logic, embedded in the landscape, that made my brain fizz.

I was standing and thinking this through when the four men returned to the graveyard, looking distinctly unsettled. The oldest wore a knit cap and walked with a slow shuffle.

'Hi there,' I called. 'Nice day for it?'

'Oh, a *great* day,' he replied angrily: the mourner's contempt for the tourist, perhaps. I couldn't really explain that I'd come to pay my respects to an older dead.

Curious about what had unnerved them, I moved through the gap in the trees myself, and emerged into blinding light. Clear of the forest, I realised the graveyard actually stood on a promontory high above the river. The scale of the landscape laid out before me was overwhelming. Sunset burned above a vast gravel valley, walled in by muscular peaks. Glowing mist wreathed the compressed blue silhouettes of the mountains along Raureka's route. But what left me awestruck was the Rakaia.

Here, finally, was one of Ngāi Tahu's great rivers in full force. Five teal-blue braids snaked across the gravel plain, each a huge river in its own right. But even they were dwarfed by the power station outflow at the bottom of the cliff beneath my boots. The water came pushing, seething, roaring out into the main flow. It was stupefyingly wide and deep. I felt like I was standing too close to the tracks while an endless freight train smashed past. No wonder the mourners had left so fast.

Unnerved, I sat on a wooden bench in terminal sunshine and pulled out my notebook. A hawk glided north, wings gleaming. This promontory was where our people had roasted moa over the embers and watched the sun sink west towards Hawaiki, the homeland and the abode of the dead. Strange to think we'd had seven hundred years of telling stories beneath these peaks, but there was nothing to alert people today: no villages, no ruins, no brochures, not even a home-made sign nailed to a tree. The remains of the nearby settlement of Tokinui had been erased in the 1860s when runholders souvenired the carved posts for garden ornaments.

Thunder rolled downriver, and I turned to see dark smears of rain above the Rakaia Gorge, where the river sawed through the foothills to the plains. They still find mysterious piles of agate pebbles down there, the last remains of moa, their gizzard stones stacked like tiny cairns. That was the way Raureka went. The foothills were ghosts, greyed out with rain.

What had I gleaned about her life so far? The mountains themselves suggested she'd known what she was doing, and contemporary scholars said she wasn't really mad; but if I was honest, my walk mostly amounted to echoes and ghosts. I was no closer to understanding her psychology or motivation. And there was still the nagging thought I'd been ignoring the whole time: perhaps she never existed at all.

The idea came from the Pākehā author Barry Brailsford. He claimed Raureka's story wasn't found in local traditions: 'its source is a mystery and its authenticity questionable.' Was she a myth? Or even the construct of European writers, as Brailsford seems to suggest? Many who'd recounted her story were Europeans who gave it their own romantic twist (strangely, Brailsford himself later wrote his own Raureka myth). On the other hand, I'd found Ngāi Tahu references to Raureka from the nineteenth century, and everyone I'd spoken to within the tribe acknowledged her as an important figure from our past. 'Te kopa iti a Raureka', the tiny purse of

Raureka, is a proverb still used for small but precious things.

Sitting above the river, trying to think this through, I struggled to concentrate. God, there was power in those waters. The turbine outflow was actually driving the main current back up the valley against the natural flow. I stood and walked to the edge and stared down at the relentless blue flood, whirlpooled and supernaturally clear. I could pick out every boulder on the bottom. Vertigo dragged me closer. I could feel the icy slap and plunge, feel my body hitting that roiling skin.

In my search for Raureka's past I'd had days of heat and isolation, days of dry riverbeds, days of a thirst that was both metaphorical and real. And now I'd finally found water—it was too much. I felt short-circuited. My eyes prickled. There was some thickening of time, some concentration of force in those waters I felt acutely but couldn't articulate beyond—power?

Something clicked. I'd been searching for the truth about Raureka, but I'd found power. A power station. The metaphor collapsed. I saw Raureka then, and I understood.

I took the small bird's-egg pebble of serpentine from Kaniere from my pocket and weighed it in my hand, ready to throw it off the edge: fool's gold for a fake river, to commemorate a futile journey into the past. A week of jostling against other pebbles had worn smooth patches in its surface. I polished away the dust. The stone glowed darker green. I held it up: a tiny luminous sun between thumb and finger. Unbelievable. It was pounamu, after all. A tiny piece of Waitaiki, the mother of the stone. The urge to hurl it into the water remained, but I slipped it back into my pocket. That wasn't a real river down there. That was a monster.

•

Walking back to the village, I knew immediately that I wanted to camp at the power station. Rather than jump the fence and trigger a national security alert, I climbed the pine-infested hill at the back and pitched my tent beneath the sizzling arcs of high-voltage lines. While daylight failed I sat on a crumbling concrete pad and drank beer smuggled from the corporate retreat that was the village's only going concern. Blood sang in my veins. It was an appalling place to camp, but it felt right. I'd been determined to follow my instincts. This was where they'd led.

I'd been trying to discover the truth of Raureka's story, but my questions had been wrong. What quickens Māori history is mana, whakapapa, whenua: the prestige and lineage of your people, and authority over the land. Power, in other words. What was real, what was myth; why she set out, where she camped, what she thought and felt—none of that was the point. All the old stories are both history and myth.

Which meant that Raureka was a person, and the personification of an event: how Ngāi Tahu first crossed the Southern Alps and gained control of the pounamu coast. She brought the stone to our door and, by marrying into Ngāi Tahu, she passed on her bloodlines and rights along with knowledge of the route. She joined the two great rivers, the Arahura and the Rakaia, and the two great lineages, Kāti Wairaki and Ngāi Tahu. She was our creation myth for how we gained power over pounamu and Poutini's coast. And like the oral map of Poutini and Waitaiki, her story contained the map of her route.

My beer bottle clinked down against the concrete. I switched off the burner and went at a bowl of hot salty laksa. Spits of rain came whispering up off the breeze, but for now the storm seemed to be moving up the coast.

With food in my belly and a shifting sense of Raureka's story, I should have felt more at peace. But I was still freaked out by that headland above the river. An empty cemetery filled with moa bones, lightning strikes, the power-station outflow: the place felt wrong. It was mauri, life-force. Boiling away down there was all the rain that had fallen on the ranges standing over me in the dark. It was hundreds of side creeks, dozens of rivers, the Waitāwhiri, the story of Raureka and Kāti Wairaki, and a thousand years of whakapapa, forced into a pipe. What came out the other side was scrambled, just the chaos of raw matter sent on to the ocean without history or name. New origin stories took over—the settling of the land by my Pākehā ancestors, the coming of electricity, the birth of modernity: new claims to authority and power.

I packed up my things and climbed into my tent. I could keep going south, but I wasn't going to find further trace of Raureka on the plains. I'd come back for the Rakaia Gorge another time, but for now, I still had a couple of days' food. I'd go north. Follow the transmission lines. Follow the power. See where it led.

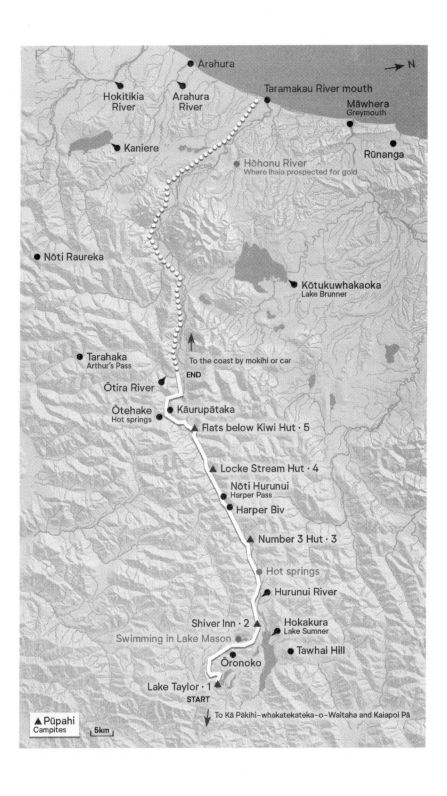

Arahura

Taramakau River mouth

Hokitikia
River

Arahura
River

Māwhera
Greymouth

N

Kaniere

Rūnanga

Hōhonu River
Where Ihaia prospected for gold

Nōti Raureka

Kōtukuwhakaoka
Lake Brunner

To the coast by mokihi or car

Tarahaka
Arthur's Pass

END

Ōtira River

Ōtehake
Hot springs

Kāurupātaka

▲ Flats below Kiwi Hut · 5

▲ Locke Stream Hut · 4

Nōti Hurunui
Harper Pass

● Harper Biv

▲ Number 3 Hut · 3

● Hot springs

● Hurunui River

Shiver Inn · 2 ▲

Hokakura
Lake Sumner

Swimming in Lake Mason ●

● Tawhai Hill

● Ōronoko

Lake Taylor · 1 ▲
START

To Kā Pākihi–whakatekateka–o–Waitaha and Kaiapoi Pā

▲ Pūpahi
Campsites   5km

2

Nōti Hurunui
(Harper Pass)

PART I: KAIAPOI PĀ, CANTERBURY COAST. SUMMER.

Dad and I stepped from the car into cool air and sunshine sharp as a blade. A crisp southerly wind shivered through the cornfields at our back. Beyond the earthen embankments and the dunes in front of us, the Pacific Ocean moved unseen. I paused and frowned. I could smell charred timber. But that was impossible: it'd been nearly two hundred years since the fire.

We climbed the embankment to a large grassed plateau. The hollows and mounds of old earthworks caught in the morning light. I imagined the great carved meeting house Pukukura standing among raised storehouses and thatched homes. The murmur of seated figures reached us, the syncopated thump of commoners pounding roasted fernroot, the rasp of gritstone polishing greenstone as carvers went about their work nearby. In those days, the five-acre settlement was protected by tidal swamp on one side, and a lagoon on the other.

We paced the perimeter, where snarls of blackberry had replaced the wooden palisades. I eyed the faint jagged line of the mountains waiting at the horizon. Above the shrill of cicadas I heard snatches of distressed shouting on the breeze. A man's voice, hoarse with rage and fear. Again, the reek of smoke. Dad paused and turned, and we held each other's gaze.

'Did you hear that?' I said.

He nodded. We listened hard.

Nothing. After a minute, we shrugged and moved on. There were farmhouses around. Someone having a bad day. But we were both unnerved.

•

The prosperous fortified settlement that once stood here was Te Kōhaka-a-Kaikai-a-waro, or Kaiapoi Pā, a Ngāi Tahu cultural and economic centre, and stronghold of the Ngāi Tūāhuriri branch of the tribe. After Ngāi Tahu took control of the West Coast, this was the epicentre of the pounamu trade. Raw stone was brought across the Alps, carved at Kaiapoi, then traded north.

Pounamu wasn't the only reason for trans-alpine journeys, nor was Nōti Raureka the only route. The easiest passage west went via Nōti Hurunui, the saddle between the headwaters of the Hurunui River and the Taramakau. The pass is under a thousand metres, the approach and descent benign. Family groups and war parties have been using it for a long time. And in 1857, a young Ngāi Tahu rakatira (chief) used the route to guide the first Europeans across the 'impassable barrier' of the Alps.

The story begins with the meeting of two aristocratic families at Kaiapoi, when chief Werita Tainui and his son Ihaia received a visit from Bishop Henry Harper and his son Leonard.

At the time, Ihaia would have been in his mid-twenties. His father and uncle were senior chiefs. His grandfather, Tuhuru, was a member of the expedition that decisively defeated Kāti Wairaki, and leader of the Ngāi Tahu people who stayed on to occupy the West Coast. Leonard, aged twenty-five, had a similarly elite pedigree. His father had just become the first Bishop of Christchurch, had a doctorate from Oxford and had been Curate at Eton before receiving the plum job of ministering to the infant Canterbury colony.

In the course of that social visit, the men's conversation turned to the old Kaiapoi Pā. Though the settlement had a rich history, settler society at this time was obsessed with its bloody demise a quarter of a century earlier.

In the 1820s a new currency had emerged in the Māori economy: guns. Ever fast to adapt, tribes engaged in strategic trade with Europeans to amass muskets, powder and shot. Traditional warfare took a fierce turn, leading to slaughter approaching a European scale.

On the pretext of an alleged taunt, Te Rauparaha, leader of the North Island Ngāti Toa tribe, embarked on an extended vendetta against Ngāi Tahu. Through surprise attacks, his forces destroyed settlements around Kaikōura, then moved south to Kaiapoi, claiming their intention was to trade. But survivors from Kaikōura, got there first, so when the Ngāti Toa chiefs entered Kaiapoi Pā, Ngāi Tahu struck first, wiping out much of Ngāti Toa's senior leadership. Te Rauparaha survived, and later returned to seek utu (payment). After a series of ruthless battles, including an ambush at Akaroa by Ngāti Toa warriors concealed in the hold of a British ship, an alliance of northern invaders encircled Kaiapoi Pā in 1831.

At the time, the fighting men of Kaiapoi were away, but ill discipline saw the Ngāti Toa attackers fire at people working in the fields, alerting the pā. Women, old men and children barred the gates, and defended the settlement until the warriors could return. They crossed the swamp to the pā via secret pathways of tree stumps just below the water line. To the astonished northerners it looked like the defenders were running across the surface of the water itself.

Sniper fire and night raids against Ngāti Toa and their allies kept the enemy at bay for months. But at last their sapper trenches reached the stockade's southern perimeter. The attackers piled brushwood against the palisade—right beside the spot where Dad and I now stood.

In a strong nor'-west wind, the defenders took a gamble. They lit the fire themselves so the flames would sweep downwind, away from the pā. But on this coast the hot nor'-wester always gives way to a strong cold southerly; as kids we were told the story of Kaiapoi Pā to illustrate the point. The defenders watched in horror as the wind swung south. The palisades burned; Ngāti Toa warriors poured through the gap. Old gods and new weapons: the settlement was razed. Many defenders were killed, some captured and bled to death, and hundreds enslaved, while hundreds more escaped. Most went to Ngāi Tahu strongholds further south. But some, as Werita Tainui told his guests, took their children west through the mountains to safety. They'd used a pass at the head of the Hurunui River.

At the mention of a pass via the Hurunui, young Leonard Harper pricked up his ears. The South Island was in the grip of gold fever; just a month earlier, Provincial Surveyor Edward Dobson had attempted a pass at the head of the Hurunui, and reported signs of gold. No European had ever crossed the Alps to the West Coast. Leonard asked his hosts if they'd be willing to show him the way.

Werita Tainui declined. The route was a taoka, a treasure, and strategically important as a pounamu highway, even more so now because the West Coast and its pounamu rivers were still in Ngāi Tahu hands. The rest of the tribe's territory had been sold, and Werita had ample evidence that poverty ensued when Māori opened up their lands.

But the chief had converted to Christianity. Perhaps it was hard for a religious man to argue with a bishop's son—especially with the bishop in the room. After much persuasion, Werita reluctantly agreed to send Ihaia and three others to guide Leonard across the pass.

The chief placed an important caveat on his decision, from one honourable family to another: he would only allow the journey if Leonard promised to keep the route secret. Leonard agreed.

•

Walking ahead of me across the site of Kaiapoi Pā, Dad looked like a retired rock star, with his mirrored aviators and close-cropped white beard. A curious, enthusiastic and gentle man, a keen tramper and a jazz musician by trade, he'd just turned seventy-three. Twenty-five years after he'd first taken my brothers and me into the Alps, I was taking him across the mountains in Ihaia and Leonard's tracks.

We left the plateau and walked back down to the road, pausing to pour water into our palms and drift it over our heads, to clear the tapu of this sacred place. Again, I could smell the tang of smoke and scorched timber on the wind. The pā's southern embankment was right in front of us. The cornfields around were full of bones. We were standing where the palisades had burned.

A house stood across the road. I looked intently, and the charred sockets of the window frames stared back. The place had been torched.

I jumped the fence and padded through the wreckage. The exterior walls remained intact but the interior was gutted, the timber skeletal. Soft ash carpeted my footfalls. I felt repulsed by my fascination. History felt too close.

We climbed into the car and followed Ihaia and Leonard's party north.

•

West of Waipara, the foothills of the Southern Alps rose around us in waves of tawny tussock. As the steeper blue ranges loomed ahead I scanned for openings, feeling a familiar sweet anticipation, but also apprehension. It was Dad's first long-distance tramp in quite a while. 'How long?' I asked.

'About thirty years,' he replied cheerfully, as if that was a perfectly normal length of time between hikes. 'We were overdue getting back.' His tone grew subdued. 'You were just kids at the time. Your mother worried I was never coming home.'

At Weka Pass, limestone outcrops rose above the road. Ihaia Tainui and Leonard Harper rode through here on horseback, past caves covered in rock art that were used for shelter in ancient times. There were six in the party: Ihaia and three other Ngāi

Tahu, and Leonard and another European settler named Locke.

In a photo from around that time, Leonard Harper is clearly young, with a high domed forehead, a neat lick of hair and round, youthful cheeks, but his eyes hold the weary, ironic gaze of a much older man. A bushranger beard hides his mouth.

The only photo I can find of Ihaia, a hand-tinted portrait kept at Arahura marae, shows him when older. He looks prosperous and astute, with a small, neat moustache, glossy hair and the same wide cheekbones as his father, Werita. Ihaia is Māori for Isaiah, the Old Testament prophet who thundered: 'Through the wrath of the Lord of Hosts is the land darkened, and the people shall be as the fuel of the fire.'

Leonard was heading into the mountains for the first time. Ihaia had been raised on the West Coast side, and had already crossed the Alps at least twice. (In 1863 he told the Pākehā gold-miner William Smart that he'd been brought through the mountains to safety as a refugee from Kaiapoi Pā.)

Past Jollie Brook, where the aquamarine Hurunui flows from the foothills through a deep gorge, and Ngāi Tahu left vine ladders in place to navigate the cliffs, Dad and I stopped at Lake Taylor for the night. Modest family cars and big tents packed the campsite. Kids whisked round on bikes beside the silver-black expanse of the lake. For centuries travellers on alpine crossings stopped here and at nearby Hokakura (Lake Sumner) to stock up on tuna (eels) and waterfowl. As we prepared dinner, modernity faded with the sun, leaving faint light in the west and the glow of fires, and the timeless murmur of families together at the end of the day.

Before dark we broke out the maps, and Dad pointed out the silhouetted landmarks. The range at our back was Ōronoko, named for its resemblance to a canoe. There were the Brothers, and the Sisters. Since we were kids he'd always taken the time to teach us the names of the mountains we passed. In Māori that process is sometimes called kanohi-whenua (literally, face to face with the land). Kaumātua Rick Pitama from Rāpaki once told me that when he was a kid, his uncles took him up the volcanic peak known as Te Poho-o-Tamatea behind their home.

'They'd point out the different mountains and hills, and tell us the names and the stories. There was a rock up the top. They said, "Lift that up." They'd hidden money under there to keep us coming back. They said, "Any time you kids want an ice cream, you come up here and there'll be money under that rock."'

As a child, Ihaia would have been taught the landmarks along this route by his parents and relations. Twenty years later, I can imagine him sat across a campfire from Leonard Harper, pointing out the same features, bringing a newcomer face to face with his home.

•

Day dawned utterly still across a clear, pale sky. Lake Taylor lay in a perfect mirrored sheet, surrounded by green hills shaped by a long-extinct glacier's retreat. We divvied up the gear.

'Here, let me take the tent and the cooking gear,' I said. 'And the fresh food.'

'Well—' Dad said.

'I'm used to carrying mountaineering gear. A bit of extra cheese won't hurt.'

'Okay.' He passed me the food bag with a good-natured shrug, but I could see that this new dynamic was as strange to him as it was to me.

We loaded our packs and walked quietly out of the sleeping campsite. Ihaia and Leonard's party followed the traditional route north-west up the valley to Hokakura, Lake Sumner, another major mahika kai. They loaded their swags into the canoes that Ngāi Tahu kept at the lake, and pulled them around the edge on horseback. Dad had visited Hokakura plenty of times, so we were going via Lake Mason instead—a detour of a few hours to the west.

Once the climbing began over the scrubby Ōronoko Range my shoulders began to ache. It was only a five-day trip, so we'd gone gourmet, with fresh meat, fruit and vegetables, and a block of cheese nearly the size of my head. Collectively it weighed quite a bit more than ice axes and a rope. The sun hit us and I began to sweat. I'd imagined exploring sublime landscapes for traces of ancient history, and here we were plodding up a steep, boring farm road. Dad seemed unfazed, climbing ahead of me with the slightly stooped gait that had once belonged to his mother, and one day would belong to me. Every time I looked up, I saw his red Alp Sports pack jaunting along in front.

I'd trotted after that pack on my first overnight trip, up the Waimakariri River to the old Anti Crow Hut. I remember following it through golden head-high grass, chattering and fossicking as I went. We were small, and the mountains made us tiny. My older brother Ben and I carried our school bags with just a sleeping bag inside. Dad cheerfully lugged everything else, including our younger brother Tim at times.

I pictured the Ngāi Tahu children being carried through here, fleeing from Kaiapoi. Perhaps this was while the settlement was still under siege; perhaps after their home had burned and many of their kin been killed. Fleeing from an earlier Ngāti Toa attack on Ōmihi, up the coast to the north, a woman named Ema Turumeke gave a chilling eye-witness account of being stalked by Te Rauparaha's warriors: at intervals her pursuers sat down and pretended to weep, calling out that they too had escaped the slaughter and needed help. If Ihaia's party was tracked into the Alps, they would lose the secret of the greenstone route and expose their West Coast kin to attack. If they were overtaken, they'd lose their children. I doubt they begrudged the weight on their backs. I swallowed my grumbling and kept on after Dad.

The day grew blindingly bright and breezy and shimmered with flies. Cattle followed us in a curious scrum. We came down onto baked river terraces beside the Hurunui's South Branch, then turned north through scrappy high country farmland, ready to swim after a beating from the sun. At Lake Mason the breeze whipped the open water into whitecaps. We stripped off beneath giant red beech trees, and I waded out, my legs sinking into peat, then launched and swam. I'd fallen in love with swimming in the mountains aged twelve, when Dad convinced me to take a heart-stopping plunge in a snowmelt tarn outside Barker Hut, in Arthur's Pass National Park.

I floated and turned to look back. Dad stood in the shallows with his back to me. His pale shanks, so like my own, rose like a wading bird from the water. He was strong—a month earlier we'd slogged up a vertical kilometre of loose shingle to reach the low peak of Mt Manakau in the Seaward Kaikouras. But when he bent to scoop water over himself, in that simple action I saw the weathered back of an old man, made vulnerable by sun and time. I floated there in the grip of a fierce protective love, made all the more acute by the knowledge that one day we would lose each other.

In the afternoon's bronze light we followed sheep tracks through acres of waving grass. On the ridge separating us from the main Hurunui valley we saw the silver river coiling out of the west. Grass flats spread in the sun like a golden road. There were no gorges or real bluffs. Even the forested ranges on either side stood back to let in the light. It was obvious why Ngāi Tahu families favoured this route.

To reach the valley floor we ignored a wandering farm track for a more direct descent, bush-bashing through steep mānuka scrub. The crushed foliage released an aroma of spiced honey, but the branches were tight as sprung steel. We laughed and swore and backtracked, then tried another line further east. The ground grew steep and loose underfoot. We were both in running shoes, our boots packed away for more serious terrain. Dad slipped and fell. My heart caught.

I rushed down to where he lay on the stones. He seemed unhurt, but that ferocious protective feeling was back in my chest, shot through with guilt. I'd brought him here. It'd been a long time since he'd carried a heavy pack. His safety was my responsibility. I thought: this must be how parents feel about their kids.

It was a relief to reach the bottom and pitch camp for the night beside a locked musterer's hut. The sign above the door read Shiver-Inn. We were both sun-scoured and wind-worn. I cooked bolognaise while Dad played the kōauau (bone flute). Though he's Pākehā, in recent decades he has devoted himself to traditional Māori music under the guidance of master musician Richard Nunns. As he played, shadows slowly filled the valley.

The tune, 'Mā wai rā', is said to have been written by a man who couldn't make his best friend's taki (funeral). The music carried, high, haunting and calm.

.

Come morning the moon still hung above the eastern horizon. The sky was a powdery haze, and the one hill on the far ridge with a European name—Niggerhead, until recently—seemed to float in an azure void. After breakfast we found the main Hurunui Saddle track. Dad was going slowly.

'Are you okay?' I asked.

'Just a bit weary,' he said. 'First tramp in a long time.'

I wasn't in great shape myself, with my guts sore from the water at the Shiver-Inn, but I took more of his meal bags to lighten his load.

Away in the distance, hazy dots grew into walkers coming our way. It was a long weekend, and the track was busy with teenage adventurers, through-hikers on the epic four-month Te Araroa Trail, and a young couple trailing three reluctant kids. Each time we reached a new group, we stopped to share news of the trail.

When Ihaia and Leonard's party rode up this valley, they might have met any number of travellers. In the 1850s that included West Coast Māori heading to Christchurch to see about land sales, families bound for baptism in Nelson or to visit Kaiapoi relations, or east coast parties returning with pounamu. The route's historical importance would have been at the forefront of Ihaia's mind. His grandfather had participated in the famed Ngāi Tahu war party that crossed Nōti Hurunui to defeat Raureka's people and ultimately settle the West Coast.

By contrast, Europeans had first come up the Hurunui two

months before Ihaia and Leonard set out. A newspaper account mentions the Māori route, and the rope ladders left in place at Māori Gully to navigate the gorge. Yet when Edward Dobson's party arrived in the upper reaches of the valley, 'the headwaters of the Hurunui were reached for the first time.' 'Firsts' always have a mythical and a political dimension. Where we choose to locate them says more about the present than about the past.

•

Past Hurunui Hut, Dad and I walked single file up the valley into a pummelling nor'-wester. We went slowly but steadily. I was grateful when the track led us into mossy beech forest along the valley's southern slope. The ground softened to leaf litter and a golden scattered light. In the gullies we hopped across side streams, or stooped in the gloom to drink from cupped hands. There was no gold in these streams, but on the West Coast, Māori travellers passed it in the rivers all the time. The mineral had no value in the Māori economy. But the second they perceived its allure to Europeans in the mid-nineteenth century, the game changed.

Ihaia Tainui introduced Leonard Harper to gold-bearing rivers, and it seems in turn Leonard introduced Ihaia to prospecting. Their party found several 'fine specimens' on the western side of the pass; later accounts suggest it was the Māori members who discovered the gold. A few months after their journey over the pass, Ihaia was already prospecting for himself. He'd grown up in pounamu country, so he'd been raised to search the rivers for precious things. Shifting the focus to gold was a profound change in cultural and economic terms, but practically was no shift at all.

Māori on the Coast took to prospecting in a major way. When a rush broke out in Nelson, to the north, Ihaia went to work among the Māori diggers, picking up gold and geological knowledge. On returning home he prospected around Kapitia Creek and the Hōhonu River. On 18 October 1862, he and fellow diggers Neri and Whītau struck gold of their own.

I imagine them up to their knees in the river Ihaia had known since childhood, passing the grainy gold from one calloused hand to the next with mounting excitement. The Canterbury Provincial Government had offered a thousand-pound reward for the discovery of a payable goldfield. Ihaia prepared to walk to Christchurch to claim the reward.

Before he left, a ship's captain named Dixon heard he was heading east, and gave him a package to deliver. It took Ihaia four days to cross the Hurunui Saddle and walk to Christchurch. He dropped off the package to a man named Captain Peter Oakes without a second thought; then, on the dot of ten o'clock the next morning, stepped into the Provincial Secretary's office. Ihaia handed over an introductory letter, and the gold.

The Superintendent was called. Officials pored over Ihaia's samples. Gold fever spread through the building. Other provinces were booming thanks to the discovery of gold. Perhaps Canterbury's time had come.

But at ten minutes past ten, Ihaia heard raised voices, and an enraged man barged into the room. It was Captain Peter Oakes, to whom Ihaia had delivered the package the previous night. The package contained another sample of gold and a letter from Dixon claiming the reward for himself.

Ihaia was astonished. He'd had no idea what had been inside. Oakes alleged fraud, accusing him of stealing from Dixon's package. The headlines named Dixon as the discoverer of gold. The

Lyttelton Times described Ihaia as turning white as a ghost when he realised he'd unwittingly carried the claim that trumped his own.

Shocking as it was to have his mana questioned, Ihaia was quickly vindicated. The seal on Dixon's package was untouched and the gold inside was clearly different. In the end, both claims were denied on technicalities. Ihaia returned empty-handed across the pass.

•

At the edge of the flats past Mackenzie Stream, the smell of sulphur drifted towards us on the wind. Dad and I followed it to where a hot spring ran down the hillside in steaming, mossy ropes. We scrambled up to a small pool nestled among ferny green tongues of blechnum and kiokio. I lowered myself into the water in a hot silty cloud. After days of carrying a heavy pack, the warm, floating sensation was bliss. I could imagine Ihaia having a soak here after the stress of being wrongfully accused of theft. I could also imagine he'd need to unwind when he learned the name of the pass ahead had been changed.

Instead of Nōti Hurunui, or any other name Ngāi Tahu might have used, from 1857 the saddle was officially Harper's Pass. Leonard Harper had promised Werita Tainui he would keep the route secret, but he published an account of his journey the moment he got back.

I hauled myself up out of the spring. The geothermal water was too hot in the blazing summer sun. I had to splash down to the river's edge and plunge into the icy freshwater to shock myself awake.

•

From Matagouri Flat we left the cattle plains and entered a head-high maze of matagouri scrub. The old growth was tough as barbed wire, and the new shoots were a soft green matrix of thorns that still razored through our clothes. I flinched every time we squeezed through a gap, and yet I loved the fact that the terrain was growing rougher with each kilometre we advanced. The bronze light, filtering through acres of this ancient, stubborn scrub, gave me the strange feeling of travelling back into deep time. There was no trace of modernity. We might have been in the year 1600 CE, or 1600 BCE.

The terrain around No. 3 Hut felt older and darker still. We stopped for the night. Drizzle hazed the valley upriver where it narrowed and steepened towards the pass. Distant ruru called their soft, sooty hoot—*koukou, koukou*. Teone Taare Tikao, the great early-twentieth-century Ngāi Tahu tohuka, said that in the old days, one owl calling through the night spoke of bad weather, two or more of storms.

When I woke in the night the sky had cleared. Moonlight sharpened the clearing around the hut, and the air was still but for the slapping hiss of an unseen waterfall. I stood beneath a lone beech tree posted like a sentry, with the mountains circling up on all sides. Was this landscape hostile or benign to the early travellers? We know they rarely walked at night because atua (spirits) were abroad. But in familiar mountains, and fearing pursuit?

Koukou, koukou, came the cry.

On their flight from Kaiapoi, did the refugees travel these hills by moonlight? I returned to my bunk and listened to my father's sleeping breath. Did they camp without fires and lie awake listening for footsteps? Hear that same waterfall, pouring away into the dark?

•

The little night owls knew rain was coming. At dawn the valley filled with mist, and by breakfast drizzle thickened the air. By the time we'd reached Cameron Stream, the rain set in hard. Flooded side streams dissolved the track into a wash of boulders. We crossed the small flats past Camerons Hut, brushing past sodden tussock grass hanging in shaggy manes, like a reddish cloak laid across the land. The Hurunui's full name is Huruhurunui, referencing a cloak of fur or feathers. Travellers wore raincapes woven from red tussock, and would have blended perfectly with the landscape round here. I paused among the undulating grass and watched as if to catch the bushes standing up, transforming into men, women and children. They gazed back down the valley then, certain they weren't being pursued, continued west.

As we gained height the valley closed in, and the surrounding peaks blurred to grey ghosts. The wide, slow Hurunui became an abrupt mountain stream. Ihaia Tainui and Leonard Harper's party left the horses here and shouldered their swags for the half-day scramble to the pass. Dad and I climbed through bands of tough subalpine speargrass, mountain flax and fern. The downpour intensified, and once we broke out into the upper valley the wind began to bite. Dad was moving slowly, and I realised he hadn't said much all day. He looked cold. We huddled in to confer beneath our hoods.

'How's it going?' I asked.

He shook his head, his face tense, rain dripping through his beard. 'Not so good. This old parka's useless. I'm soaked.'

We checked the map. Harper Pass Bivvy had to be close, and we could pause there and rest. Ahead of us, two teenagers emerged from the gloom, drenched from coming over the pass. The first Pāhehā guy looked miserable, scowling through the rain, and passed with barely a nod. The second, a handsome young Māori guy, was having a ball.

'How far to the biv?' Dad asked.

He cracked a massive grin and turned theatrically to his right. 'Ta-daaa!'

The orange emergency shelter was right behind us, tucked in among the ribbonwoods. It looked as simple and welcoming as a child's drawing of a house, with just two bunks, a tiny bench, and room for one person to stand at a time. We brewed tea and sat chatting with our heads ducked and the door open while the rain smashed down. The only view was up. Vertical gardens ascended into cloud. Within minutes the deluge grew harder still.

'Timed that well,' Dad said. He looked around the tiny hut, colour returning to his cheeks. 'I stayed in a place like this the first time I got taken into the West Coast bush.'

A family friend had taken him deerstalking in the hills behind Harihari, south of Hokitika, when he was eighteen. They hunted during the day and at night dossed down on bare earth inside a tiny aluminium shed. It rained torrentially for three days, but Dad loved every minute—that vivid feeling of being alive in the hills. He had introduced me to that feeling, in turn. I was pretty sure Ihaia had felt it too, given how much of his life he spent out here.

•

After Leonard Harper publicised the Hurunui route, initially the only Europeans to come this way were a handful of surveyors and prospectors. Small finds hadn't materialised into a viable goldfield. Explorers returned with 'a dismal narrative of gloomy skies, and incessant rain, of a country kept in perpetual solitude, incapable of occupation, niggardly of promise'. The newspapers were blunt: 'Mr Harper has discovered no country of value.'

Then, in midsummer 1864, two of Ihaia Tainui's contemporaries, Haimona Tuakau and Iwikau Te Aika, found a two-tonne boulder of pounamu in the Hōhonu River, a tributary of the Taramakau. Finding greenstone wasn't news in the colonial press, but when the two men prised the slab from the riverbed what they found underneath made headlines.

It must have been a beautiful moment: the men's excited breath, the icy silk of the Hōhonu dragging at their legs, the lustre of greenstone, and when the muddied waters cleared, a rich scatter of gold underneath. Their find finally sparked a full-scale rush to the West Coast.

For colonial society on the east coast, until now the Alps had been a jagged line behind which the sun set. Some appreciated their beauty, but Leonard's brother Henry W. Harper called them an 'impassable barrier' to what Leonard described as an 'uninhabitable' place. If those peaks symbolised one thing, it was the hostility of the new land.

Now, thousands of colonists headed straight for them. Here was settler society's first mass encounter with Kā Tiritiri-o-te-moana, the Southern Alps. The empty, rainswept riverbed we could see outside the biv door turned into a mess of people and packhorses and flocks of sheep being driven across the snowy pass. The swamps were so churned by hooves that horses sank to their nostrils and drowned. Butchers' tents sprang up along the river flats like a gruesome travelling circus, full of greening mutton scribbled with flies. It rained and it rained. The rats were so fierce that travellers found toothmarks in the lead shot.

Provincial Geologist Julius von Haast crossed this pass at the height of the rush, in 1865. He met people returning from the West Coast 'covered with rags, and whose hollow features showed only too plainly traces of the unaccustomed privations they had endured'. Many crossed expecting to buy food on the Coast, only to find there was nothing to buy, and no one to buy it from. Others failed to respect the rivers and drowned.

Ngāi Tahu, and those with back-country experience, did better, and soon enough boomtowns sprang up to service the diggings. Demand for land spiked. Three years earlier Ihaia's elders had sold most of the West Coast to the Crown, and now they were pressured to give up more of what little they'd retained. This was precisely what Ihaia's father, Werita Tainui, must have feared when he resisted showing Leonard Harper the route.

·

Once the rain subsided we emptied Dad's old red pack and loaded most of the remaining contents into mine. I shouldered the new load and we set off on the winding climb towards the pass. Near the top visibility dropped to twenty metres. The morning swirled around us, cold and windy and wet. I realised we were following the track cut for the diggers in the 1860s, which bypassed the actual pass. I looked down on the short swampy saddle where earlier travellers had crossed from east to west.

For Ngāi Tahu residing on Te Tai o Poutini (the West Coast), the Alps acted as a fortress. Later, in colonial times, that same difficulty of access helped keep the greenstone rivers in Ngāi

Tahu hands. Even now the mountains offer protection. A Māori-language teacher once told me that she and her students had been in Fiordland, in the south-west of the island, when an earthquake hit. The kids were petrified: they were still recovering from the quakes that had devastated their hometown, Christchurch. Their teacher pointed to the snow-capped wall of the Southern Alps.

'You see those mountains?' she said. 'Those mountains are your ancestors. They're standing strong between you and the fault line, and they're protecting you from earthquakes. You're safe here.'

'They calmed down just like that,' she told me. 'You should have seen their faces. It was totally real for them.'

The protection of the mountains was real for the children brought across from Kaiapoi, when their families put the peaks between them and Te Rauparaha's men. But a quarter of a century later, when Ihaia stood at the pass with Leonard Harper, how did he feel, guiding a stranger through this break in their fortress walls, against his father's better judgement? As if he was giving up some ancient protection? Or sharing knowledge as a way of building relationships with the newcomers? Perhaps both.

The temptation to drop down to the pass and stand where Ihaia had was strong. But Dad was walking on ahead in silence, and I knew he was hurting. The southerly wind whipped rain into our faces. The mountains offered no protection today.

PART II: NŌTI HURUNUI (HARPER PASS), CANTERBURY ALPS. SUMMER.

Before we descended, the cloud began to lift, and we could see the Taramakau River curl away beneath us, swinging north at a range of hills built from heaped-up mist. Cloud scarved the ridges, and heavy West Coast bush spilled into the river below. Seen from above, before you plunged in, the land offered hope.

We plunged, down a steep spur that dropped us to the valley floor through one long, twisting archway beneath the trees. After the monotonous cattle flats of the east, the bush was a magnificent shock of ferns, creeper and tall hardwoods. Raindrops hung orbs of light in the spiders' webs. I spared a thought for the hundreds of parties that had come up this slope with pounamu boulders on their backs. Down we went and up they came, muscles straining, breathing hard.

Out in the stream bed the track disappeared and we were free to make our own way down, wading here and there up to our knees. I was content: I'd take this over cattle flats any day. But Dad had strained his Achilles on the descent. It pained me to watch him limping over the loose boulders. He'd keep going indefinitely unless I intervened.

'How about a lunch stop?' I said.

'No, I'm okay,' Dad replied, as predicted.

'No, seriously. You need to rest your leg.'

Reluctantly, he put down his pack.

Near the traditional camping place known as Whakamoemoe, I made elaborate sandwiches beneath a grey robin's bobbing gaze. Afterwards I took all of Dad's remaining spare weight, and we meandered west.

In the premature dusk that comes to steep-sided valleys, we sloshed up the steps of Locke Stream Hut with the river in our boots. The long, low red-tin building looked like a remnant of the gold rush. The hand-adzed floorboards felt exquisite under bare feet. We ate pad thai and enjoyed quiet conversation by the fire, and resolved to go extra slow the next day.

For Ihaia Tainui and Leonard Harper the journey down the Taramakau was arduous. Days of heavy rain brought the river and side creeks into high flood, forcing the men into long and brutal detours to find safe crossing points. Their food supplies ran out, so Ihaia and his friends went back to their usual practice of catching birds. Days passed waiting out storms under canvas. I wondered if Ihaia and Leonard had talked much over the drumming rain. Beyond their immediate cultural differences, they had plenty in common; in fact, their later lives would parallel each other's in uncanny ways. First and foremost, they'd both been groomed for leadership, and would go on to take responsibility for the land they'd explored as young men.

After his goldmining days, Ihaia became secretary of the Rūnaka (Māori council) at Arahura, and a trustee for the Māori reserves—the small parcels of land that Ngāi Tahu retained on the Coast after the sale. Though the tribe had wanted to keep two hundred thousand acres, they ended up with only ten thousand, and the gold rush eroded even this. Māori land was always preferred for new roads and railways, because it could be taken with little or no compensation. More than half of the remaining reserves were put under government administration, then leased to settlers in perpetuity. Much of the rental money never reached the owners.

Fighting for what land remained took up more and more of Ihaia's life. His correspondence includes magnificent, biblical letters demanding justice. Like so many of Ngāi Tahu's leaders, year after year he petitioned the government, and year after year they rejected his case. In 1877 the committee charged with hearing such petitions simply sent their rejection letter from the previous year. Perhaps that insult spurred Ihaia's decision to enter politics himself. In 1879 he was elected to the House of Representatives, where he learned first-hand how settler society dealt with Māori land.

When European settlement had begun in earnest, from 1840 onwards, the pressure on Māori to give up their land grew apace. In the North Island powerful tribes and alliances began to resist further encroachment, until London sent imperial troops to put down resistance and clear them from their lands. From the early 1860s, the British Empire was engaged in full-scale wars against Māori in the North Island, first in Taranaki, then in the Waikato and beyond.

In parliament Ihaia sat on a committee investigating the legality of land dealings during these wars. Tribes who had resisted encroachment were deemed in rebellion and had their lands confiscated, while settlers who fought against Māori received a share of the confiscated ground. He also advocated for the followers of the prophet Te Whiti, who had been imprisoned indefinitely without trial in southern jails. Ihaia resigned from parliament the following year to make way for his fellow Ngāi Tahu leader

H. K. Taiaroa. He continued to petition the government every year until his untimely death.

Leonard Harper's rise to prominence and responsibility was just as swift. Returning from his explorations, he swapped his swag for a lawyer's wig. By the late 1860s he was representing large runholders in the Supreme Court. With his family's impeccable connections, his Christchurch-based law firm became the conduit for incoming capital: as the *Poverty Bay Herald* put it, 'there is a large class at Home to whom New Zealand means Canterbury, and Canterbury [means] Harper and Co.' Funds were loaned to the settler elite to buy significant property across the South Island. Vast estates passed through the firm's books or were held in trust for absentee landowners.

Leonard became a runholder himself. His mansion Ilam ('the hills') was once the largest private residence in New Zealand. He too ended up in parliament, serving from 1876 to 1877 and 1884 to 1887.

The two young men who set out from Kaiapoi in 1857 both made the transition from exploring the land to holding it in trust for others. Each was a pou (a pillar) in their respective houses. Each carried a lot of weight.

·

Dad and I had worked hard to eat all the luxury food, so when I shouldered my pack the following morning, I wasn't carrying much weight at all. And while I wanted to take some responsibility for the land I loved by writing about it, right now my only responsibility was to ensure Dad got safely home.

We moved slowly, taking breaks and napping more than we walked. When it came time to cross the main branch of the

Taramakau, Dad and I linked arms and dropped into the river, angling towards the far bank. Deep blue light shimmered off the eddies, and the chill water climbed to our thighs. We hit the main channel and the current pulled hard, carrying each raised boot in exaggerated strides. My walking pole shivered against the flow. I gripped Dad's bony shoulder and he gripped mine, and we forged on to reach the bank.

Towards late afternoon along the northern edge of the Taramakau, we found the river had devoured its banks, and with them the track. We waded along in the river instead, clinging to sapling tōtara trees for balance, then headed back to dry land where the bush thinned. An arcade of tree ferns cast a filigree of light across our faces and hands. In one section the only way through the tangle was balancing along the top of an enormous fallen red beech.

When we reached Kiwi Hut on an old moraine terrace, we found it was a gloomy shed surrounded by chainsawed stumps. Dad and I looked at each other.

'Shall we camp out?' I said.

'Let's.'

The grassy clearing at the foot of the terrace was a glorious natural campsite. We flopped down on our backs to test the softness of the ground. The blue sky above was a river of thistledown drifting past. Nā rere kā puāwai, the saying goes: thistledown is flying—meaning that news from elsewhere is on its way.

At dusk I brushed my teeth and slipped into a fuchsia grove to spit. I found myself in a junkyard of scattered deer ribs and skulls.

'Look at this,' I called.

'They hang them up from the trees,' Dad said, looking over my shoulder. 'Gut them, take the back legs and leave the rest.'

•

In 1891 Leonard Harper left New Zealand for good. Two years later the truth came out: his law firm was bankrupt, and more than two hundred thousand pounds was missing. Scandal ripped through the upper echelons of colonial society. The firm had been bankrupt since the mid-1880s. The Christchurch *Press* raged: 'Had they...heeded their difficulties manfully and declared their insolvency tens of thousands of pounds would have been saved from the whirlpool...it is impossible to acquit Messrs Harper and Co. of culpable weakness and moral cowardice.'

By that time, Leonard Harper was long gone. In 1894 Scotland Yard found him living in the holiday destination of Jersey, in the Channel Islands. He was arrested on charges of stealing his clients' money and deported to New Zealand to face trial. Harper insisted it was pointless charging him, because the money was long gone.

In a series of trials that polarised the public along class lines, witnesses outlined an impenetrable tangle of dishonest paperwork that hid underlying financial ruin. The first trial ended with a not-guilty verdict on a technical point. An epic retrial was abandoned with a hung jury. The third and final trial, held in Wellington to escape local bias, and before a special jury of businessmen, delivered not-guilty verdicts on the first two counts, and the Crown abandoned the rest. A low-ranking accountant got two years' hard labour on a minor charge. Leonard Harper denied all wrong-doing and returned to England. He'd lost hundreds of thousands of pounds of his clients' money. He made no apology.

Trying to wrap my head around the case, I'd waded through pages of nineteenth-century legalese with a growing sense of disquiet. It was the total abstraction of Leonard Harper's world:

mortgage documents, loan schemes, titles and deeds. Aged twenty, descending the Taramakau with Ihaia, he'd given up his boots for pāraerae (flax sandals), letting New Zealand's rivers flow between his toes. By the time he left for England, for him New Zealand had become the manipulation of numbers in ledger books. The business collapsed and, in his mind, that was the end of it. But the land remained.

·

I woke to find our tent becalmed in a sea of ground mist. We'd slept for ten hours. I unzipped the tent, energised and ready to move. By the time the coffee had brewed, the fierce midsummer sun showed itself at the shoulder of the Main Divide, and we set off into another day of strange purity. No wind, no clouds. Rangi Taipō and the blue hills of the Bald Range shimmered in the early heat, flat as paper cut-outs. A seagull circled overhead and I sensed the valley opening out, the Taramakau sweeping west towards the ocean.

We found a good ford and waded across to the south bank, then paused at the confluence with the Ōtehake River. With his sore Achilles, Dad was going to continue along the flats. I'd race south on my own, up to the Ōtehake hot springs, over the saddle to the traditional camping spot at Kāurupātaka (Lake Kaurapataka), then back out to the Ōtira River, where we'd meet that evening. We hugged and went our separate ways. I cinched my boots tight and splashed off up the Ōtehake. I'd have to move fast.

At the entrance to the Ōtehake Gorge the river deepened to a forceful aquamarine. I waded into the flow. The surface was placid, but the current beneath pushed against my thighs, then my belly, then my chest. The water froze my breath. I crossed armpit-deep pools from the safety of one gravel beach to the next.

Past the gorge, in an empty flood channel of the Ōtehake, I sank into a steaming silver pool. Water from the tectonic plates, I thought; boiled by the grind of continents. I lay back and gazed up at the bony spires above Whāiti Stream. It was one of my favourite places on the West Coast: a few hours from the highway, the perfect combination of rugged, remote and luxurious. When I got too hot, I crept barefoot to the river and whooped and splashed into the snowmelt, then returned, shivering, to the pool. My thoughts escaped in strings of bubbles like pearls.

•

On the way back, I scaled a small waterfall onto the disused flood track above the gorge, then clambered over greasy rocks and fallen trees with the river blasting away below. The climb wasn't normally so tough, but I didn't usually do it straight after an hour in the hot springs. My legs felt leaden. Like generations of coast-to-coast travellers, I paused at Kāurupātaka to rest, then sped on through a cathedral forest of ancient red beech trees. Shafts of sunlight fell between the dark pillars of the trees. Where Pfeifer Creek rejoined the Taramakau, the valley before me looked grim. The flats had burned recently. I followed an old farm track through twisted black skeletons of gorse. The western horizon glowed white with heat.

At the appointed hour I reached the grey shingle expanse of the Ōtira riverbed. No sign of Dad. I couldn't see the Ōtira but it was a serious river which turned tramping parties back all the time. I didn't think Dad would have crossed on his own with an injured leg. I dropped my pack and searched the head-high gorse, hoping to catch a glimpse of his red pack. I shouted his name. Through

my binoculars all I could see on the far side was the farmhouse at
Aitken, and a few cars sweeping down the highway towards the sea.

•

Once Ihaia and Leonard's party crossed the Ōtira, they spent a day
cutting and binding rushes to construct a mōkihi, the unsinkable
white-water rafts Ngāi Tahu used to descend the South Island's
rivers. Unlike canoes, mōkihi float in rather than on the water.
From here down, the Taramakau becomes too deep to cross on
foot, and the banks become cliffs. Early European explorers lost
ruinous weeks trying to negotiate these West Coast gorges on
foot, but in a mōkihi, the coast was only hours away.

With the raft ready, Ihaia's party camped in the dry riverbed
beside the main channel. It rained hard in the night; by dawn,
their campsite was a small island surrounded by a torrent carrying
uprooted trees. The Taramakau is frightening in that state. Leonard wanted to launch immediately; Ihaia and his friends protested
that it would be a desperate act. Rivers went down just as fast as
they came up, and they only had to wait. Leonard insisted. The
flood carried them south.

•

In later life Ihaia, like Leonard, stumbled under the weight of
his burden. Most of what I knew was gleaned from newspaper
articles, and conversation with James Russell and other kaumātua
at Arahura. But, strangely, I'd also found an account written by
Leonard Harper's brother, Henry Harper junior.

Henry Harper served as Anglican minister in Hokitika. Ihaia
was the chief Anglican lay reader at nearby Arahura, so the two
men would have known each other well. In a letter dated 10 July
1868, Harper wrote of receiving a deputation from Arahura, led

by 'their Chief, Ihaia Tainui a man of recognised birth, and also of
personal influence...a specially fine specimen of a Māori'.

Ihaia and his people had come to Henry Harper on a matter
of honour. During a recent visit by family from Kaiapoi, Ihaia had
found three of their horses among his oats. In his anger he chased
them out and flung his tomahawk after them, hamstringing one.
The animal had to be destroyed. At a tribal court Ihaia pleaded
guilty and was fined the value of the horse.

When Henry Harper asked if that was the end of the matter,
Ihaia replied:

> Do you think so? It is this: I am the Chief of my tribe;
> I pride myself on my blood and birth; I am the native
> representative in Parliament...Do you think it is enough
> that I have paid the legal fine...? I have disgraced myself
> in the eyes of my people; it is not a question of so much
> money; I have given way to anger, and shown myself
> unworthy of my position. What am I to do?

Henry, impressed by Ihaia's character, wrote out a confession for
him to read in church: 'This Rangatira, Chief of his tribe...stood
before his tribe and made confession of his fault with the simple
sincerity of a true Christian...these are the sort of men that we,
who pride ourselves on the superiority of our race, may well stand
before, cap in hand.'

When I read that, a shiver ran through me. The letter appeared
to have actually been written much later, after Leonard Harper's
disgrace. I couldn't help thinking that Henry was writing with his
own brother in mind, for refusing to show remorse or take responsibility for what he'd done.

And what's more, while Ihaia hamstringing a horse was a good story, instinct told me that it wasn't true. The dates are wrong. And the letter ends with a feast and celebration, with Ihaia restored to his rightful place. It sounded like a benign Victorian parable masking a darker truth.

This is what really took place. On a Sunday night in October 1885, having devoted his life to the exhausting fight to protect Poutini Ngāi Tahu's land and reserves, Ihaia Tainui called a meeting of his people at Arahura. He stood before them and confessed that he had broken the law.

He'd been given money by a man named Hungerford, who wanted to quarry stone on tribal land at Māwhera. Ihaia hadn't apportioned the money among the tribe, but kept it for himself. Earlier that day he'd seen Hungerford in a coach, and felt certain he was about to be exposed.

When the meeting ended and everyone headed for bed, Ihaia was in a highly distressed state. He begged his friends to take care of his family should anything happened to him.

In those days, there wasn't a traditional meeting house at Arahura. Ihaia's descendant James Russell later told me that public meetings were held in Toker's Hall, a building attached to the local hotel. Although the hall had no carved pou representing the ancestors as a meeting house did, it is still significant that it's where the tribe gathered.

They found Ihaia Tainui inside the hall the following morning. He had left a note. A translation read: 'Do not blame anybody for my death. I hanged myself; this is punishment for my misdeeds in dealing wrongfully with land and appropriating the money. I have not slept till 5 o'clock this morning.'

He had tied a handkerchief over his eyes. The amount he'd been given was twenty pounds.

'He was asked to account for the money,' James Russell told me, 'and he was three pennies short.'

•

I reached the Ōtira River feeling worried. But the last two days had been free of rain and the Ōtira was at normal flow. I had to assume Dad made the crossing alone.

I sloshed my way through each of the river's braids and clambered up the steep far bank, watching for a flash of red pack. Returning from another Ōtehake trip, at exactly this spot I'd once come across the wizened old farmer who owned the run. He'd fallen down the bank and couldn't get up, but lay there in his tiny shorts and gumboots, gazing into the middle distance, pretending he was having a rest. He looked like he would rather die than admit that he was too old to be out burning gorse on his own. It took ages before he agreed to a hand up.

I put the thought aside. Dad would be fine.

When I crossed farmland to reach the small car park beside the highway, I found Dad reclining in the shade of a giant flax bush, leaning back on his elbows, bare feet stretched in front of him. He seemed bored from waiting, but pleased.

'We made it,' I said. 'From the east coast to the west.'

He looked up with a smile, blue eyes tired but warm. 'Not bad for seventy-three.'

I shed my pack and flopped down beside him. He sat in comfortable silence looking back up the valley while I rabbited on about hot pools, and as I felt the sweat cooling in the small of my back I wished that the route hadn't ended, that we could put our packs back on and keep going together. Five days in the hills with your father is a precious thing.

·

Half an hour later, Dad's sister picked us up. Hilary is a bright-eyed, energetic historian, whose book about Henry Whitcombe and Jakob Lauper's ill-fated alpine crossing in 1863 had sparked my engagement with Pākehā mountain history.

We flowed west by car rather than raft, winding with the river above its southern bank, past the flats at Inchbonnie, the old pā site at the mouth of the Hopeakoa (Taipō) river, the Māori reserves along the Taramakau once under Ihaia's care. Below us in the gorge, Ihaia and Leonard had spent three silent hours drifting with the current beneath cliffs dripping with kareao and tātarā-moa vines, until they reached the small village of Taramakau at the coast.

As we drew near, I switched on my phone and called Leigh. Since I'd returned from Nōti Raureka, we'd Facebook-stalked each other and swapped a few texts.

'I'm back on the Coast,' I said.

She sounded excited. 'Where are you?'

'Heading for the mouth of the Taramakau, then going to find a campground. What about you?'

'*At* the mouth of the Taramakau.'

'Seriously?'

'I'm looking at it out the window right now. I'm housesitting for Dad, and his place overlooks the lagoon. Come for dinner if you like. There's a spare room too, if you want to stay.'

'I'd love to. Uh...is there room for my dad? And my aunt?'

·

After dinner, Dad, Hilary and I gathered at the river mouth near where the Taramakau village once stood. Across the river the sand stretched north to the slate-blue Paparoa ranges, a jumble of sharp ridges, some sun-struck, some silhouetted, all dissolving west into sea mist. Up that way was Rūnanga, where, after the final battle against Kāti Wairaki, it was decided that Ihaia's grandfather Tuhuru and his people would stay to occupy the Coast. To the south, white-gold light caught the tips of Ihaia's oldest ancestors, the Alps.

The inquest after his death made it clear that Ihaia had done no wrong: 'the deceased was under a misconception, thinking that the slight irregularity that he had committed was a grave breach of the criminal law.' But if there was ever absolution, I felt it was in the calm vigil of the peaks.

For Ihaia and Leonard, stepping from their mōkihi onto this beach meant very different things. Here was the outer limit of civilisation for Leonard Harper. The rest of his life was a retreat from this apparently wild place. After being taken south along the coast by Ihaia's uncle, the chief Tarapuhi, he went back over the pass to the east coast, back to Christchurch, and ultimately kept going, all the way back to England by ship. He died in the Channel Islands in 1915.

For Ihaia, this river mouth was where he would have arrived to safety from Kaiapoi, as a baby. He was a couple of hours' walk from where he was raised, at Māwhera, and half a day from the Hōhonu, where in a few years he would be prospecting. A few hours south was Arahura, where he would be chief, and would be buried, and where, today, his carved figure holds up the meeting-house roof. Ihaia Tainui was home.

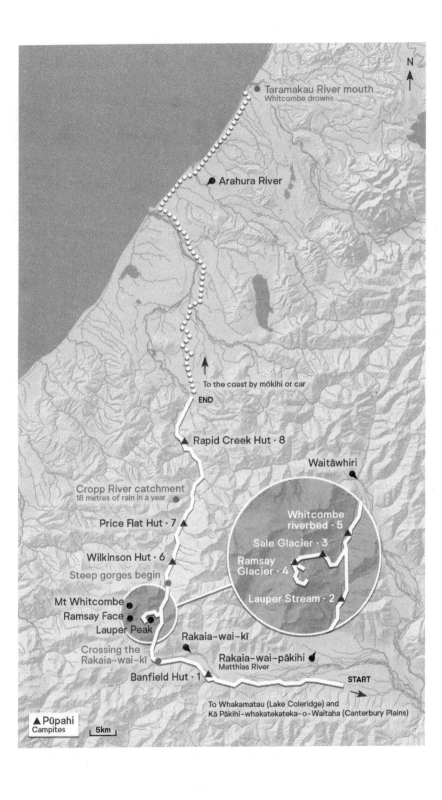

N

Taramakau River mouth
Whitcombe drowns

Arahura River

To the coast by mōkihi or car
END

Rapid Creek Hut · 8

Waitāwhiri

Cropp River catchment
18 metres of rain in a year

Whitcombe
riverbed · 5

Price Flat Hut · 7

Sale Glacier · 3

Wilkinson Hut · 6

Ramsay
Glacier · 4

Steep gorges begin

Lauper Stream · 2

Mt Whitcombe
Ramsay Face
Lauper Peak

Rakaia-wai-kī

Crossing the
Rakaia-wai-kī

Rakaia-wai-pākihi
Matthias River

Banfield Hut · 1

START

To Whakamatau (Lake Coleridge) and
Kā Pākihi-whakatekateka-o-Waitaha (Canterbury Plains)

▲ Pūpahi
Campites

5km

3

Rurumātaikau
(Whitcombe Pass)

Jon and I were two tiny travellers moving up the wide shingle
valley of the Rakaia-wai-kī (Rakaia River South Branch). We
were just west of where Raureka first came out of the hills. Snow-
dusted blades of rock rose above Jagged Stream, with the icefalls of
the Butler Range beyond. Each time I looked up from my boots,
shape-shifting cloud had revealed new vistas and hid the old. I
rested on my walking poles and watched, as if to catch the peaks
moving.

After a couple of easy lowland walks, I felt the sweet, nervy
anticipation of heading into the higher Alps with a pack full of
mountaineering gear. As always, it was like carrying a sack of

concrete covered in knives, but that weight was freedom. We could explore wherever we chose between here and the West Coast.

Below Prospect Hill we crossed one small braid of the Rakaia-wai-kī. The milky-blue water bore down hard and cold against our calves. With skin tingling, we wandered on across the millions of boulders below Washbourne Creek. The landscape felt empty.

'Mister Whit!' Jon said. 'I thought we booked the whole valley!'

Beneath his leather stockman's hat, Jon's tanned face wore an exaggerated frown. A botanist, surveyor and mountaineer whose acerbic humour masked the quiet, thoughtful man underneath, Jon was pointing upriver with his walking pole. I thought I could make out faint movement in the distance.

'Damn them, Lauper,' I said. 'I thought we were here first.'

'Me too, Mister Whit. Shall I go tell them to piss off?'

Each branch of the Rakaia held a Ngāi Tahu story and route across the Alps. The next major valley west from where Raureka descended was Ōtūtekawa (Mathias Pass), recalling the chief Tūtekawa, who played a dramatic role in Ngāi Tahu's settlement of Te Waipounamu. Today, our destination was Rurumātaikau (Whitcombe Pass), easily the wildest of the three Rakaia routes. But beyond a few scattered nineteenth-century references, a key discovery in a cave, and a rumour that it was accidentally used by Tūtekawa's son Te Rakitāmau, little is known about it.

The geography tells a story, though. Just before the Ramsay Glacier, you sight an obvious low gap in the Main Divide, at the head of Lauper Stream. Travel is easy. You ascend Lauper Stream to the airy saddle at the pass. From there the way down looks straightforward. You commit.

But instead of exiting west to the Tasman Sea, the valley runs north, parallel to the Main Divide like a giant gutter, and shuts in beneath cliffs and vicious scrub. The only way down is in the Whitcombe River, over thirty relentless kilometres of boulders, waterfalls and gorges, before the valley opens out and the swamps begin. Travel is torturously slow, and the rivers rise fast. The Cropp River, which holds the New Zealand rainfall record of eighteen metres in a year, is just one small tributary of the Whitcombe. (Melbourne's annual rainfall averages 65 centimetres.) Early Māori explorers and all subsequent travellers—likely expeditionary war parties and pounamu hunters—would have needed careful preparation and brilliant bush craft to survive.

In March 1863, a young British civil engineer named Henry Whitcombe led a government expedition up the Rakaia in search of a rumoured Māori pass. At the time, the Canterbury Provincial Government was desperate to find a pass suitable for a road to the West Coast goldfields, to prevent the gold from being whisked off to Melbourne by ship. On finding a suitable pass in the upper Rakaia, Whitcombe was to return and report. His orders were clear.

But Henry Whitcombe had ideas of his own. When they reached the upper Rakaia, Whitcombe sent his men home. With just one companion, a Swiss mercenary and goldminer named Jakob Lauper, he reached Rurumataikau and kept going, heading for the West Coast.

What happened next was an unmitigated disaster. At its conclusion, Whitcombe drowned at the mouth of the Taramakau.

Lauper survived, thanks to Poutini Ngāi Tahu and a European surveying party, but the experience broke him.

Earlier European explorers on the West Coast depended largely on Māori guides for survival. The guides knew the terrain; knew how to build shelter, how to hunt, fish and forage, and how to navigate local customs as well. In 1846, New Zealand Company Artist and Surveyor Charles Heaphy, journeying down the coastal pounamu route used by Kāti Wairaki, wrote that his guide Kehu

> appears to have an instinctive sense, beyond our com-
> prehension, which enables him to find his way through
> the forest when neither sun nor distant object is visible,
> amidst gullies, brakes, and ravines in confused disorder...
> until at length he points out to you the notch in some
> tree or the foot-print in moss, which assures you that he
> has fallen upon a track, although one [with] which
> he had not previously been acquainted.

Whitcombe's superiors understood the importance of such guides. The expedition budget explicitly included funds for two Māori members of the party. Yet for some reason Whitcombe chose to take none.

•

Over the next ten days, Jon and I planned to retrace Whitcombe and Lauper's footsteps, but to do so through the eyes of the Māori guides who should have accompanied them. Armed with food-gathering and bush-craft accounts from elders in the early twentieth century, plus Jon's botanical expertise, and Andrew Crowe's Field Guide to the Edible Native Plants of New Zealand, we'd eat our way to the West Coast. Would there have been enough calories in the bush to supplement the travellers' rations? What Māori strategies might have helped them survive? And what made an English gentleman with no back-country experience tackle such vicious terrain without local help?

Our other guide to the terrain was Lauper's own account of the ordeal, republished as *Pushing His Luck*, a new translation and commentary by my aunt Hilary Low. Though an official report, it's a compelling read.

From the pass, Jon and I would detour to climb Lauper Peak and the razorbacked black massif of Mt Whitcombe. Along the way we'd interrogate the heroic stories that inspired our European ancestors to sail into the unknown—and look at what happened when those stories ran aground on the Southern Alps.

•

In the past, heading into the bush, I'd always felt a sense of home-coming. But walking with a botanist, I realised I didn't know much about New Zealand's native vegetation at all. On a 4WD track heading west through matagouri scrub, Jon pointed out plants I'd passed over a thousand times.

'That's an epilobium,' he said, brushing a hand across a small fire-coloured shrub growing in a shingle slide. Tūtāhuna, or 'veg-etable sheep', were large cushions of sage-coloured matting that preserved the imprint of every boot. Crouched to inspect a tiny white pimelea flower, I felt tiny myself, overshadowed by the mountains on all sides.

Past Washbourne Hut the peaks and icefields that barricaded the head of the valley swung into view. The outflow of Lauper Stream lay on the opposite side of the valley, which meant crossing the main branch of the Rakaia-wai-kī. The first braid ran milky and swift, making a faint choppy whisper where it ran over the boulder bed. Jon and I linked arms and stepped in. A quarter of the way across we stopped.

'I don't like it, Mr Whit,' Jon said.

'Me neither, Jakob.'

We were already thigh deep and getting deeper with each shuffled step. Standing waves spoke of boulders and holes in the riverbed ahead. The current was numbing and fierce, too strong for us to turn around. We backed out, careful and slow, then stood dripping on the bank to take stock.

.

I remembered the first time I'd sat down to talk about the mountains with Tā Tipene O'Regan, the senior Ngāi Tahu chief, historian and company director who'd spearheaded our Treaty claim against the Crown. Though in his late seventies and recovering from heart troubles, he was as imposing as ever: impeccable tan suit and black boots with Cuban heel, a hei matau pendant of filigree whalebone at his throat. His knowledge of tradition and history is second to none.

'We were all round the Raki-ihia,' he told me, 'which is the real name for the Rakaia.'

'Rakiihia?' I said. 'Was that—'

'No, not the ancestor. I think the ancestor was named after the river. It's all about the way to cross the river. Like that.'

He lifted his tokotoko (carved staff) towards me and grasped it with both hands. I grasped the other end.

'That's how people crossed the rivers,' he said. 'Raki-ihia, or Raki-ahea. I'm not sure of the precise sense, but I know it refers to how we crossed those rivers.'

I let go of the end and he returned the tokotoko to the floor. I'd watched Tā Tipene give speeches, lead huge events; heard dozens of stories of his clashes with government ministers. It was good to be out there with him at the foot of the Alps, crossing the Rakaia, even if it was only in our heads.

•

Twenty minutes upriver at the real Rakaia, Jon and I found a better ford and tried again. We linked up—Raki-ihia—and this time the current helped sweep us across.

Against the icy ramparts of the Main Divide, there was no mistaking the gentle V-shaped valley that held Lauper Stream. There was no track, but we made good progress shadowing the riverbed, with just the odd boulder scramble and thicket of sharp scrub. On nightfall we bivvied below the pass in light rain with a stiff westerly worrying at our clothes. Like Whitcombe and Lauper, we'd chosen to leave the tent behind. Drizzle pattered against my bivvy bag. A three-quarter moon hung over the Martius Glacier, electrifying the thick mist about the pass. I squirmed down into the earth, shifting stones beneath my hips. Nestled my head under a small overhanging rock to keep the rain off my face. Grinned to myself. So far, so good.

•

When Jakob Lauper entered the upper valley of the Rakaia-wai-kī in 1863, the view reminded him of Switzerland. 'I strode quickly, absorbed in thoughts of my homeland. These mountains and glaciers were a vivid reminder of my youth, when so often I would roam about, light-hearted and carefree, in country just like this. Oh, how much has changed since then!'

As a boy, Lauper was a free spirit who loved practical jokes.

Decades later, when he arrived in New Zealand, he had become an 'imposing figure...a giant of a man with an aura of strength and energy'. Gold prospecting and soldiering across Europe's colonial empires had hardened him. He'd served in the Swiss Guard at the Vatican, then disappeared for five years, doing something that made him write of experiencing warfare and death. He had fierce, sad eyes set in a weathered, deeply tanned face, with a long beard reaching nearly to his waist.

When he and Henry Whitcombe and the rest of the party advanced up the Rakaia Valley, Lauper noticed 'a deep cleft in the mountain range—a side valley leading west. Here a powerful stream came down in a raging torrent'. This looked like the pass they'd been searching for. Their instructions were to travel to the pass, then return and report.

Lauper writes that Whitcombe took him aside. 'All at once he asked me whether I would be afraid to go alone with him to the West Coast. He had decided to go all the way down to the coast and return by the Taramakau.

'I said that I was not at all afraid, but I did not see how I could carry everything on my own. "We won't take much with us," he replied, "only enough for fourteen days."'

Henry Whitcombe had never been to the West Coast. He dashed off a series of breezy estimates: at most it would be fifty miles to the coast; at the very worst they'd travel five or six miles a day, making the whole journey ten days at the outside. Once on the coast they'd find food easily. 'It's simply a question of getting us down,' he said. 'The rest would take care of itself.'

Whitcombe and Lauper planned their journey after dinner, with full bellies. They took some mutton and sugar, four small

birds, and two ship's biscuits per person per day. Having enjoyed
a perfect east-coast day, they decided to leave the tent behind.
Whitcombe hoped the weather would hold—but, with rationed
food, he was firm that they'd push on regardless. Next morning
they set off up the side valley towards the pass.

When I read that, I realised the depth of his ignorance. He
thought bad weather meant walking in the rain. A guide would
have told him that the rivers would be lethal in a matter of
hours.

•

Dawn lit the top of Lauper Peak with a rusty glow. From where I
lay I could just see the south ridge, where it jagged above hanging
glaciers to a summit frosted with new snow. We'd be standing up
there in two days. I slithered free of my sleeping bag and stuffed
my gear into my pack, hungry to move.

Higher in the valley we hauled ourselves over waterworn boulders like giant knucklebones. Climbing with heavy packs among
wet rock, we each slipped, but were safely caught by the dense
scrub bordering the stream. Jon paused over a creeping shrub
with fine, fleshy, pointed leaves. He gave me a handful of crimson
berries tipped with fat green nubs.

'Snow tōtara,' he said. 'Try 'em.'

The sweet, piney berries made a good snack on our ascent. At
the top I stood with hands on hips. The pass was a wide boulder
field dotted with tarns.

'This is *it*?' I said in a bad English accent. 'That was easy, Jakob.'

'We'll be down at the coast in half an hour. Shall we stop
for lunch and a pipe?'

We strung up our damp sleeping bags like giant windsocks and collected handfuls of blood-red coprosma berries and the tiny, translucent white star-shaped fruit of the pōhuehue (muehlenbeckia) vine. They seemed too beautiful to eat, but their sweet rosewater bursts made them too good to leave.

With or without guides, Whitcombe and Lauper wouldn't have stopped to gather berries. Near the pass,

> At about 11 o'clock, before we had time to think about it, a dark cloud drifted over the mountain tops and almost at the same moment it began to pour with rain. We thought it was just a passing thunderstorm, but the rain became persistent and heavier. Then it started snowing. The snowflakes were as big as your hand, and soon everything was covered.

One of the other men had helped carry their provisions to the saddle. He turned back before the snow became too deep, leaving Lauper to take the full load on his back. He and Whitcombe trudged on into the blizzard, hoping to find shelter and firewood before nightfall.

Two Māori guides would have allowed the party to carry more supplies, guns and tents. More importantly, while sudden storms are always possible in the Alps, anyone who's spent time in them knows there are often warning signs. If the guides had spotted thickening high cloud, hogsbacks, the swirl of the nor'-wester turning south, they may have cautioned against going on. With no feel for the mountains, Whitcombe and Lauper committed themselves to crossing the Divide in a major storm.

Jon and I followed them across to the West Coast, feeling the slope shift downhill, seeing trickles of water begin to flow west.

We looked ahead to where the valley, bisected by huge spines of moraine, curled out of sight. There was no way of knowing what was down there, or how far it was to the bush, but it looked easy enough. Whitcombe and Lauper had marched on down. For now, Jon and I began climbing steadily through the moraine fields of the Sale Glacier, en route to Lauper Peak.

.

The Sale Glacier unfurls from the north face of Lauper Peak in a sinuous reverse-S, then funnels between ramparts of black rock before spilling into the Whitcombe below. In an hour, the landscape had dissolved into an infinity of smashed rock. It was like climbing through the static of an old television set. Mist hovered on all sides. The unstable moraine made us stagger as if drunk. Jon crested the glacier above me, silhouetted black against the tongue of white ice. We broke out the crampons, then plodded on up, glad to be off the ankle-breaking moraine.

As we climbed through the mist, we glimpsed icefalls to the north and west, until fog closed the view down to thirty metres. The breeze stiffened; the temperature dropped. It was only 5 p.m. but a strange twilight glow descended. From the map, we knew the terrain was about to get steep.

'Let's find a 'schrund or a slot to camp in,' Jon said. 'Somewhere to get out of this wind.'

Peering into the bergschrund—a large crevasse formed when moving glacial ice pulls away from permanent ice or rock above—I could see plenty of places to shelter, but none we could get out of alive. While I kept searching, Jon started hacking out a platform between two deep blue slots with his ice axe. I must have looked unconvinced.

'Better than nothing,' he yelled over the wind in a theatrical voice. 'Just don't roll over in the night!'

The site looked mildly desperate, but it beat wandering round in the gloom. Besides, we were confident the weather would improve in the morning. But just in case, we anchored everything to the ice before bed, including ourselves.

•

Whitcombe and Lauper's first campsite west of the pass was also less than ideal:

> it grew dark before we could gather any firewood, and we had no choice but simply to sit down...It snowed solidly the whole night. Many times we had to shake our blankets when they became too heavy with snow. It was too wet to lie down, so we sat the whole time.

Lauper says they were in good spirits because they thought the worst was over. I suspect the optimism came from Whitcombe alone. With a grandfather who'd been a private attorney to British royalty, and a wealthy lawyer father, Whitcombe clearly backed himself. As Provincial Road Surveyor in the Canterbury colony he was liked and respected, but could also be cavalier, 'impulsive, off-hand, even arrogant'. He'd hired Lauper for his West Coast experience, but when Lauper suggested they bring another man and more supplies, Whitcombe dismissed the idea. Things would work out fine.

Lauper, on the other hand, knew there was worse to come. He and another man had recently returned from an abortive trip to the Buller goldfields, 150 kilometres north of Hokitika. Where Leonard Harper had been safely guided down the Taramakau by

Ihaia Taihui, Lauper's unguided journey was such an ordeal that the papers wrote it up as a warning to others.

> Rain, rain, all the while, no cessation night nor day, blankets and clothes all soaked through, their powder and matches both useless, their flesh and clothes torn to rags, crawling through the scrub, and for seven days they travelled up the [Taramakau] river bank without fire, or food of any description but one wood hen they managed to kill and...devour raw.

With that experience still fresh in his mind, Lauper wrote: 'It was a long night. But this was just the beginning of our woes. At least we had good food. It was true that the biscuits had become soft from the rain and snow, but they still tasted good and we still had meat.'

Jon and I lay in our sleeping bags in our whited-out eyrie reading Lauper's account aloud. To the explorers the day's journey had felt like fifteen miles, but they'd walked fewer than five: the geography had reeled them in. Lauper was reeling us in, too. He tells us the worst is over, but foreshadows there's far worse to come. Here was the first hint of Lauper as not just adventurer but adventure writer.

I flicked off my head torch and bade Jon good night.

·

I woke to find the dark sawtooth ranges around us crisp beneath the mass of southern stars. I rolled over in my bivvy bag, feeling precarious but happy on our little ledge. Icefalls to the west broke away in gleaming shards. We stretched and gazed around without the need to speak.

When we began our climb, the ranges fell away beneath us to an open western horizon: that way lay the Tasman Sea. We belayed each other across fractured snow bridges on the upper slopes, and took turns balancing across the upper 'schrund, arms out, core tensed, stepping over the emptiness with a scrape of crampons onto solid rock.

At the top of the Butler Range, we passed through a cleft in the ridge, and our view opened onto ziggurats and spires of black rock ringing a sweeping ice basin. Erewhon Col and Erewhon Peak stood off to our right. Their name is almost 'nowhere' backwards. If Nowhere was ever an actual place, this magical, desolate kingdom of ice was it.

'Erewhon' comes from the title of a satirical novel by the English writer Samuel Butler, published in 1872. It's about a mysterious civilisation reached by crossing an alpine pass. In Erewhon the sick are arrested and punished, and the murderous are nursed back to redemption. Among the city's towers and spires, machines begin to achieve sentience and dominance, until the humans destroy them all in a vicious war.

Beyond Butler's anticipation of *Terminator*, what interested me was his dramatisation of the search for a pass through the Southern Alps, and the role of Māori guides. As a young man, Butler had come to New Zealand to take up a high-country run on the Rangitata, not far to the south. In 1861, while out searching for more grazing land, he became the first European to lay eyes on Rurumataikau. He and a friend reached the saddle two years ahead of Whitcombe and Lauper, but turned back when the infernal nature of the terrain on the other side became clear.

In his imagination, though, Butler kept going. In *Erewhon*, set in an unnamed southern colony 'previously uninhabited, save by a few tribes of savages', an ambitious Englishman named Higgs wonders what easy wealth might lie over the great range. He asks a native chief, Kahabuka, for information about a route.

Like Werita Tainui, Kahabuka chooses to withhold knowledge: 'He became uneasy, and began to prevaricate and shuffle... no efforts or coaxing could get a word from him about them.'

Kahabuka is clearly Māori. His name sounds remarkably like the common European mispronunciation of Te Whakataupuka, the famous southern chief who was described in 1827 as 'the most complete model of strength, activity, and elegance I had seen combined in any man'.

When the sealer John Boultbee wrote those words, Ngāi Tahu were still masters of their own lands. Beyond localised property disputes, relations between Europeans and Māori were good.

By the early 1860s, attitudes had changed. Butler's Māori chief gibbers and points. He is devious, cowardly, 'a great liar', 'exceedingly ugly', a violent drunk with an 'impenetrably stupid nature'. Higgs plies Kahabuka with alcohol, hoping he'll reveal the route, then gives him a good kicking when he refuses. Finally Kahabuka relents, and the pair set off into the hills. But as they draw close to what is clearly Rurumataikau, the native man runs away, leaving the European hero to forge on by himself. So much for Māori guides.

•

Jon and I stood under a hot blue sky, studying the terrain for a long time. Across the bowl of the Ramsay Glacier, one long, jagged ridge ran south from Erewhon Col to the top of Mt Whitcombe, then down to Menace Gap. Fresh snow highlighted every contour

of the black rock. The pinkish slabs of Lauper Peak rose at our
back. We'd climb that first, then Mt Whitcombe the following
day.

We scouted a route for Lauper Peak, running a couple of
pitches up the north ridge to get a feel for the rock, then turned
in early. As we lay in our sleeping bags in the twilight, a huge
avalanche poured down the Ramsay Face of Mt Whitcombe. The
roar echoed long after the ice had settled onto the glacier below.

Jon had climbed much harder peaks than Mt Whitcombe and,
according to its grade, a route via the north ridge was within my
capabilities. Now I could see it, I wasn't so sure.

•

If Whitcombe or Lauper had doubts as they continued down the
valley, it seems neither said a word. Snow fell all day, leaving just
the dark line of the river threading through a white landscape.
Already the river had turned into a series of waterfalls crashing
over huge boulders into deep pools. The banks became nearly
vertical. Between the snow and the spray, they were drenched. A
full day's scrambling gained them three miles.

After a long struggle Lauper got a fire going. As their chests
dried, falling snow soaked their backs. Their sugar had liquified
and run all through Lauper's possessions. 'We laughed about that.
We could easily live without sugar, but we were seriously concerned about the biscuits. They had become a mass of wet dough.
We could already see that they would not last long in this state.'

The next day they trudged through a hallucinatory world of
rainbows, thrown up by sunlight hitting waterfall spray. At a huge
landslide they climbed out of the riverbed and finally managed an
hour's sleep in the sun. They woke to find blowflies had laid eggs

through their clothes and Whitcombe's possum-skin rug, which hatched into maggots in a few days.

The rain returned, hard and relentless. The river swelled and was already dangerous to cross. Though the boulders grew bigger and more slippery, they kept their spirits up. 'We trusted the roughest part of the route was well behind us and that it would soon improve.'

Then, at noon the next day, Lauper reached 'a cliff as high as a church. I looked straight down into a pool that was like a tank of boiling water. There appeared to be no way of crossing. I said nothing and laid down my swag.'

•

Jon and I rose and made coffee before dawn. The moon was down; the stars were veiled, just the burner's blue flame alive in the pitch. As we crunched our way over the ice, the mountains emerged above us like a photograph in developing solution. The Ramsay Face was a beautiful, monstrous presence; the glacier below, a sooty smear.

We hiked snow slopes to reach our chosen line up the south ridge, stowed crampons and axes, and stood at the base of the rock face leading to the summit. A roseate glow now filled the eastern sky, brushing the stone chimneys of the Arrowsmith Range away across the Rakaia Valley. I could see Aoraki to the south, and a hundred other summits pricking the dawn.

Our mood was playful, knowing we had an easy climb ahead. It'd been several years since Jon had been mountaineering, and he was visibly happy to be back in the sky.

'Good climbing,' we told each other. 'No mistakes.'

Straight up, the terrain was loose and sharp-edged, with snow and ice plastered in each crevice. We scrambled without the rope, but as the line steepened and the rock grew more fractured, we roped up again. Finding reliable placements for gear was hard. With the coast so close, the freeze-thaw cycle destroyed all but the strongest rock.

'Pure Weet-bix, Lauper,' I said.

'Yeah, choss-fest, Mr Whit,' Jon replied, referring to the shattered consistency of the rock underfoot.

We inched our way up the side of Lauper Peak like Gulliver on his travels, scaling the crumbling form of the Swiss giant himself.

Two pitches in, we rounded the south ridge and trended out towards the east face. The drop to the ice below was suddenly severe. It was easy climbing but bloody awful rock. Leading took concentration not to dislodge anything onto Jon below. Coming up behind me, he cleared footholds by sending rocks spinning down the cliff. Bounce, clatter, silence—then the distant dull *thump* of them hitting the glacier below. It was disconcerting, but I trusted Jon. He was older, tougher, more experienced. I was the relative novice: the question was more whether he should trust me.

Jon reached my belay and there was worry in his eyes. 'I'm doing the old sewing machine,' he said with a half-laugh.

'The what?'

'Legs shaking. I hate this rock. You know, when I left, Anna said: "Make sure you come back alive." I never worried in the past, but—' He broke off to look at a bank of dark cloud building up at the Divide. He returned his gaze to mine, eyes serious. 'All I can think about is how we're going to get down.'

I'd woken up with the summit clear in my mind, and now I felt a powerful momentum to push on. I tried to force it down.

'We can turn back at any point,' I said. 'Just say the word. We're almost past the steep stuff, though. From the map, it looks like the ridge will level off soon. If we want to do another pitch, I'm happy to lead.'

Jon rubbed his chin. 'Okay,' he said. 'One more pitch.'

'You want me to lead?'

'No, I'm good.'

Jon climbed past where I was wedged into my belay stance, and placed and clipped a cam above his head. He found good hand holds, set his foot on a large slab of rock, then stepped up. The entire slab cracked and slid several inches with a sudden hollow rasp. Fine rubble skittered away into the void.

'Fuck!' we both exclaimed.

Jon turned back and locked eyes with me. 'Let's go down.'

I nodded. 'For sure.'

I resolved not to let my disappointment show. We didn't have to be here: the burning need to keep climbing is always in your head. I was confident we could make it if we pushed on, but I kept the thought to myself.

•

Jon and I took our time heading back down, joined by a rope but alone with our thoughts. Darkness had hidden the Ramsay Glacier on our ascent, but by daylight it curled away beneath us, a leviathan streaked with debris off the Ramsay Face. The wind had been at us all morning, and by the time we reached camp it'd grown icy against my cheeks. Thick cloud poured over the Divide from the west.

We'd planned to camp on Erewhon Col, ready to climb Mt Whitcombe the next day, but it didn't take long to agree that this was a bad idea. Whitcombe was a bigger ask than Lauper Peak, and with no tent and the weather coming in, there was no point in sticking around. We decided to return to the river, and pick up the trail of Jakob and Mr Whit.

'Thanks for coming down back there,' Jon said as we strode down the Sale Glacier. He told me about a climbing partner who'd refused to retreat even when conditions turned seriously bad. Jon had had to make the tough call to leave him up there on his own.

'Fair enough,' I said. 'That kind of stubbornness is the best way to get yourself killed.'

John nodded. He pointed his ice axe at the swirling cloud that now engulfed the top of Lauper Peak. 'I'm just glad we didn't get caught in that.'

As we left the moraine and approached the riverbed, life began to reappear among the stones. We pocketed handfuls of tapuka (snowberries) shaped like delicate pink bells, to garnish our muesli the following day.

Just before dark we bivvied beside a huge boulder sitting in the riverbed like a fallen asteroid. There was just enough of an overhang to keep our heads out of the drizzle. Kea called back and forth in the mist, and I glimpsed one of the alpine parrots watching us from the lip of the boulder above. The Whitcombe River rushed away endlessly to our right.

On the verge of sleep, I heard Jon's voice in the dark. 'Running water,' he said. 'I'll never forget that sound.'

I didn't know Jon that well, but adrenaline and reliance on each other made us want to talk. He told me about the day he was airlifted off the Tasman Glacier with a friend who had broken his leg. When the chopper landed, an ambulance was waiting for his friend, but the police were waiting for Jon. They broke the news that his father had died.

That night he stayed at the Alpine Club lodge, just out of Mt Cook Village. It was the dead of winter: so cold that they had to leave the bathroom taps running so the pipes wouldn't freeze. Water gushed all night. Jon lay awake till dawn, listening to it splashing away.

He tailed off, then drifted to sleep, and I listened to the river alone. My parents were still alive. I'd never lost a close friend. I'd had the odd near miss, but I'd never felt in real danger. I thought about my desire to push on to the summit of Lauper Peak; my confidence that everything would go well. I realised that, like Whitcombe, my confidence was that of the novice, based on nothing at all.

PART II: WHITCOMBE RIVERBED TO THE MOUTH OF THE TARAMAKAU RIVER. EARLY AUTUMN.

If Whitcombe had taken the two guides that his superiors had budgeted for, he would have descended the river with someone like Ihaia Tainui, or his relations from the Kāti Māhaki hapū in South Westland, who worked with Europeans at the time, keeping them on track, fed and sheltered, alive. Ihaia and his contemporaries would likely have known the place names along this river that had been bestowed by Raureka's people, Kāti Wairaki. Even if they hadn't used the route before, for Māori raised on the Coast the combination of rapids and pools, narrow gorges, dense bush, and heavy rain would have been familiar.

But Whitcombe and Lauper, sealed off from the land, dependent on what they could carry for survival, were fighting a hostile wilderness and losing. Whitcombe had only the optimism of the novice to keep him going. Three days into their journey downriver, his optimism started to crack. Peering over a waterfall's lip, shouting over the thundering slap of the river hitting the pool below, the two men weighed their options, and decided to push on.

Lauper lowered himself into the seething pool using their rope. Whitcombe followed him down with a knife between his teeth. He cut the rope and slid the last of the way. It was pointless continuing—their task was to find a route for a road, and Whitcombe admitted that it would be impossible to build one through such hostile terrain—but now there was no turning back.

That night, in relentless rain, Lauper struggled to light a fire. They ate sodden dough and attempted to dry the rest beside the blaze. Adrenaline and reliance on each other seemed to have brought them closer as well, because despite their fatigue and their class differences, they talked into the night.

Whitcombe was despondent. 'He said to me,' Lauper wrote, 'that he felt exhausted and very weak, and that he had not thought it would be so dreadfully rough...We chatted for a long time. He told me about India, the war and so on.'

Whitcombe had worked as an engineer for the East Indian Railway Company, and was overseeing the building of a bridge when the Indian Mutiny broke out in 1857. Nine of his fellow engineers were killed, and dozens more from the lower ranks. His Indian labourers walked off the job, leaving him scrambling to find workers to finish the bridge before the monsoon floods arrived.

The mutiny challenged the legitimacy of the British Empire: the myth that native peoples loved their colonial masters. Retaliation was fierce. The British razed Delhi and Lucknow, burned whole villages, hanged and bayoneted the mutineers or blasted them from the mouths of cannons. By the end, a hundred thousand Indian troops and untold civilians were dead.

The effects rippled across the Empire. Colonisers began to see native peoples as 'half-devil, half-child', as Kipling later put it. By the time Whitcombe and Lauper were talking by the fire, six years after the Indian Mutiny, fear of native rebellion had arrived in New Zealand.

As northern iwi began armed resistance to European surveying and settlement of their lands, outlying farms on disputed land were attacked. Newspapers denounced 'brutal and unprovoked murder' by the 'ruthless savage'. Panic swept through Auckland that whites would be massacred in their beds. The rumours were false, but they enabled Governor Grey finally to convince London to send Imperial troops. In early 1863, preparations were nearing completion for all-out war against Māori in the central North Island. I couldn't help thinking that all of this influenced Whitcombe's decision not to take Māori guides on his expedition.

After their conversation, Lauper sat up all night in the snow, tending the blaze while Whitcombe slept. After a disgusting breakfast of sour, mouldy dough, they set off downriver, only to reach another waterfall higher than the first.

Once again, Whitcombe despaired, and Lauper got on with the job: he led them straight up the near-vertical north bank, hand over hand up through the scrub, to skirt the waterfall. By dark they'd managed two hundred yards. They couldn't get a fire to catch. Dinner was a little dough and the last of their meat. They were desperate for food. Hunting wasn't an option, because Whitcombe had decided against taking a gun. They slept huddled together against the cold.

·

As Jon and I descended the increasingly rough riverbed, we left the sub-alpine world of small tough shrubs and tussock grasses behind and entered the bush. We began studying the plant life in earnest, wondering what Ihaia and his fellow nineteenth-century guides might have found to eat. On this side of the pass, the vegetation was riotous and lush. Jon plucked various leaves and passed them over his shoulder.

'Here—hen and chicken fern,' he said. 'That's good to eat.'

I took the handful of mouku, a fractal fern whose seedlings

grow fully formed on the leaves of the parent plant. They were regarded as the best fern to eat, so we filled a Ziploc bag. The hanging green fronds of the kiokio were just as prolific, and another welcome addition to dinner that night.

'How much has the bush changed since we were last here, Jakob?' I asked.

'It's basically the same, Mr Whit,' Jon said. 'I haven't seen a weed since we left the Rakaia.'

Ahead, what looked like a ruined monastery rose from the riverbed, complete with arches and nave. The crumbling stone walls looked uncanny, a Tintern Abbey somehow built deep in the tangled West Coast bush. Our map labelled the natural formation the Gateway.

'Gateway to what, Mr Whit?' Jon said.

'Erewhon,' I said. 'I bet you ten pounds that this is what gave Butler his ideas.'

We splashed past in the shallows, then stopped for lunch at Neave Hut. Jon made an experimental lichen sandwich.

'How many of them would you need to survive?' I asked.

He spat. 'Ptah! A lot!'

There's no record of our Māori ancestors eating lichen, but ferns and other greens were regularly served as a kīnaki (side dish or relish), and would offer small sustenance to starving travellers. As would the greenish-black berries of kāpuka (broadleaf), eaten purely as a survival food. I plucked a handful, chewed one and threw away the rest: a tooth-cracking seed in a purse of bitter flesh.

The real prize guides would have searched for was aruhe (bracken fern root), 'te tūtanga tē unuhia', the staple that never fails. As Joseph Banks, the botanist on Captain Cook's Endeavour, said: it was 'to them what bread is to us'. In addition to growing wild, bracken was often planted in clearings every two days along the old trails to provide sustenance for travellers. We kept an eye out as we descended the river after lunch.

North towards Wilkinson Hut, the terrain that ruined Whitcombe and Lauper began. The river plunged from pool to pool through a rubble-choked gorge, changing colour to a rich cobalt blue as its depth increased. Jon and I had the benefit of a rough track cut high above the north bank. Each time I looked down into the gorge I spared a thought for the early Māori travellers, and for Lauper, clawing their way up and down these banks.

At the junction with the Wilkinson River, past where the silvery cliffs and waterfalls of Mt Evans descended from cloud, we paused to scout the dank, mossy interior of Cave Camp. Climbers in the 1930s used the large cave as a base for attempts on Mt Evans. There were other natural rock shelters around; Uncle Peter Ramsden, a kaumātua from Koukourarata, had told me that as a young man out deer culling in the Whitcombe, he'd discovered a pair of pāraerae in a cave. It was the first physical confirmation I'd heard of Māori using the route.

'What did you do with the sandals?' I asked.

He raised his eyebrows. 'Left them there, of course.'

'And you're not going to tell me where the cave is, are you?'

He laughed. 'You have to find it for yourself!'

Jon was a caver as well as a climber, and loved prospecting for new systems. We'd been ducking off the track whenever we spotted overhangs and nearby cliffs, but the bush was so dense you'd have to either get lucky or spend weeks on the hunt.

When we reached the hut we ate our selection of crunchy,

faintly astringent steamed fern heads, augmented with delicious freeze-dried packet slop. While we ate, I read up on how aruhe was prepared. The preferred method was to dig up and dry the deep roots, then soak and dry them again, at which point they could be stored long-term. On the trail they were roasted in the fire, pounded and eaten as a sweet, cake-like meal—apart from the inedible fibrous pulp, which was spat out.

'Sounds like a lot of work,' I said.

'True,' Jon said. 'But listen to this.'

He held up the packet of freeze-dried pasta and began to read: 'Durum wheat flour, dehydrated vegetables, thickener 1442, maltodextrin, herbs and spices, hydrolysed vegetable proteins from maize and soy, sugar, salt, acidity regulator 296...'

I laughed. Maybe fernroot wasn't so complex after all. But finding the roots, as well as catching birds and eels, drying and preserving them—it all took time. Whitcombe and Lauper had no tent, and were determined to keep moving every day.

I thought about the many Pākehā explorers who'd been exasperated by their guides' refusal to budge from a good source of food. Thomas Brunner's guides Kehu and Pikawiti and their wives would build a shelter and stay put until they'd caught, preserved and packed all they could carry. In unfamiliar terrain you never knew when you'd find your next meal.

Survival out here wasn't just about food. It was also about time. You had to let the land determine the pace of travel. You couldn't just push on.

•

We woke early, to a loud, drumming darkness. The famed West Coast rain had come. Muffled thunder rolled. Warm in our bunks, we took a while to summon the willpower to move. But once out the door, I felt liberated to be finally walking in the mist and rain. We headed down the valley with our view limited to a single veiled spur emerging from under cloud. The river had risen fast, roaring and dirty. Whitcombe and Lauper suffered ceaseless rain, and we'd had almost none. Thank god for engineering, I thought at Wilkinson Bridge, watching the torrent whipping beneath our feet.

Heading downriver, Jon showed me two more species of edible fern: huruhuru whenua (shining spleenwort) and pāraharaha (hound's tongue fern). We crouched beside three electric-blue mushrooms.

'Can you eat these, Jakob?' I asked.

'No idea, Mr Whit. They're either so poisonous or so good that no one's saying a word.'

In pouring rain I used Jon's ice axe to hack off a length of tātarāmoa (bush lawyer), the vicious climber that hooks your skin and won't let go without drawing blood. The sweet berries are cousins to blackberries, and a fat two-metre length of vine gives a cup of nutritious, nutty-flavoured sap. I stood there gnawing at the severed end while Jon looked on and cackled. You'd need a much thicker vine to get anything useful, and it's unlikely you'd bother, given the abundance of mamaku (black tree fern) around.

With its cousins kātote, punga, nīkau, kōrau and pītau, mamaku fills the West Coast bush with reliable food. The white pith is baked in an umu or on the coals, turning char-sweet, rather like turnip or baked apple; else it's sliced thin and dried in the sun. When there wasn't much in the way of birds or eels, explorers like Charles Heaphy subsisted on mamaku harvested by their Māori guides.

Jon and I weren't about to turn lumberjack, but where the

track passed through storm damage we found freshly snapped kātote stumps. I placed my lips over the fleshy centre of one and sucked. Even raw, it had a succulent sweetness like coconut flesh. I dug out a section with my knife, and stashed several fat fronds for dinner that night.

With the right skills, we could have caught birds, fish and eels in the lower valleys. Later, I would learn how to make traps and snares using flax, sticks and vines, from a bushcraft expert who'd studied traditional Māori hunting methods. For Whitcombe and Lauper, with no gun and no guides, the land was barren. Their only hope was to find people on the Coast—local Ngāi Tahu, government stores, a supply ship—to feed them, and fast.

Between the botanising, the cave prospecting and the rain, Jon and I were moving slowly. The track was little more than a rough staircase of boulders, landslides and roots. We lowered ourselves down chains and gut-crawled beneath fallen trees. It was like trying to climb a slippery head-high boulder with a bag of concrete strapped to your back, over and over, all day long.

At the next hut we baked the mamaku, steamed a range of baby fern fronds and ate them with 'Māori bread', slow-cooked in a camp oven above the fire. The hard flat loaves were similar to nineteenth-century biscuits, so our dinner was what Whitcombe and Lauper might have eaten if they'd had guides and kept their rations dry.

The other party in the hut, a pugnacious old tramper and his downtrodden son, looked on, bemused. We'd hadn't harvested enough mamaku to make a meal, nor cooked some of the greens for long enough. I tried not to grimace as I chewed.

'I wish we'd caught a weka,' I said.

As a survival effort, it was laughable. But it was a taste of knowledge and history. People had survived in the West Coast bush for centuries. This nutty sweetness, this crunchy bitterness, were among the flavours that had passed their lips.

.

For the road surveyor and his hired man, each day became a night-marish repeat of the last. The river's banks were so steep, the side streams so swift, that they had to climb through miles of scrub just to find safe crossing points. Each night they forced down a hand-ful of rotting dough and got a little less sleep, huddled beneath a wet blanket or a maggot-infested rug.

Strangely, they never tried to build a shelter, as guides would have done each night. Other European explorers were astonished by the speed and skill with which their guides could build a water-proof shelter from whatever materials were at hand. Sleeping out of the rain would have made a huge difference to Whitcombe and Lauper's strength and morale.

Where the Hokitika River joined from the north, the hills opened out and the two men knew that at last the coast was near. Guides would have shown them how to make a mōkihi to raft down to the beach in a matter of hours, as Ihaia Tainui did for Leonard Harper. Instead, for three days Whitcombe and Lauper waded across some of the country's worst swamps. They heard the booming surf due west, but there was no travelling in a straight line.

The biscuit sack tore and they lost more dough. At nightfall, 'with scratched hands and battered faces, bruised and dead tired, we lay down to sleep, and froze the whole night.' It rained con-stantly, hard and cold. Whitcombe gave Lauper their last handful of dough. He was confident they would soon be saved by Poutini

Ngāi Tahu. Lauper forced down that foul morsel. Their food was gone.

Roughly thirteen days after crossing the pass, Henry Whitcombe and Jakob Lauper staggered onto the beach at the mouth of the Hokitika. A wide horizon and glittering sea, smooth sand underfoot. The sun warm on their faces. Lauper had been here once before, and had been fed by Ngāi Tahu at Arahura Pā, less than a day's walk up the beach. 'We were starving but in good spirits—our troubles would soon be over.'

At Arahura, their hopes were crushed. The pā was empty, everyone gone to the gold diggings. Overwhelmed, Whitcombe went to sleep in the sun, leaving Lauper to forage in the pā's plantations for hours. The resourceful Swiss hadn't once looked for edible plants in the bush; for him, food came from gardens. He found a handful of tiny potatoes.

'Jakob, you've lost a good deal of flesh,' Whitcombe said, staring at Lauper while they waited for the potatoes to cook. 'How do I look? I feel so very weak and hungry.'

'I told him he did not look so bad. But to be honest, you would have barely recognised him. His eyes were sunken in his head, his lips were white and his face yellow, like a wax figure. You could see his teeth through his cheeks, so to speak.'

Lauper suggested they wait for low tide to expose the mussel beds along the rocks. Whitcombe refused. They would push on to the pā at Taramakau, where someone would give them food. They waded into the Arahura but the high tide forced them back. The rain returned, and they sat waiting in the downpour. Fleas and sandflies feasted on their flesh, 'busily finding their long-denied nourishment'. Lauper understood the irony of the hungry being eaten, but Whitcombe was maddened.

'We must put an end to this misery as soon as we possibly can,' he said.

They finally forced a crossing of the Arahura, and staggered along the beach in the dark. 'And so around midnight we arrived at the fatal Taramakau.'

·

Jon and I passed the next day and a half in intense concentration in that steep narrow channel between the mountains. The world became a single boulder covered with slippery moss. Icy streams cannoned into our legs among bush so dense we could have been walking in the middle of the night. The sun rose to touch the mountaintops, and sank to a misty gloaming on dusk.

Like Whitcombe, I kept wanting to believe that 'it must get better soon' and that civilisation was close. We were also bound for the Taramakau: Leigh had invited us to stay where she was housesitting at her dad's. Twice my mind wandered to her smiling face, and twice I slipped and fell, my heavy pack slamming me into the dirt. Rurumataikau permitted little thought beyond the placement of your boots.

Past Rapid Creek, we winched ourselves over the torrent in a lurching metal cage. As we approached the coast, rain and plant life proliferated. Jon paused to quiz me on the plant names I'd learned along the way. I'd point with my walking pole: mahoe, miro, horopito. What was once 'the bush' had begun to separate into different identities, each with its own niche and taste.

'You must eat, Mr Whit,' Jon said, handing me a small red and green marbled fruit. 'You've lost a lot of flesh. This will make you strong.'

I cracked the horopito berry between my teeth, and fire seared my mouth. I walked on, spitting and spitting, while Jon chortled at my back. Kareao (supplejack creepers) reared into our path like snakes, and I snapped off their astringent pinkish tips and chewed.

Then suddenly we were out in the open, pacing out fence lines and farm roads. The western horizon stood clear to the coast.

'Hurrah, Jakob—we are saved!' I said.

Jon turned and shook my hand formally. 'Great mission, Mr Whit.' He looked as buggered as I felt, but his skin was tanned from our time on the glaciers, and his eyes shone clear.

'I couldn't have done it without you, Jakob,' I said.

'You're not done yet. Haven't you got a date?'

'It's not a date. Leigh's—'

'With the Taramakau.'

.

Near Hokitika, Leigh picked us up in a giant silver 4WD. 'It's my Dad's,' she said, climbing down from the cab. 'I feel like I've borrowed someone else's life.' She looked energised but under-slept from working long hours.

'How's the book?' I asked.

She beamed. 'We're celebrating. I got a deal with Hachette!'

'Incredible. Congratulations!'

We hugged, and after so long in the bush, the floral scent of her shampoo and soap was alarming. 'Sorry,' I said. 'I haven't had a shower in ten days.'

'Mmm,' she said. 'You actually smell good.'

I blushed and stepped back. 'Uh, Leigh, this is Jon.'

Jon was watching us with a smile. 'Call me Jakob,' he said in his worst German accent. 'I've heard all about you. Tell me, in this land, do you have fish and chips?'

•

After dinner, while Jon caught up on the TV news, and Leigh and I shared celebratory beers at the dining table, a blinding storm came in off the Tasman Sea. The three of us stumbled down the beach to where Whitcombe and Lauper had attempted to cross the Taramakau—the same place where Ihaia Tainui and Leonard Harper ended their journey. I fell behind the others to tie a shoe-lace, and imagined that the two grey blurs ahead of me, leaning into the teeth of the gale, were Jakob and Mr Whit.

It took grim patience to light a fire in the rain. When the kindling finally caught, we piled up driftwood till we had a blaze. Huddled under a scrap of tarpaulin, I clicked on my head torch and opened my aunt's book. As the swollen black Taramakau pushed out into the sea, I read Lauper's words aloud.

'All life seemed to be extinct.' That's how the Swiss juggernaut felt when dawn revealed the scene at the river mouth. No people, no canoes, no sign of the government supply ship that had been dispatched to ease the pressure on local Ngāi Tahu, who were having to feed so many starving Europeans. They could see the pā across the river, but it seemed deserted.

Mr Whit was beside himself. 'We must get across the river or we'll starve to death.'

Lauper demurred. The Taramakau was in full flood, far too deep and fierce to wade across. The previous time he had crossed in a good boat with a party of five, 'including a Māori', and even then they'd barely survived.

'I've swum in worse places than this,' Whitcombe replied.

Once across, they'd be in Nelson in no time, where he'd buy Lauper as much food as he liked.

He wandered the beach. 'Hurrah, Jakob, hurrah!' he cried. He'd found two tiny rotted canoes, both broken, one without gunwales. A lunatic determination took hold of him. They'd tie them together and float across.

Lauper now argued for his life. He couldn't swim. The canoes were useless.

But Whitcombe refused to listen. It 'won't be dangerous at all,' he said. 'Besides, I'm a good swimmer. If we get into difficulties I can help you.'

Lauper was clearly sick at the prospect, but for some reason—his status as a hired man, exhaustion, a soldier's training to follow orders unto death—he gave in.

On the bank of that torrent, he bound the two canoes together with flax rope to form a makeshift outrigger. The first reach was a calm backwater. Like children playing at explorers, they made their way out using boards as paddles, with a branch for a rudder and a tin mug as a bailer. The tops of the canoes were an inch and a half above the water.

As they approached the small island that marked the beginning of the real current, water began to come over the side.

'Ah, Mr Whit, let's go back,' Lauper begged.

'It's going really well. Couldn't be better.'

They rounded the island. Water poured into the bottom of the canoes.

'Jakob, bail! The canoes are full up!'

Lauper bailed frantically with his leather hat. The canoes filled and began to sink. The current sped them towards the monstrous surf. Only now did the reality hit Whitcombe.

'Jakob, we're lost! It's my fault! Get out of the canoes! Swim to this side...Follow me, quickly, or you'll drown!'

The Englishman stripped off his jacket and took a mighty dive over the side. He made five or six powerful strokes towards the near bank and Lauper lost sight of him. The Swiss went under, despairing. 'I had no doubt that he would reach safety, but I was doomed.'

•

Huddled metres from the scene, I paused to separate pages stuck together by rain. Squalls flattened the fire, leaving just the roaring glow of the coals. The surf boomed in: the same surf that pounded Lauper to the point of death.

He tethered himself to the canoes by winding the end of the flax rope around his hand. Over and over he was tumbled and hurled and dragged down, and over and over the canoes lifted him for another breath. They battered his body and cracked his head so hard he thought his skull was split.

Gradually, the waves calmed. For hours he drifted out to sea. His clawed hands were fixed to the canoes as if nailed. 'Black thoughts of despair overwhelmed me...I have stared death in the face before, both in raging battle and in perilous situations, but I had never seen it so horrible and so close. And yet I could not drown. Almost against my will, I remained in this state for some time.'

The canoes struck against something. *Bump.* And again. *Bump.* It was too dark to see, but it had to be land. The sea had given him back.

Daylight found him paralysed, one eye buried in sand. With the other, he could see only his hands, black with sandflies, red with his blood. Slowly he regained the use of his body. An animal staggering; a freshwater stream. Muzzle in the water, vomiting and shaking. Still on the wrong side of the river. Roaming about, searching for mussels.

Further along the beach, he found a scrap of his blanket, then Whitcombe's rotted possum-skin rug. Next, the canoes, and the biscuit sack—and a pair of shoes sticking out of the sand. 'To my horror, there lay Mr Whit himself, his head and torso buried, his legs and feet lying free.'

Lauper dug him out. The younger man's waistcoat was drawn up over his head, his pockets weighted with sand, his face untouched but for a smear of dried blood. Too weak to carry him, Lauper fashioned a skid of driftwood and dragged him beyond the reach of the surf.

There he slowly scraped out a grave with his hands. 'As I performed this sad task I became quite emotional and I felt tears running down my cheeks.'

He laid Mr Whit in the ground with his head facing south. He covered him with sand, and laid driftwood over the mound to keep wild dogs away.

Lauper was alone.

He managed to strike a spark with his knife, and torched an enormous pile of driftwood. 'I was warm enough all night, yet I shook the whole time, and even now as I write this I still feel slight fits of trembling from this horror.'

•

I walked back along the beach, alone and without a torch. Leigh and Jon had already gone back to the house. The gale hounded me on, shoving me in the small of the back. Ahead through the rain I saw no lights, no buildings, heard nothing above the roar of the surf.

Back at Leigh's I sat at her kitchen table while the storm picked up force outside. The floor-to-ceiling windows bowed under the gusts, making the room's cosy reflection shimmer and distort. My hands reeked of smoke; it'd taken an age to kindle that fire, and a few handfuls of wet sand to put it out. To reach the forest and find no food, to survive the waterfalls and gorges and find swamps, to reach this coast and find only death, and still to keep going: I felt respect for Lauper, and sadness. The ordeal had been unnecessary. If Whitcombe had taken guides, they would have enjoyed more food from hunting and harvesting, and from what two extra people could have carried on their backs. They would have camped out of the rain, and so been able to sleep, and rafted out to the coast, saving days of slog. All this would surely have kept them from desperate acts. But whether Whitcombe would have taken his guides' advice to let the land dictate their pace—I had my doubts.

·

The adventure stories that drove men like Whitcombe and Lauper out across the colonial empires all have happy endings. Robinson Crusoe, whose story Lauper loved as a child, avoids the cannibal hordes and returns home to find himself rich, thanks to gifts, plantations and slaves. In Jules Verne's *Among the Cannibals*, inspired in part by Whitcombe and Lauper's expedition, the heroes flee man-eating tribes, marry and live happily ever after. Samuel Butler's hero in *Erewhon* gets the girl and escapes the natives by hot-air balloon. Even Whitcombe was honoured in death as a hero.

But the reality was quite different. For European explorers on the West Coast, the natives were their saving grace. Lauper was helped by Poutini Ngāi Tahu parties, who fed rather than ate him, and gave him a ride across the river. A government survey party took him in, and lent him a horse for the journey back across the Alps. But he never really recovered.

A year after the ordeal, an anonymous notice in the Christchurch *Press* claimed that Lauper could be found walking 'about the streets of Christchurch, old, maimed, and almost starving'. The writer excoriated local crowds for paying to see an exhibition celebrating the failed Australian explorers Burke and Wills, while leaving their own pioneer 'Swiss Jakob' to rot. But perhaps Lauper's fate isn't so surprising. A story about eating mouldy dough, shivering all night in the rain and burying your friend in a shallow grave inspired neither adventure nor romance.

Lauper died alone and poor. But in death, his legend was free to grow. In his Swiss home town they say he kept wild Arabian stallions, and drove them through the terrified village at full gallop. Rumours that he left a fortune in New Zealand became as good as fact, and in the 1920s his grandson initiated a long and fruitless search for it.

But the best story about the story of Jakob Lauper comes from a pub in New Zealand in the 1880s. A crowd of drinkers had formed around a man recounting the harrowing tale of two adventurers descending the Whitcombe Pass. Further along the bar, a heavy-set, elderly stranger sat watching and listening intently. The storyteller finished with Whitcombe's death, and Lauper's survival.

'Have you heard that story before?' the storyteller asked the stranger.

The old gentleman smiled sadly. 'Sir,' he said with a thick accent, 'I was that man.'

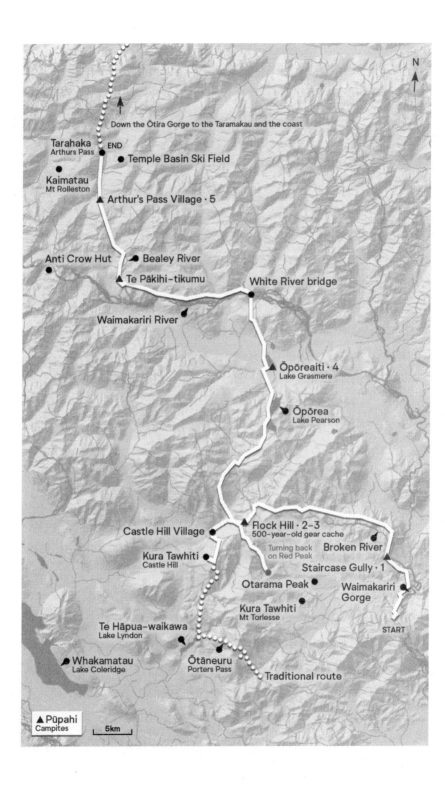

N

Down the Ōtira Gorge to the Taramakau and the coast

Tarahaka
Arthurs Pass
END
Temple Basin Ski Field

Kaimatau
Mt Rolleston

Arthur's Pass Village · 5

Anti Crow Hut
Bealey River

Te Pākihi-tikumu
White River bridge

Waimakariri River

Ōpōreaiti · 4
Lake Grasmere

Ōpōrea
Lake Pearson

Castle Hill Village
Flock Hill · 2–3
500-year-old gear cache
Broken River

Kura Tawhiti
Castle Hill
Turning back
on Red Peak

Staircase Gully · 1

Otarama Peak
Waimakariri
Gorge

Kura Tawhiti
Mt Torlesse

Te Hāpua-waikawa
Lake Lyndon
START

Whakamatau
Lake Coleridge
Ōtāneuru
Porters Pass
Traditional route

▲ Pūpahi
Campites
5km

4

Tarahaka
(Arthur's Pass)

PART I: TARAMAKAU RIVER MOUTH. EARLY AUTUMN.

The day after Jon and I arrived at Leigh's place, I farewelled him at the bus stop at the nearby town of Kumara, then returned to Leigh's to write. We worked in silence at opposite ends of the long open-plan house. Every now and then I stole a glance at her. She typed furiously, hair pulled back in a messy bun, the patter of her keyboard the only sound. Though originally a journalist, for years she'd supported her travel and writing habits through table dancing, and was finishing a memoir about her former life in strip clubs around the world. 'I told them I'd have the second half written in six weeks,' she'd said the previous night. 'Three weeks to go!'

I'd never met a stripper before. All I knew were the cliches of oppressed women struggling to make rent, or party girls who spent their money on drugs. Leigh had spent hers cycling from London to Nepal, and the length of New Zealand, and much of Australia as well. She'd also bought a house, and put herself through a writing degree and yoga-teacher training, though I suspected she'd done her share of partying, too. In conversation her manner shifted between dreamy and hard-nosed. While I sneaked glances, she never once looked up from her screen. I liked her focus.

That night she made seafood marinara with the slow precision of a person who rarely cooks but is making an effort. The smell of grilled garlic and fresh mussels filled the house.

It turned out we'd lived a few blocks apart in Melbourne for years, and had both come home to write. We cracked open a bottle of wine, and talked about being back after more than a decade away.

'I'm always slightly on edge in the Australian bush,' I said. 'I love it, but I don't understand it. Everything clicks when I've got big rivers and mountains and storms.'

'It's the West Coast beaches for me,' Leigh said, placing a steaming bowl of pasta in front of me, and sitting opposite with her own. 'The deep blues and greens, and seeing the mountains in the distance. I feel at home here. Though I don't know if I belong.'

'How come?'

'I mean, my family's from the Coast, on both sides, and we've always worked in fishing and mining and pubs—but I've always known that we're from somewhere else. My grandmother still talks about our ancestors from Lancashire and Scotland. It must be different if your ancestors are from here.'

'Yes and no. My ancestors are mainly from down south; in

the mountains, it's as much my Pākehā side that makes me feel at home. They're the ones who took me tramping. You must feel like you belong somewhere.'

'Not really. Maybe when I'm on the road? Or, actually, at Temple Basin. That's my happy place.'

Temple Basin is a tiny ski field in Arthur's Pass National Park. There's no cafe or chairlifts, or even an access road: just a snowy bowl surrounded by jagged peaks, reached by a steep foot track. Leigh had been going there since she was a kid.

'Snap,' I said. 'Arthur's Pass is my happy place as well. Our cousins have a bach there. I've never skied at Temple, but I have climbed Blimit, up the back. Out the door, straight up.'

She nodded, recognition in her eyes. 'Things are steep, they're high, they're wild. There's something *sudden* about it.' She wrinkled her nose. 'And, I don't know, it was a place of first loves, first kisses. I spent a lot of time up there as a teenager.'

'Me too! The first time I went away with a girlfriend on my own was to Arthur's Pass. Our initials are still carved into the table at the bach...I'm actually walking there next.'

'What, to Arthur's Pass? Along the highway?'

'Highway and train line, and farmland. The plan is to trespass as much as I can.'

Leigh tilted her head. 'How come?'

'To find out how it feels to be unwelcome on land you love.'

I told her how Arthur's Pass was a Ngāi Tahu trans-alpine trail, and the Waimakariri Basin, east of the pass, a mahika kai full of seasonal hunting and fishing camps. After European settlement it all got drained, fenced and farmed, and a rich culture of walking in the high country all but disappeared. I wanted to look at that culture, and what was being done to get our people back into the hills today.

'Who are you trespassing with?' Leigh asked.

'I'm meeting one guy along the way, and interviewing people beforehand, but it's mostly just me. Everyone's too busy running the tribe, or they're not into tramping. We used to walk everywhere, but now it's mostly seen as a Pākehā thing. So maybe I'm looking at what tramping would be like if it was a Māori sport.'

'And?'

'Well, it wouldn't just be me. I think my ultimate would be a mission with all my relations down south. Anyway, I'll be stopping off at the bach in Arthur's Pass along the way. If you're still around in a month or so, come visit.'

'To see your initials carved into the table?'

'Nah, to climb Temple Basin and check out where you had your first kiss.'

'That'd be sweet,' Leigh said. 'But I'm heading back to Melbourne. I'm nearly done on this draft.'

'Ah, well. Another time.'

I stood to clear the plates, and between the ten-day slog and the fact that I never drank wine, I realised I was exhausted. I wondered where the night was headed. I liked Leigh a lot, but after misjudging things so badly with my old friend, I didn't trust my ability to read a situation.

Leigh poured two whiskies, then turned shy.

'I've got a surprise,' she said. 'I made you a bath.'

I laughed. 'What do you mean, you made a bath?'

'I thought: what would I want if I'd had ten days in the bush? So I bought an old bath and set it up outside.'

Nestled among the ferns, overlooking the estuary and the distant Paparoas, Leigh had built a small wooden platform with a bath perched on top. We bucketed hot water from the bathroom in the twilight, then stood watching the steam lifting on the briny breeze. It was perfect.

'Who's going first?' I said after a while.

Leigh rolled her eyes and started to undress. 'Get in,' she said.

PART II: WAIMAKARIRI GORGE, FOOTHILLS OF THE CANTERBURY ALPS. AUTUMN.

The foothills of the Torlesse Range rose above me in sinuous white curves of new snow. In the gorge below, the immense Waimakariri River coiled south towards the plains. It was still autumn but the air already tasted bitter and exhilarating, of the winter to come.

Two steps ahead of me a hawk startled from the underbrush and shot skyward. She wheeled and climbed out of the shadows, then seemed to burst into flame as the late-afternoon sun caught in her wings. She hung motionless on an updraft and we watched each other carefully. Against the depthless blue I couldn't judge scale; her wingspan could have been huge. There's an old story from these mountains about a giant eagle that hunted men to feed its chicks.

A distant murmur grew to a roar, and a train swung round the corner and slammed past: lit windows, starched shirts, passengers reading tablets or staring into space. Two teenagers in the rear viewing car did a double take and waved, then the TranzAlpine hissed away round a bend. Silence returned. God, it felt good to be out here on foot. I just had to make it across the gorge at Staircase Creek before dark.

As day faded I followed the burnished rails into twilight, jogging past stacks of rotting sleepers with my pack bouncing on my back. At Staircase Creek I halted at the edge of the ravine. The railway line crossed on an airy lattice of steel, then disappeared into a tunnel on the far side. I could scramble down eighty metres of steep rock, then climb about twice that height to get out the other side. Or I could trespass across the viaduct like a tightrope walker, then creep through the tunnel, bracing for a wind of diesel and steel. It looked like I had some scrambling to do.

Deer often find the best routes in the Alps, and sure enough a track led down into the ravine. Towards the bottom the trail steepened, turning into loose shingle over rock slabs. I slithered down as if walking on marbles. A slip wasn't serious here, but if I fell while climbing out the much steeper other side, I'd die. Better to camp at the bottom and wait until first light.

Deep in the gorge I pitched my tent on an icy river terrace, gathered armfuls of driftwood, and sparked a bonfire. Looking up at low cloud whipping overhead, I felt like I was camped at the bottom of a well. The night grew freezing and I built the blaze higher, till the heat scorched my cheeks. The moon rose, projecting a line of shadow down the disintegrating bluffs, until it came full over the ridge, striking a blue gleam off each river stone.

The following day I was meeting the veteran wilderness writer Kennedy Warne at Flock Hill, fifteen kilometres to the west. We were off to climb Kura Tawhiti (Mt Torlesse) in the snow. After that, I'd detour west across the valley to the other site known as Kura Tawhiti, the spectacular limestone fortress at Castle Hill, to investigate claims that it was the spiritual centre of Māori culture in the Alps. Then I would continue north to Arthur's Pass. On impulse, Leigh was flying over from Melbourne to meet me. I couldn't wait. I turned in, ready for an early start.

•

In the small hours I snapped awake to find my tent flooded in pewter light, and with the total certainty that there were people outside. The wind was up, flapping the tent walls hard. I sensed the visitors standing very still, listening as I listened, holding their breath as I held mine. I somehow knew it was a travelling party, all of them armed, wondering who I was and why I was there. I didn't dare open the tent fly and find their tattooed faces gazing in; nor could I bring myself to dispel the illusion and unzip to find empty ground. I lay silent in my sleeping bag, straining to hear something above the wind. At some point I drifted back to sleep, and to wild dreams.

At 5.45 a.m. I woke, bemused by my overactive imagination. We have stories about patupaiarehe, fairy people who visit travellers, and whose fires leave no trace. Some part of me had believed in the vision enough to feel a twinge of fear. But when I emerged from the tent, I saw that I had been visited in the night—by snow. I gazed around at the white veil covering my tent and the cliffs and the riverbed, then looked down in wonder. Stark against the white landscape, a perfect black circle lay at my feet, where I'd built my fire. Right where I'd imagined the people standing.

Ahikāroa, 'the long-burning fires of occupation', refers to the authority and guardianship that comes from occupying land. In the complex Māori system of collective land tenure, property rights came through discovery, marriage, conquest or inheritance, but all had to be backed up with ahi kā, the fires of occupation. Here in the high country, that meant annual seasonal visits to mahika kai. My map, from Ngāi Tahu's head archivist, Takerei Norton, showed lines of foot travel heading this way as dense as a London Underground map. Taruwahine, Te Kauaka, Te Notī,

Te Awa-a-Tutu: each was a station on the inland line to the high country, and the West Coast via Tarahaka, Arthur's Pass. I was walking to Arthur's Pass to learn more about Ngāi Tahu's culture of travelling, and ahi kā.

•

By first light I was packed and ready to go, energised for the day ahead. I paced up and down the riverbed, scanning the cliffs for a good line, then waded across the icy river and began to climb. Snow fell with an insistent wet hush against my hood. I wormed hand over hand through scrub, then scrambled up a steep rocky rib. Soon I was standing high and breathless above the viaduct, looking down on the gorge through a haze of falling snow. I pulled up and over onto flat ground, and sped north, scrambling over slippery snow-covered tussocks in running shoes, with the mighty Waimakariri rushing away below.

Before lunch I reached the point where the gorge opened onto the broad golden tablelands of the upper Waimakariri Basin. A tawny Sphinx-like hill stood watch over Slovens Stream. The cloud had started to lift, leaving the line of mountains above me frosted white. Silvery birdsong rang from nearby stands of beech.

This landscape lies under the protective cloak of Ngāi Tūāhuriri, the hapū of Ngāi Tahu based at Tuahiwi, and before that at Kaiapoi Pā. Joseph Hullen, an easygoing whakapapa expert with dreadlocks, a dry sense of humour and an astonishing knowledge of Ngāi Tūāhuriri and Ngāi Tahu history, had given me a vivid description of the scene in the old days.

Deep-green forests of massive tōtara trees flanked the mountains, ringing the golden-brown basin of harakeke (flax), raupō (rushes) and hebe, interspersed with dry patches of inaka and matagouri scrub. Moa grazed the open areas. Limestone outcroppings, so stark today, were largely hidden by bush, but had small swamps and ponds at their bases.

The flanks of Kura Tawhiti (Mt Torlesse) were known as Te Māeaea, and they were rich in kākāpō. These chubby flightless night parrots had a booming call; their iridescent green feathers were used to make beautiful cloaks. When the hapū arrived in the region, the sons of leading chief Tūāhuriri each wanted Te Māeaea for their own daughters.

Three of the sons—club-footed Tūrakautahi, Moki the war-leader, and the eldest, Tanetiki (who later led an expedition over Nōti Raureka, and drowned at Māhinapua)—walked into the foothills to hold a taunaha, a verbal competition between chiefs. A taunaha blurs the lines between person and place. You lay claim to a landscape by likening it to your body: that ridge is my elbow; that lake is the cup of my hand.

To make a strong claim, you need details of the landscape in question. In one version of the tale, Tūrakautahi, with his club foot, knew he'd reach Whata-a-rama (Otarama Peak) too late to compete with his brothers. Instead, he had his slave climb a tree and sight Kura Tawhiti above the forest canopy. Tūrakautahi then claimed the entire mountain by making it one with his person: 'Ko Kuratawhiti te mauka kākāpō. Ko au te takata.' (Kuratawhiti is the mountain of the kākāpō. I am the man [who claims it].)

Kura Tawhiti stands visible right across the Canterbury Plains, and its flanks were just one among thousands of mahika kai: literally 'food-making-places'. Each mahika kai had multiple own-ers, and each hapū, whānau and individual had rights to multiple mahika kai. Some were occasional stopping places; many were

semi-permanent villages and seasonal camps. In the densely popu-
lated east, there were three for every kilometre of coastline. Around
South Canterbury, the camps were spaced on average every fifteen
square kilometres, and every twenty-four up in the Waimakariri
Basin. That meant roughly a five-kilometre walk from one to the
next. The entire high country was dotted with such places.

The esteemed Ngāi Tahu archaeologist Atholl Anderson,
author of numerous books about the tribe, and an emeritus professor at the Australian National University in Canberra, says the
preferred site was a 'stretch of flax-bordered stream where eels
and other fish were procured, ducks caught, and fern root or tī
kōuka [cabbage-tree pith] obtained'. To live well, travelling parties
needed little more than a spear and a gaff. It wasn't subsistence living, either. In the winter months the high country tussock teemed
with weka, plump with their winter fat. Parties lived inland for
months, catching, preserving and packing hundreds of birds to be
eaten over the rest of the year. 'They'd depot stuff,' Joseph Hullen
said, 'then use Broken River to ferry it down through the gorge on
mōkihi. It's gnarly now, but there were very different flow volumes
before the land was drained.'

Here in the south, where it was too cold for imported Polynesian crops, mahika kai were essential. The first and most basic
meanings of travelling in those days were sustenance and ownership. Travelling parties moved through on foot, following the
seasons, harvesting and tending, keeping the fires burning in each
place.

·

Striding down a muddy farm track cut into the side of Bold Hill,
I saw the Avoca Homestead waiting below. The farmhouse was

freshly painted, cream with red trim, and framed by neat box hedges. Someone had left an axe sunk into a chopping block out front. Standing at the door, I felt like I should knock. Avoca is now a public hut, but it was once the most remote high-country station in New Zealand.

I shot the bolt, swung open the door and sat at the scarred wooden dining table, half-expecting to hear the scuff and scrape of boots outside. After eating sandwiches made with clumsy, thawing hands, I charted my course to where I was due to meet Kennedy Warne.

The traditional route into the Waimakariri Basin came up and over Ōtāneuru (Porters Pass). My route via the gorge would only have been used when returning to the coast in mōkihi; I had chosen it for the westward journey because it allowed me to travel long distances on private land. Hundreds of inland mahika kai became off-limits in the 1860s with the erection of fences during the high-country farming boom. Over the next couple of days, I wanted to capture a little of how that lockout might have felt.

I set off to the west, wading through the numbing waters of Broken River and climbing out onto the flanks of Broken Hill. A series of broad tussock terraces would take me twelve kilometres across a working high-country farm.

Out in the open, I was watchful and alert. I crouched to inspect hoof prints and tyre tracks, trying to gauge their age, wondering where the shepherds were. It's not uncommon to have to cross farmland to reach the start of a track in New Zealand, but you always get permission first. Without it, I imagined armed land-owners and angry dogs over every rise. I took my breaks crouched out of sight.

Go fast, I told myself. Faster.

The feeling of trespassing in this landscape, of being watched, was very old. As I contoured around the side of Flock Hill, I saw two kāhu (hawks) dipping and circling in the icy blue. The tale of the man-eating pouākai would have been recounted by any travelling party coming this way.

•

The pouākai, or Pou-a-Hawaiki, was a giant eagle that nested on the side of Kura Tawhiti and preyed on travellers passing into the Waimakariri Basin via Ōtāneuru. Walkers had to be alert to the circling shadow, the blotted sun, the sudden whistling strike. The creature carried off its victims to feed its chicks.

Among the local people there was a famously fast runner named Hautere. He hatched a plan. At the base of Ōtāneuru, at Kōwai Stream, the people built a house with windows but no door, and draped with nets. The strongest warriors hid inside. Then Hautere went out to attract the huge predator. When the pouākai appeared overhead, circling on outstretched wings, Hautere sprinted for the house. The eagle folded its wings and dived, but Hautere reached the house and leapt in through a window.

The eagle jammed one wing through the window, then through another, trying to get at the men inside. There was a violent tussle, feathers flying, giant tendons cracking. The men entangled the poukai in their nets and beat it to death. Tired and bleeding, they emerged from the house, but they still weren't safe. The eagle had a nest, and the nest had chicks. The warriors climbed the ridge from Kowai Stream, heading up towards the summit of Kura Tawhiti, and crept close to the nest. They lay in hiding, listening to the chicks' strange song, carefully memorising the notes. Then they pounced and killed the fledgling pouākai. The people were safe to travel into the Waimakariri Basin, and still are today.

•

The story is rooted in this specific landscape, and it shows the importance of the route and the inland mahika kai. It's also ancient: versions of the tale are told right across the Pacific. It was carried here in the memories of the first arrivals, the Waitaha people. Yet, when they stepped ashore, the legend of the pouākai became true.

New Zealand was then home to the largest bird of prey ever known. Called the Haast's eagle in English, the real pouākai had a wingspan of three metres, weighed up to sixteen kilograms, and preyed on moa, the large flightless birds that grazed the high country and plains. Kennedy Warne's description of the kārearea (New Zealand falcon), a modern bird of prey evolved to hunt in the same terrain, suggests what pouākai were capable of: 'prolonged chases through dense bush, contour-hugging prey searches, screaming dives...and surprise attacks, where prey are plucked out of the sky literally without knowing what hit them.' The fossil record shows a striking pouākai could punch its talons clean through a moa's pelvis, with an impact like being hit by a block of concrete thrown from an eight-storey building.

Joseph Hullen told me that when moa became extinct, there's a good chance pouākai may have prey-switched to humans; we have four separate oral traditions on this point. I've seen drawings on cave walls in South Canterbury depicting the eagle hunting overhead. The old story probably started its life far away as history, arrived here as myth, then perhaps taught our ancestors how to fight a real predator; before slowly becoming myth once again.

•

Further west, the land opened out and the light turned gold. My paranoia was for nothing: as the kilometres clicked over I saw no one, and save for the glassy eyes of a wild pig's severed head, no one saw me. This late in the season, the ground was frozen solid. The shepherds had moved all the stock to lower ground, leaving the land looking unused. *Waste-land*. I smiled to myself. That bulky hill to my right was my shoulder, the descending ridge my arm. Perhaps I could claim the farm as my own.

The declining sun pulled the valley into shadow, and the air began to bite. Night came on as I circled the base of Flock Hill, a slanting plateau several kilometres across, spiked with thousands of rock pinnacles. I flashed my head torch across the weathered limestone escarpments above.

'Cooo-eeee!' I called into the silence.

No reply. I checked the map to confirm I was in the right place. I'd sent Kennedy Warne a message saying *Meet me here!* along with the co-ordinates for where a cache of fifteenth-century tramping gear had been found. The spot was immediately above me.

For an hour, I wandered among the eerie rock towers, hoping to find Kennedy while staying hidden from the landowners. The limestone forms loomed from the dark like the half-buried bones of giants. Frosted tussock crackled underfoot. I clicked off my light, hoping to catch the glow of a campfire. No sign. A faint breeze curled through the limestone chimneys, whispering in my ear. 'Hello? Kennedy?' I called.

Something moved in my peripheral vision. I turned sharply. Slowly, steadily, the first sliver of a huge yellow moon climbed from behind a nearby tor into the sky.

Beneath a deep limestone overhang, I made camp and lit my
stove. Firelight flared across the surrounding walls. Several hundred years ago, just thirty metres from my perch, a Māori tramper
had stashed an ingenious and beautiful backpack of woven flax
with a round wooden frame and broad shoulder strap. Inside were
kākahi shells, used as knives; feathers and fine cordage; unfinished
paua-shell pendants; and bones. Underneath the pack was a pile
of dry firewood and kindling. The stash was uncovered in 1983,
and is now held in the Canterbury Museum.

I sat warming my hands over the burner, delighted at the
beauty of my eyrie, but also tired and strangely anxious from a
day spent on someone else's land. Beneath that, I had a creeping
sense of how much knowledge about these valleys had been hidden, or lost. There was something intimate, and sad, about a bunch
of kindling kept dry for five centuries. It anticipated a campfire,
warmth, belonging: ahi kā. I thought about the traveller who had
placed that tinder into the rock, and why they'd never come back.

Plenty of individual whānau still drive up into the high country
to gather mahika kai and keep traditions alive. Ngāi Tūāhuriri people still have their wakawaka (allocations of harvesting grounds)
up around Kura Tawhiti. But it has been generations since the
majority of the tribe regularly walked our once-vast network of
fisheries, lakes, rivers and hunting grounds. Why?

•

In 1848, under intense pressure from settlers, Ngāi Tahu chiefs
sold twenty million acres of land in this area to the government,
for the Canterbury colony. The chiefs still drove a hard bargain:
the sale would only proceed if the tribe could keep land amounting to approximately one acre in every ten, including all villages

and settlements, large tracts of farmland to stock with sheep and cattle, and all of the mahika kai. Capital from the sale and two million acres of reserves would ensure the tribe could thrive in the new world.

Henry Tacy Kemp, who negotiated the purchase for the government, had official instructions to reserve 'ample portions for [the tribe's] present and future wants'. But he had private instructions as well: to agree to large reserves, but insist they be marked out to Ngāi Tahu's satisfaction *after* the sale. That way, reserves would be seen as 'a boon conferred by the Government', not as Māori reserving from sale what they already owned. This misconception, that reserves were 'given' to indigenous peoples, is still common in former colonies around the world.

Once the sale was concluded with the signing of Kemp's Deed, the job of marking out the reserves went to a minor public servant and later politician named Walter Mantell, who was quietly told he could make whatever reserves 'he may consider necessary'. Mantell was to consolidate reserves into blocks to avoid the 'evils' of inconveniencing future settlers. And Governor George Grey, a passionate advocate for getting natives off their land and into 'civilising' labouring and domestic work, had privately authorised a maximum of ten acres per head.

Walter Mantell thus set off on an infamous journey in the history of New Zealand walking. On his two-month trek south down the east coast of Te Waipounamu, Walter Mantell relied on Ngāi Tahu guides and hospitality; but, when laying out reserves, he rejected the chiefs' instructions with a 'high hand'. The Ngāi Tūāhuriri people at Tuahiwi instructed Mantell to reserve a hundred-thousand-hectare strip through to the West Coast, so as to retain their mahika kai and access to pounamu—including much of the trail I was walking. They got five acres per head. (On the same journey, Mantell allocated a single European settler, John Jones, a 2,650-acre block.) At Kāikanui, near the mouth of the Waimakariri, Werita Tainui and ten others were allocated a total of two acres.

Mantell demanded whole populations move and blackballed anyone who dared argue, reporting them to the government as 'sullen and evilly disposed.' Old chiefs who'd fought the rival iwi Ngāti Toa to protect their ancestral lands were forced to beg an arrogant young stranger for scraps. Mantell should have reserved two million acres. At the end of his walk, he had reserved for the entire tribe a total of 6,359. Those were days of rage and disbelief, and the beginning of a fight that would last seven generations.

And although the right to keep all mahika kai was enshrined in the deed of sale, the Māori version signed by the chiefs vanished into the colonial archives, lost for over a century. The English version was enforced, and it translated mahika kai as merely plantations. It was a simple but effective deception. Ngāi Tahu's vast network of food-gathering places collapsed into a few domestic gardens. The high country was sold off to farmers. The last great inland walk was in 1871, when the prophet Hipa Te Maiharoa led two hundred followers into the Waitaki Basin, where they asserted their ownership by peacefully occupying ancestral lands. For two years they farmed at Te Ao Mārama (Ōmārama), harvested mahika kai and taught the spiritual traditions of the interior. Then the colony's Armed Constabulary evicted them at gunpoint, burned their village and sent them back to the coast.

So that's what happened to Ngāi Tahu's travelling culture in the high country. Without right of access to land, walking didn't affirm belonging or ownership. Walking was trespassing. Many fires went out.

PART III: FLOCK HILL, WAIMAKARIRI BASIN. AUTUMN.

I woke to a sublime view of the Craigieburn Range framed between two dark limestone tors. The land rippled and gleamed each time I moved my head. Raw frost cloaked the basin below, while ruby light tipped the encircling peaks. I dragged myself out of my warm cocoon and set off to find Kennedy Warne. Kura Tawhiti was up there on the range to my left. I hoped we'd still have time to climb it.

Before leaving Flock Hill, I paused to create a gear cache of my own. I stuffed my sleeping and cooking gear into a dry bag, and lodged it in a cleft in the limestone, close to the location of the original stash. Wandering away, then looking back to memorise the spot, I wondered what future archaeologists would think if something happened to me on the climb. It looked like hardcore survival gear. Would they guess these were luxury items used in a leisure pursuit? The original flax backpack told us little about the pleasures its owner took from walking in the Alps. But on a pure, windless morning, pacing through a world seemingly snap-frozen, I found it hard to imagine our ancestors didn't take joy from visiting, and feel the loss of access as a physical pain.

At the boundary of Flock Hill Station, next to an enormous NO TRESPASSING sign, I threw my pack over the hurricane fencing and climbed after it. Back on public land for a few hours, I finally relaxed.

There was only one car in the Cave Stream carpark: Kennedy

Warne's well-loved Toyota Surf. It was empty. I made breakfast, and half an hour later the man himself came strolling up from the direction of Broken River Gorge, smiling a little wearily beneath wispy greying hair. In his late fifties, he looked sinewy and strong, with the comfortable dishevelment of a man used to living outdoors.

'What happened to you?!' he said, giving me a big hug.

'I was going to say the same thing!'

Somehow, we'd mixed up the co-ordinates. Kennedy had spent a freezing night out on Gorge Hill instead, with just a tiny remnant tōtara tree for cover.

'I need a coffee,' he said. 'You want one?'

He opened the tailgate of his truck to reveal an espresso maker. Climbing could wait.

•

Kennedy Warne is perhaps New Zealand's most high-profile advocate for the idea that, beyond individual recreation, walking is politically and spiritually significant: it's how we belong to this land. He's Pākehā, with a profound sense of place, and in recent years has turned to te ao Māori, the Māori world, the better to understand his connection to the bush. His book *Tūhoe: Portrait of a Nation* (2013) tells the story of the North Island's Tūhoe people and their unbroken relationship with the mountainous Urewera area. He founded *New Zealand Geographic* and travels the world for *National Geographic*, writing about wilderness, economic development, and the relationship between humans and nature.

'In modern societies, that relationship has become distant and strained,' he has written. 'I have come to think that addressing the land is an essential task if the relationship between people and the natural world is to be restored.'

By 'addressing the land' he means immersing yourself in your environment, leaving tracks behind, moving slowly, swimming in tarns, drinking from streams, listening and feeling and tasting your way through the bush. This is closer to customary Māori ways of travel, and it resonates with pretty much every tramper and climber I know. Certainly my Pākehā family's sense of belonging is closely linked to walking in the bush.

After coffee in the early-morning sun, we packed boots, ice axes and crampons, and set off to address the land.

'Haven't used these in a while!' he said.

'All good,' I said. 'It's just a plod up in the snow.'

We left the sunlit tussock and descended into the frozen gorge of Cave Stream, boulder-hopping across the water where it poured out from a limestone cave system. We picked our way beneath cliffs hung with icicles, breath pluming from our mouths, then climbed out and over Gorge Hill.

Ascending towards a spur that would take us onto Red Peak, we were immediately back on farmland, jumping barbed-wire fences and watching for shepherds, talking about the difference between owning and belonging to land. For our earliest Pākehā ancestors, walking in the high country was about ownership. Like Tūrakautahi and his brothers in the taunaha, they came to claim what they saw. The first generation of settlers wore out their boots clearing, burning and fencing, and it was only later that tramping became a way to belong.

Kennedy has argued that Pākehā can leave this exploitative model behind and become takata whenua (people of the land) through conversation with Māori, and with place. 'The land will naturalise us if we will let it. The land will make us "native"— a nativeness of soul.'

After lunch, our conversation turned to Māori spiritual connections to place. Like any good journalist, Kennedy pumped me for information.

'So, what are the important things you've learned from your walks so far?' he asked, striding ahead.

'Uh,' I said, feeling put on the spot. The spiritual dimension was everywhere, in conversations with friends and elders, in books and manuscripts, in my increasingly vivid dreams, but the whole thing made me acutely uncomfortable. I mumbled something noncommittal.

Kennedy looked back over his shoulder with a mysterious smile, and said, 'So, what do you think "wairua" means?'

I shrugged. 'Spirit, or soul. The essence of a thing.'

'It's two words,' Kennedy said. '"Wai" and "rua"—literally, "two waters". What if it meant there were two waters flowing through everything, like a physical and a spiritual side? So every tree or bird or stone has a spirit of its own? I don't know, but it's fun to think about.'

'Hrmm,' I said. 'Could be.'

'You know,' Kennedy continued, 'more and more I find myself wanting to spend time with indigenous people. We've got so much to learn, especially about how they relate to the land.'

I paused and watched the back of Kennedy's head as he strode away. His sentiment was fine, but he'd unwittingly included me in the camp of non-indigenous people who have a lot to learn. Maybe that wasn't surprising, given how I look—and when he'd spent so much time with native-speaking Tuhoe people with full-facial tā moko. And I *did* have a lot to learn. It still stung.

We tracked south-east, all the while trespassing as we approached the muscular lower flanks of Red Peak. At the edge of the valley basin we stopped at the last fence. Just five strands of wire separated pastureland from the beech forests of Korowai / Torlesse Tussocklands Park, but the difference was profound. The sound of tūī and korimako (bellbirds) shimmered through the canopy on the other side. It was the most intense native birdsong I'd heard in years. For some time we stood listening and watching the chase of iridescent wings.

It was half-past one. We'd been talking a lot faster than we walked, but now, after hours of boring farmland, the fun was about to begin. The summit of Red Peak stood a thousand vertical metres above us, followed by a ridgeline traverse in the snow to reach Kura Tawhiti.

'Ready to climb?' I said. 'We'll be fine getting up, though we'll be coming back in the dark.'

Kennedy hesitated.

'It's a full moon tonight,' I said. 'It'll be awesome. We can rest up on top for a couple of hours until the moon rises, then come back by moonlight. John Pascoe did it all the time in the nineteen-thirties. It'll be bright as day up there.' Invoking the famous local mountaineer would, I hoped, make my plan seem less rogue.

'I'd better not,' Kennedy said. 'I thought I might keep driving, head through to Nelson tonight.'

'Okay, cool.' I nodded, not letting my disappointment show. We turned and ambled back down towards Gorge Hill. The only time we used our ice axes was climbing a steep patch of frozen dirt to get out of the gorge. I remembered turning around on Lauper Peak with Jon and thought: next time, I'll push on alone.

•

Kennedy and I hugged goodbye in the car park, then he gunned his truck and pulled onto State Highway 73. I recovered my cache of gear, and returned to trespassing. It took me an hour wandering the gnarled limestone galleries on top of Flock Hill to find the perfect campsite: sheltered, invisible to farmers, and with thought-annihilating views. I finally found a spot beside two pinnacles like giant chess pieces. It was a beautiful, cracking cold night, but I was frustrated by the last couple of days.

I was out here looking for traces of Ngāi Tahu's travelling culture, but so far I'd really only seen evidence of European farming, and the absence of the wetlands that once made this place so rich in food and resources. The people who could interpret what was still here were all back in the cities, too busy to come walking; without them, the landscape was largely mute. I'd missed Kennedy the night before, we'd failed to climb Kura Tawhiti and our conversations had got my back up. I was grateful he'd come for a walk, but I realised that, right now, I didn't want to be out here speculating about how Māori spirituality could help Pākehā feel like they belonged. I wanted to be walking with the Ngāi Tahu people who already belonged, and to think about how more of the tribe could, too.

And if I was honest, talk of spirituality made me uncomfortable because I *was* interested, but deeply wary of bullshit after what had happened to the last person who'd undertaken a project like mine. Back in the 1980s, another writer had fixated on the Ngāi Tahu mountain trails. He'd dug out the same manuscripts as I had, talked to elders, walked many of the same routes, even written his own book about it. His interest in the technical aspects of the trails gave way to an obsession with the spiritual. He'd come to believe that he'd been chosen to fulfil an ancient prophecy that centred on the other Kura Tawhiti (Castle Hill). And tomorrow, on my way there, I would pass his house.

•

As I detoured south from Flock Hill along the highway, the limestone battlements of Kura Tawhiti (Castle Hill) rose from the valley floor like a ruined mediaeval fortress. I paced my way up a pale, dusty path, through hundreds of standing boulders. Low sun threw their shadows far ahead. More stood watch on the ridgelines to my left and right, weathered into soft curves. I saw the glinting figures of tourists atop the highest walls of the main outcrop, posing for selfies with the basin at their backs.

Roughly a kilometre across, and containing thousands of these stone formations, Kura Tawhiti always captured my imagination as a child. On the way to and from Arthur's Pass, we'd twist in our seats to watch it from the back of the car. It was the closest thing we'd seen to Europe's stone ruins. To the Western imagination, it clearly evokes the work of human hands; in the nineteenth century, the Reverend Charles Clarke thought the stones looked like 'the circling seats of a vast amphitheatre; and...the gigantic monoliths of Stonehenge'. Kura Tawhiti is also important to Ngāi Tahu, sharing its name with the landmark peak east across the valley. It's an obvious and spectacular camping place for parties come to gather mahika kai, or en route to the West Coast. A stream runs through the centre; the limestone is riddled with caves, the caves marked with sacred rock art.

Reaching the centre of the plateau at its heart, I drew crisp air into my lungs and gazed around. Up here, the view of the surrounding snow-capped peaks disappeared behind limestone tors on all sides. The wind dropped; the day grew hushed. Even crawling with tourists, it was a humbling landscape.

In his book *Song of Waitaha* (1994), Barry Brailsford details how the earliest of Ngāi Tahu's ancestors, the Waitaha people, lived peaceful spiritual lives centred on this place. They knew it as Te Kōhaka (the nest, or 'the birthplace of the gods'). These limestone galleries once echoed with sacred chants. The stone formations dotting the hillside were the remains of giant statues like those on Easter Island. Some marked the rising and setting positions of sacred stars. The largest statue was of Rākaihautū, founding chief of Waitaha and the first person to cross the Alps. His bones lay somewhere here. Trails radiated off in all directions, linking settlements on either side of the Alps. Tramping those trails was more than travelling: it was the key to sacred knowledge. *Song of Waitaha* suggests that if I wanted to understand Māori walking culture and spirituality, this was the place to start.

•

Song of Waitaha is perhaps the most widely read book on Māori spirituality ever written. I frequently spot copies on people's bookshelves, and I look it up in public or university libraries wherever I travel around the world. Often, it's there on the shelves. It's remarkable that the book has travelled so far, because, according to Ngāi Tahu leaders and scholars, very little in the book is true. It's not a book about Māori spirituality; it's a book that uses Māori spirituality to justify the European desire to belong in the places that you love, but that your ancestors effectively took.

Barry Brailsford was a Pākehā educator who'd written two
valuable books on Ngāi Tahu history. His *Greenstone Trails* (1984)
details the tribe's routes through the Alps. In the late 1980s he and
another man, Peter Ruka, were chosen to write a book on the
history of the tribe, going back to Waitaha, the earliest people to
arrive in the south. In addition to his earlier books, Brailsford had
given evidence for Ngāi Tahu at the Waitangi Tribunal's investi-
gation into the historical loss of land. When he asked the senior
elder Pani Manawatu for his blessing, the old man said yes. With
support from the Ministry of Education and several major corpo-
rations, the book would go into libraries and schools nationwide.

I'll never forget the day *Song of Waitaha* arrived at our house.
I would have been around fifteen. A package addressed to Mum
arrived. In our hallway she slipped the book from its protective
packaging and turned it to the light. *Song of Waitaha: The Histories of a Nation.* It was exquisite: a pure-white hardback embla-
zoned with a kārara (lizard), the emblem of the spiritual world.
Here was the knowledge of some of Ngāi Tahu's most respected
tohuka. Pani Manawatu's blessing greeted the reader, followed by
photos of esteemed nineteenth-century elders.

Mum opened the book and began to read. An unfamiliar look
crossed her face: disbelief, followed by rage.

Gone was the history of Ngāi Tahu; in its place, Brailsford
had written solely about Waitaha, who he claimed were a totally
separate people from Māori. They had no weapons, no warfare, no
cannibalism, and lived lives of perfect spiritual peace centred on
Te Kōhaka. They'd arrived in New Zealand more than a thousand
years before Māori, and somehow remained hidden until now.
What's more, their advanced civilisation was a nation of many

peoples from the Pacific, Europe, Asia, the Americas and Africa. And, like Brailsford, their founder, Rākaihautū, was white.

In Ngāi Tahu whakapapa, Rākaihautū is a big deal. He was the first ancestor to set foot in Te Waipounamu. Ahi kā begins with him, as the saying goes: 'Ko Rākaihautū te takata nāna i tīmata te ahi ki ruka ki tēnei motu': Rākaihautū was the man who lit the fires of occupation in this island.

In the story we tell, he and the Waitaha people arrived in the Uruao canoe at Whakatū, near Nelson, at the top of the island. Under the leadership of his son Te Rakihouia and his son's wife, Tapuiti, half of the crew explored the east coast in the Uruao, discovering and naming the land as they went. Rākaihautū led the rest of the crew through the interior on foot, where he used his kō (digging staff), Tūwhakaroria, to hew out the major glacier lakes: Takapō, Pūkaki, Ōhou, Hāwea, Wānaka, Whakatipu Waimāori, Whakatipu Waitai, then down to Te Ana-au and the Waiau River. He left two spirit guardians in the south, Notī and Notā.

The party returned north via the coast, digging the eastern lakes as they went. At Waihao they had a joyous reunion with Te Rakihouia's party, then came to Kā Pākihi-whakatekateka-o-Waitaha (the Canterbury Plains). To show his labours were done, he renamed his kō Tuhiraki, and planted it on top of a nearby mountain (Mt Bossu today). You can still see the footrest of the kō from the Akaroa pub.

Today, the fires that Rākaihautū lit are kept burning by Ngāi Tahu. Many of us have Waitaha whakapapa. Part of our mana whenua (authority and legitimacy over the land) lies in tracing descent from Rākaihautū. Brailsford had written that our ancestor Rākaihautū wasn't even Māori: he was European. Māori

were 'invading warrior tribes' from the Pacific who had butchered
and eaten the Waitaha people. In this telling, the true colonisers
of New Zealand were Māori.

.

Leading Ngāi Tahu scholars denounced the book as fantasy.
Associate Professor Te Maire Tau, a direct descendant of Pani
Manawatu, and now the Upoko (head) of Ngāi Tūāhuriri Rūnaka,
wrote that: 'one feels as if one is reading the saga of the smurfs
and their migration to the land of the hobbits. The writer could
find little that could qualify as authentic tradition.' Dr Atholl
Anderson called it 'the latest mutation of a virulent myth', the
racist nineteenth-century falsehood that Māori had wiped out a
peaceful Moriori people, while Tā Tipene O'Regan attacked it
as 'mystical and invented nonsense' deployed for political ends.
Other respected Pākehā historians and archaeologists, including
Michael King and Michael Goldsmith, weighed in. No physical
evidence of a pre-Māori people has ever been found. The formations at Kura Tawhiti are natural, the stones carved by water and
wind. Joseph Hullen told me that nothing in our manuscripts or
traditions suggests major spiritual significance at the site, beyond
it being a stopping place on the inland journey with good shelter
and fresh water, and perhaps a place where people met to trade.

But with Brailsford's earlier accolades and apparently strong
Māori endorsement, the book struck a chord. In the early 1990s,
New Zealand was finally confronting its colonial past. Ngāi Tahu
was at the Waitangi Tribunal, laying out the Crown's default on
land sales such as those under Kemp's Deed. Nationwide, Māori
were increasingly vocal and staunch. Myths about New Zealand
having the best race relations in the world collapsed. Pākehā

anxiety about belonging in this land increased. Faced with this complex new political reality, *Song of Waitaha* offered a soothing fairytale. If you weren't Māori but felt a deep connection to this land, it was because your Waitaha ancestors had been here for two thousand years. You were the real indigenous people of this land.

•

Barry Brailsford lives just over the ridge from Kura Tawhiti, at Castle Hill Village. Now in his eighties, he's short and balding with a kind, florid, round face, grey beard and hopeful, lopsided smile. On my way past the village that morning I'd peered through the trees at the black, grey and green chalets, wondering which was his. He wasn't home, spending autumn and winter further north, but we'd spoken on the phone.

In conversation he was generous and engaging, with the true gift of the gab. When we discussed his earlier archaeology work, his stories were rich with details, names and dates. When we turned to Waitaha and his spiritual writings, though, the conversation was like chasing smoke. His sources were 'the old ones' who'd chosen to reveal their wisdom to him alone. He'd earned an MBE for services to Māori history. How, I wondered, did he leave Māori, and history, so far behind?

Brailsford's collaborator, Peter Ruka, who turned out to have fabricated his Ngāi Tahu whakapapa, started feeding him new-age pap derived from the 'plastic medicine men' of the United States: people falsely claiming to be Native American healers and elders, widely condemned by genuine Native groups for commercialising their spirituality. One of the most infamous was Sun Bear, known for selling fake prophecies of peace to sincere but naive white people. His disciple Wallis Black Elk visited Brailsford while he

was working on the book. Brailsford started talking about such
a prophecy here in New Zealand, only one that was Polynesian:

> And our tūpuna [ancestors] looked behind the rising
> waves of pain and out to the stars, and in words of bind-
> ing prophecy proclaimed...the day will come when the
> taonga will be revealed once more. And we will walk tall
> with the knowledge in the kete [basket] and find joy in
> the colours of the rainbow...And people of all colours
> join to bind what was broken and live in hope.

Believing that this prophecy was about him, Brailsford organised a tramping trip across Nōti Raureka. The party spent their
days travelling up the Arahura River searching for portals, which
looked like rocks. Once each portal was unlocked, the sacred
knowledge of the Waitaha people could be revealed. As the group
followed Raureka's trail, Brailsford claimed to develop the ability
to 'mind-fly', sending his consciousness along the track to scout
the way ahead, and to 'time-shift', vanishing round corners then
reappearing hundreds of metres away. The group's hike turned into
an epic spiritual quest. Brailsford was their tohuka, their shaman,
their guide. From this point on, everything he wrote changed.

When a draft of *Song of Waitaha* surfaced, Ngāi Tahu scholars
started asking questions. Nothing in it bore any resemblance to
the work of the Ngāi Tahu tohuka who were its supposed sources.
Brailsford wouldn't reveal his actual sources; the 140 'elders of
the Nation of Waitaha' who apparently supported him 'to the
death' weren't prepared to give their names. The tribe withdrew
all support for the project. Pani Manawatu, the Ngāi Tahu elder
whose blessing fronts the book, died three years before it came

out. He'd never read what he was supposed to have endorsed, but Brailsford used his words anyway. 'Apoplectic with rage' is how Mum describes some of Manawatu's relations at the time. Instead of listening to the tribe, Brailsford took himself off on speaking tours around the world.

This was why I was reluctant to engage with others over Māori spirituality in the mountains. Whenever I had a strange dream, or a surreal experience like being swallowed by storm clouds on top of Nōti Raureka, or heard someone talk about becoming tangata whenua through spiritual tramping, I thought of Barry Brailsford walking the pounamu trails, convinced that he could teleport from place to place, unlocking portals to other worlds.

Kennedy Warne is different: he understands that Māori spirituality and connection to place are inseparable from the loss of those places, and the need to see justice done. Our chiefs agreed to European settlement with certain conditions. Legitimacy and belonging come from knowing those conditions are being met: that deeds of sale are honoured, that Māori are equal partners under the Treaty, that amends are made for past breaches. It may be less romantic than belonging to a secret ancient civilisation, but it's real. We will all feel a deep sense of belonging when we have a clear conscience about who owns the land beneath our boots.

•

That afternoon the nor'-wester sprang up and refused to die. At Ōpōreaiti (Lake Grasmere) I went down to the water's edge, jostled along by a scrum of curious heifers, and pitched camp in the meagre shelter of a stand of poplars. The wind howled through the branches and threatened to flatten my tent. Grasmere was where William and Dorothy Wordsworth lived, in the Lake District, the epicentre of English Romanticism. Just as my Māori ancestors brought names like Waimakariri and Kura Tawhiti and thousands of others from Eastern Polynesia, my European ancestors brought Oxford and Cambridge and Grasmere. This Lake Grasmere was surrounded by vast bulwarks of shingle left by departed glaciers, watched over by higher peaks to the north.

Come dusk, last light struck clean off the lake and the black hills ran a ring around the horizon. The migrating autumn stars were so different from those of summer: Puaka directly above, Tautoru sinking to the west.

The crystalline alpine air of the Waimakariri Basin drew Māori up here to observe the stars that had guided the voyaging canoes. To the first generation of European settlers, the stars in the Southern Hemisphere were upside down. To their kids, the stars had never been any other way up. At some point we forgot there was another Kura Tawhiti, another Waimakariri, another Grasmere. This was the only one.

·

Acute morning light caught every fold of the dry golden hills. I walked up the valley towards Goldney Saddle and the snowy spines of the Polar Range beyond. Trespassing made the land seem a little wild; it made me a little wild too, tramping along in ditches and shitting in the fields. Scratched, scuffed and happy, I waded a half-frozen swamp with barbed wire on one side and Grasmere's wind-ruffled waters on the other.

From the crest of Goldney Saddle, the braided Waimakariri spread out below. The wide shingle valley still contained all of the river's old channels, enough for hundreds of rivers past. To the west, a scruff of thick cloud was massing at the Main Divide. A nor'-west storm was due after lunch and there were flood warnings. The old Ngāi Tahu trail followed the northern banks of the Waimakariri, where the Bealey and Hawdon rivers would be impassable after heavy rain. I picked up the pace.

Across Mt White Bridge I struck out west through thickets of wild roses ripe with orange hips. The grass beneath my feet had been flattened by earlier floods. Cicada song shimmered on all sides and the sun was warm on my back. I moved from farmland to tussock and on into savanna-like matagouri scrub. The mountains grew closer and the markers of civilisation dropped away. In moments like this walking offered a perfect mental wilderness, free from thought.

An hour later, a freezing wind raked through the tussock. At sunset a circus of threatening orange and purple clouds formed overhead. The Waimakariri forced me to the northern edge of the valley, the railway line my only way forward. Thirty seconds after committing to the tracks, a rising metallic hiss sent me scrabbling down the bank. I clung to the undergrowth with the river surging beneath my runners and the TranzAlpine thundering overhead.

With the storm holding off, the Bealey River posed no threat. I waded across to Te Pākihi-tikumu, a mahika kai area stretching up the Bealey, over the pass and down to Ōtira. I pitched my tent in the campground beside the highway at Klondyke Corner and kindled a fire as the first raindrops fell. But the wind was wild and changeable, whipping smoke into my face no matter where I sat. I doused the embers and stood with sooty hands on hips to watch the storm swallow the peaks overhead. North-west up the Bealey, what looked like peaks were actually boiling clouds. The true horizon lay open, suggesting a pass.

•

I'd officially made it to the first wilderness of my childhood: Arthur's Pass National Park. The track to Anti Crow Hut, where Dad took us on our first tramping trip, was two kilometres south. A few hundred metres up the road, I'd set out on my first proper alpine exploration, at age twelve, to Barker Hut. Both routes follow the Waimakariri up towards its source at the Main Divide.

In the late 1840s, Ngāi Tahu had wanted to keep this land as part of a hundred-thousand-hectare strip running through to the West Coast. Walter Mantell ignored their instructions because the proposed reserve included significant grazing land. Eighty years later, the pristine scenery trumped grazing rights. Instead of a native reserve, it became a nature reserve, to protect the land for future generations. Arthur's Pass National Park was created in 1929. As a member of those future generations, I was grateful. But what if Ngāi Tahu had been allowed the reserve, and New Zealand's walking culture had developed with Māori still owning the land? What kind of hybrid traditions might have emerged if Kemp's Deed had been honoured, the mahika kai preserved?

With two million acres of land and serious capital to develop it, Ngāi Tahu would by now have been an economic powerhouse for seven generations. There would be thriving seasonal settlements beside all the inland lakes and rivers and wetlands—flashing past your car window every minute or two—with houses that were part traditional Māori whare (house), part alpine chalet. High-country sheep stations would have carved wooden posts and gates out front, and generations of shearing gangs would sleep in Māori meeting houses beneath the peaks. There would be vast wetlands and forests supplying weka, tuna, kākāpō, kiore (native rats) and kiwi to a thriving Māori and Pākehā middle class who'd come up for weekends of eeling and birding, storytelling and mountain biking, and of course tramping.

Tramping wouldn't be just from hut to hut, but between mahika kai. Part of the joy of walking would be harvesting your own food along the way, and it would be common to meet large family groups on the trail in Gore-Tex and merino hiking gear with white pails full of weka swinging from their hands. The highlight of the trip, the thing every kid would look forward to for months, would be white-water rafting back to the coast on updated mōkihi. Everyone would go out into the hills with their maps showing Māori and English names, and with knowledge of the stories behind each one. And whereas in Europe we might look to ruined castles for a sense of history, here we'd find it in those names, and in the ground beneath our feet.

The tribe is on its way to realising this vision. Through the Waitangi Tribunal process and the courts, Ngāi Tahu finally forced the Crown to acknowledge it had defaulted on Kemp's Deed, and eight others, and had systematically excluded Ngāi Tahu from land, payment and resources. Compensation paid in 1997 was worth less than one per cent of what was owed, yet tribal businesses have since turned that sum into assets worth over NZ$1.5 billion. Some of the proceeds are being used to rekindle the inland fires.

Ngāi Tahu has bought three high-country stations and runs a range of inland tourism businesses—updating the long tradition of guiding visitors through our domain. The Dark Sky Project at Takapō (Tekapo) is an observatory that combines Western and Māori astronomy. Local rūnaka host or run host or run a range of walking and history programmes, and are revegetating wetlands and lakes across Te Waipounamu. Seventy-two nohoaka (encampment) sites approximate traditional mahika kai beside rivers and lakes, with tribal members allowed to camp for more than half of each year.

Multiple walking programmes combine Ngāi Tahu values with Pākehā tramping culture. Te Ara Whakatipu leads a group of high-school students across the Hollyford pounamu trail. Manawa Hou sees teenagers spend four days in the bush in a different part of our territory each year. The tribe's main leadership programme, Aoraki Bound, brings twenty-five people into these mountains on a cultural-immersion bootcamp. An annual alpine expedition sees four Ngāi Tahu don crampons and climb to Ball Pass, right beneath the great ancestor-mountain Aoraki himself.

Collectively, we were taking that kindling left in a cleft at Flock Hill five centuries ago, and lighting a bonfire that would be visible from every mountaintop in the land.

·

Morning brought the rain's steady hammer and the muffled roar of the Bealey River rising. I stuffed my sodden tent into my pack, and took to the bush between the river and State Highway 73. Driving this stretch of highway requires total concentration through gloomy forest and tight bends; the landscape passes unseen. Out in the riverbed, on foot, I could see the route was easy: large parties with kids could have come this far. I brushed through grass flats and open beech forest, with just the odd patch of boggy ground sucking at my shoes.

I paused at the confluence of the Mingha and Edwards rivers to scan the rain-shrouded valleys ahead. The valley walls narrowed and steepened on either side. It was a foul day, horizontal sleet lashing my face, but I was happy enough. Leigh was arriving from Melbourne tomorrow. I turned north-west and headed for Arthur's Pass village.

An hour or two later I breached the long wet grasses and splashed up the highway into civilisation. The township is a handful of one-room workers' cottages at the base of a deep V-shaped valley. I tramped past the Department of Conservation headquarters, the railway station, the tiny stone chapel with its altar window framing a boiling waterfall that suggested, today, an angry god. Squalls of rain strafed the road around me with such ferocity that people had gathered in the window of the general store to watch.

Everywhere I looked trails led off into the mountains, and the past. This was one of my most beloved homes-away-from-home. I caught the familiar blue tang of coal smoke streaming from a dozen chimneys.

The route continued north to the pass, then down the Ōtira River to join the Hurunui Saddle trail, reaching the West Coast via the Taramakau. Pounamu parties went west that way, but returned via the Hurunui: you had to swim the Ōtira Gorge, and that was impossible when carrying pounamu boulders home. With the rivers in high flood, my plan to descend the Ōtira and swim through the gorge would have to wait.

•

There was a ritual to arriving at Rākauiti, the former Christchurch Ski Club hut that my cousins owned, where we'd stayed since we were kids. You opened the door, kicked off your boots and padded into the main room, with its green paisley curtains and photos of Kaimatau (Mt Rolleston) peeling from the walls. You turned on the water and the power, split kindling, filled a tin bucket with coal. After building a nest of twigs in Little Dorrit, the potbelly stove, you struck a match. Ahi kā. It was good to be back.

Before bed, I turned on my phone and checked my messages. The lively voice of Donelle Manihera, from Ngāi Tahu's Iwi Capability Development team, filled the room. Was I interested in joining the annual alpine expedition to Ball Pass in a month's time, then doing Aoraki Bound next summer? There was also an email from Maurice Manawatu, convener of the tribe's wānaka pūrākau, a small group that meets regularly to learn traditional history and whakapapa. Maurice confirmed that I had a place at the next hui (gathering). I slumped in an armchair and exhaled, then leapt up and did a little shuffling happy dance.

·

The next day, Leigh came straight from the airport. It'd been more than a month since we'd seen each other. We stood kissing in the doorway with the rain pelting down outside.

'It's exactly how I imagined it,' she said, dumping her pack and collapsing onto the bench seat by the fire. I had lamb shanks bubbling on the stove, and the last sixpack of beer from the general store cooling in the fridge. She leaned forward to read the name plate on the stove. 'Little Dorrit. We had one of these at our place when I was a kid, only bigger.'

'I need to install one at my place in the bush,' I said, referring to the freezing mudbrick cottage north of Melbourne where I went to write.

'I'll give you a hand if you like. They're great—it's almost too hot in here.'

Smart-arse replies about wearing too many clothes flashed

through my head, but I stopped myself. 'Thanks,' I said. 'That'd be sweet.'

We ate, and lost hours in conversation while the rain eased to a slow spatter on the roof, then crawled into bed.

Sleep was warm and deep, until I dreamed of the white face of a glacier looming overhead, and heard a distant rumble that swelled into a thunderous roar that shook the whole hut, sending me swimming towards consciousness with the screaming thought: *Avalanche! Move!*

A blade of yellow light passed across the room, thrown by the headlights of a freight truck coasting past outside. I was lying half-under my pillow with the white fabric pressed against my face. Beside me, Leigh lay asleep, one tattooed arm curled above her head.

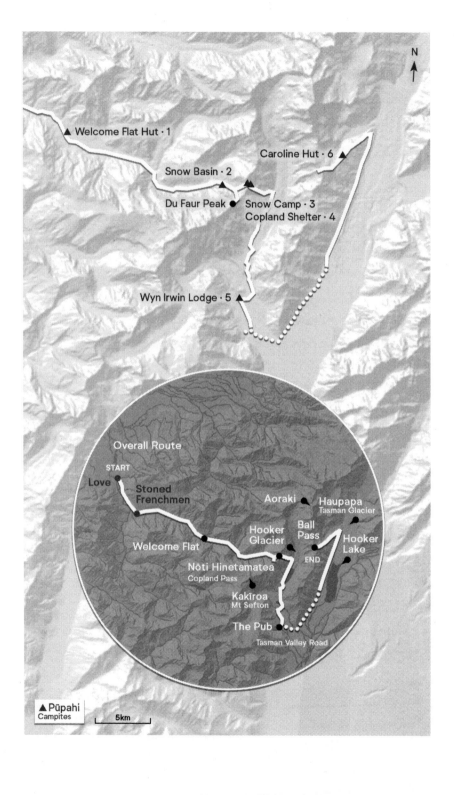

N

▲ Welcome Flat Hut · 1

Caroline Hut · 6 ▲

Snow Basin · 2 ▲

Du Faur Peak ● ▲ Snow Camp · 3
Copland Shelter · 4

Wyn Irwin Lodge · 5 ▲

Overall Route

START
Love
Stoned
Frenchmen

Aoraki   Haupapa
              Tasman Glacier

Welcome Flat

Hooker   Ball
Glacier   Pass   Hooker
                     Lake
Nōti Hinetamatea   END
Copland Pass

Kakiroa
Mt Sefton

The Pub
Tasman Valley Road

▲ Pūpahi
Campites   5km

5

Nōti Hinetamatea
(Copland Pass)

**PART I: COPLAND VALLEY, SOUTH WESTLAND.
LATE AUTUMN.**

It was dark when we stepped from the car, unfurling limbs cramped from the long drive down the West Coast. With the engine running and headlights on high beam, my brother Tim pitched the tent. Leigh helped me unload the gear. We worked fast, hunched against a storm wind that had already plastered the lower half of the island with snow.

When we were done, Leigh came and tucked herself into the crook of my body, her head under my chin. I buried my nose in her hair.

'I'd better get going,' she said.

'Soon,' I replied.

Neither of us moved. She had a long drive to get back to the Taramakau; soon after, she was flying out to Melbourne again, with no plans to return. We'd just spent a couple of weeks in calm but focused bliss, going for runs up Avalanche Peak or hiking to Temple Basin in the mornings, writing during the day, luxuriating by night. But neither of us had any real plans, beyond finishing our books. Hers was well on its way, while mine had barely started. I'd been on the road so much I was keen to be in one place, while she was restless, accustomed to difference, to change. It'd been a sweet summer and autumn, but I had a feeling we'd go our separate ways.

She said something softly, her words muffled into my chest, and they took a moment to register above the wind and the purr of the car's engine: 'I love you.'

I could just make out her face in the refracted glow of the headlights, eyes wide in the gloom, her face raw with cold. We'd only known each other a short while. It felt sudden, precarious.

'These last few months have been perfect,' I said. 'I'm just not there yet. Give me time?'

She nodded. I stood stiffly, hating the words that came out of my mouth. I'd been up for the sparky conversation and companionship and sex, but hadn't really considered anything beyond a summer fling. Now winter was on its way, and we were saying goodbye.

Leigh turned to go, into the glare of the headlights, the wind whipping her hair around her face.

•

Down in the dense South Westland bush, two small pīwakawaka (fantails), nimble as hummingbirds, flitted around my head. Air and feathers brushed my face. In the cool darkness of the under-storey one flashed through a patch of morning sunlight, then the other; then they vanished into the gloom along the trail. Tim and I lumbered after them, as if they were leading the way.

I heard voices on the trail ahead. '*Putain—que c'est magnifique.*'

In a small clearing, three magnificently stoned Frenchmen sat smoking a joint and exclaiming over the baroque mossy forest and the peaks visible through the canopy. Tim and I paused for a snack. They eyed our enormous packs, dangling with ropes and axes and boots.

'Where are you going?' one asked.

'Aoraki,' I said, gesturing east with a handful of peanuts. I noticed the Frenchmen were all wearing street shoes. One had a small backpack like you might take to school. The others were empty-handed. 'What about you guys?' I asked.

'We walk to the hot spring and stay in the hut,' he said. 'Do you think it is okay if we have no booking?'

I shrugged. 'I'm sure they won't make you sleep outside.'

On second thoughts, I wasn't so sure. Located next to a natural hot spring, Welcome Flat Hut is the most popular hut on the West Coast. Its forty bunks are booked out months in advance.

'Ah, you know we don't have a booking either,' Tim reminded me when we continued up the track. Tall, lean and strong, reserved but warm, with an absurd sense of humour, he is five years younger than me, but we're close. He's a superb rock climber and taught me everything I know about off-track navigation. He's also the voice of reason whenever I get carried away.

'True,' I replied. 'But we've got a tent. Those guys don't even have sleeping bags.'

'Or food...Hey, check that out.'

Perched above us in a silver beech, a stout tui with teal breast feathers and white throat tufts graunched out her distinctive, angular notes.

We heard the same rough silver music several times through the day, and glimpsed the birds flitting through the trees. Higher up the valley, curious bellbirds followed us, whistling and chiming in the mamaku. Tomtits were constant companions. As we lunched beside Tatawhaka Creek, another pair of pīwakawaka fought a playful dogfight around my head. This really was the valley of the birds.

•

Later in the week Tim and I were due to meet up with two other young Ngāi Tahu for the annual Ball Pass expedition into the snow on the shoulder of Aoraki / Mt Cook. The mountain, the highest in New Zealand, is the focal point Ngāi Tahu's creation stories, and the symbol of our mana.

Tim and I had decided to approach the mountain on foot. We'd also heard murmurs about an old Ngāi Tahu route that crossed the Alps from South Westland to Aoraki via Copland Pass. South Westland is the territory of the Kāti Māhaki branch of Ngāi Tahu, so we'd gone to visit two of their senior people to find out more.

Susan Wallace and Paul Madgwick welcomed Tim and me into their offices in Hokitika. Over tea and biscuits, I asked if Copland Pass had ever been a Ngāi Tahu route. They looked taken aback.

'Absolutely,' Susan said. In her early fifties, friendly and direct, Susan was Kāti Māhaki's elected representative on the main tribal council. 'Our people used Copland Pass,' she said. 'We tell an old story about its discovery by our ancestor Hinetamatea, and her two sons and their wives.'

'It was handed down to us in our oral traditions,' Paul said. He was the chair of the Kāti Māhaki Rūnaka, editor of the West Coast's daily paper, and the author of a Māori history of the area, *Aotea*. 'The story's also recorded in a manuscript from our elders. The pass wasn't used often, but it was used on a key migration from here to a place on the eastern side called Pōpātea, then on a return journey west several generations later. We're not totally sure of Hinetamatea's whakapapa, but it's an ancient story.'

That manuscript was written in 1897, when eight men and women gathered to discuss the landscapes of the south-west. They were all descendants of the great southern chief and tohuka Tūtoko, and were experts in back-country travel; as I'd later find out, they formed part of a dynasty of Ngāi Tahu mountaineers. A Pākehā surveyor recorded their conversations about the local histories of the tribe, the alpine passes used, the names of rivers and mountains, and some of the old tales.

One of those tales was the story of their ancestor Hineta-matea's discovery of Copland Pass:

> Hinetamatea and her two sons Tatawhaka and Komaru-peka were up the Karangarua when they saw a tui fly down from the mountains and eat the red totara berry & they thought it must be a good land where the tui came from so the old woman her two sons & their wives went on up the river to try and see where the tui came from. The name of the place where the tui flew down was Popatea. Hinetamatea died on the journey and was

buried under [Aoraki] and the brothers and their wives went on until they came to a good land where there were no Māoris & plenty of kiwis wekas & kakapos...

As they journeyed on they saw a rainbow and thought that the Taipo [an evil spirit, a goblin] had sent it to stop them & they stopped & made a Māori oven to drive the Taipo away. They lived on fern roots aruhe & stopped there for a long time until there were two or three hundred of them. Some came back to Mahitahi Bruce Bay Okarito everywhere, & others stopped on the other side.

The story fascinated me: migration to a land of abundance, guardian spirits and evil forces, an ancestor buried beneath a sacred mountain, the importance of ritual—all played out in the theatre of the high Alps.

Hinetamatea's route via what is now called Copland Pass had once been the classic alpine crossing for trampers. From the west, it took in the hot springs, the severe Swiss Alps grandeur of the upper valley, a stiff climb to perpetual snow at the 2,200-metre pass, and an airy descent down Copland Ridge beneath Aoraki's south face.

Dad had done 'the Copland' twice, and rated it as one of his favourite trips. I'd always wanted to go myself, but the route was now effectively closed, being considered too dangerous thanks to a collapsing moraine wall on the eastern side. But now, with a Ngāi Tahu ancestor to follow, we had the perfect excuse to give it a crack.

We told Paul and Susan our plan to walk to Aoraki via the pass. Paul looked thoughtful. 'Can you let us know how you get on?'

Aoraki and Kirikirikatata (Mount Cook Range) at sunset, with Aroarokaehe in the foreground.

Whakarewa (Lake Browning), the source of the Arahura River, at Nōti Raureka (Browning Pass).

Geoff Low descends to the Hurunui River, en route to Nōti Hurunui (Harper Pass).

Opposite top: The Waimakariri Basin seen from Flock Hill, with Red Peak and Castle Hill Peak behind.

Opposite bottom: Jon Terry, channelling Jakob Lauper, fords a braid of the Rakaia–wai–kī, heading for Rurumātaikau.

Above: Kaharoa Manihera and Donelle Manihera ascend Ball Ridge beneath the Caroline Face of Aoraki, with Haupapa behind.

Below, clockwise from top left: Geoff Low; Donelle Manihera and Kaharoa Manihera; Leigh Hopkinson; Jon Terry.

Tim Low and Kaharoa Manihera climb a hogsback cloud, Aoraki / Mt Cook National Park.

TE WAIPOUNAMU

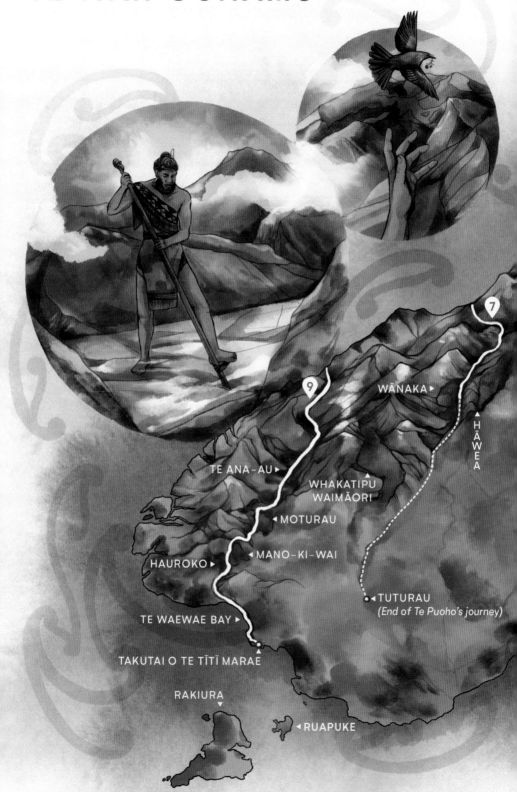

7

9

WĀNAKA ▸

HĀWEA

TE ANA–AU ▸

WHAKATIPU
WAIMĀORI ▴

◂ MOTURAU

◂ MANO–KI–WAI

HAUROKO ▸

◦ TUTURAU
(End of Te Puoho's journey)

TE WAEWAE BAY ▸

◦

TAKUTAI O TE TĪTĪ MARAE

RAKIURA ▾

◂ RUAPUKE

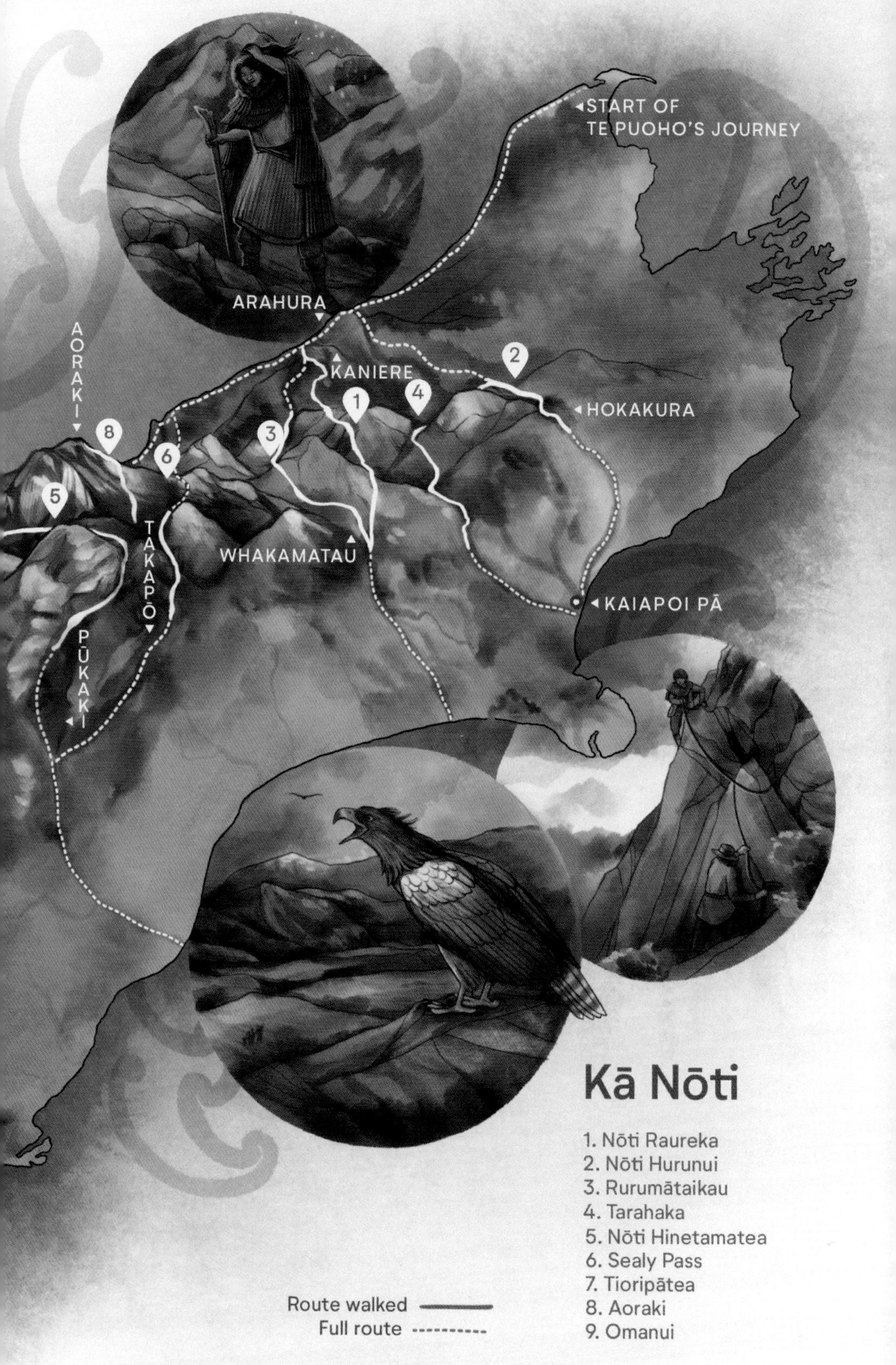

START OF
TE PUOHO'S JOURNEY

ARAHURA

KANIERE

2

1

4

HOKAKURA

AORAKI

8

3

6

5

WHAKAMATAU

TAKAPŌ

PŪKAKI

KAIAPOI PĀ

Kā Nōti

1. Nōti Raureka
2. Nōti Hurunui
3. Rurumātaikau
4. Tarahaka
5. Nōti Hinetamatea
6. Sealy Pass
7. Tioripātea
8. Aoraki
9. Omanui

Route walked ————
Full route ----------

Sunrise on Aoraki's shoulder, at the base of the Summit Rocks on the Linda Glacier route, with Haupapa (Tasman Glacier) belo

Above: Paddling across Pūkaki towards Aoraki on Ngāi Tahu's Aoraki Bound programme.

Opposite, clockwise from top left: State Highway 6 in South Westland, built to commemorate the journey of my ancestor Kawiti, heading towards Tioripātea; Bridget Reweti and Nic Low transporting pounamu the easy way, across Te Ana-au by waka; Dave Taylor tries to light a match in a storm above Hauroko, Murihiku; Koro Graeme Pepper (right) bound for Aoraki, by bus.

Below left: Bridget Reweti wades the Milford Track.

Right: Tim Low and Dave Taylor tackle the Murihiku bush.

Tim Low and Dave Taylor descend towards Hauroko (Lake Hauroko), with Ōkākā (Hump Ridge) behind on the left.

Walking the beach at Te Waewae Bay, Murihiku, heading for the Waiau River mouth where John Hunter plied his trade.

Tim Low feasting on coprosma berries.

he asked. 'We'd like to know if it might be an option for Aoraki Bound.'

The highlight of the Aoraki Bound leadership programme is a crossing of the Alps. It's currently Nōti Raureka, but Paul told us that Kāti Māhaki were keen to host the group in future years. They wondered if Hinetamatea's route was feasible, given stories about the dangerous moraine descent.

'For sure,' I said. 'We'll let you know what we find.'

•

A week later, at Welcome Flat, halfway up the Copland Valley, I lowered myself into the springs at the end of the first day's walk.

'Oh my gosh,' I said to no one in particular.

In the aftermath of the previous days' storm, the contrast between the freezing air and the hot water was profound. My aching shoulders started to relax.

An evening chorus from unseen bellbirds rippled through the trees. I counted four generations of visitors chatting in multiple languages as they soaked away the day.

'How's it going with Leigh?' Tim asked.

I sighed. 'I don't know. She's a writer, and she's ambitious, and generous, but—'

'But she's not a highly strung workaholic, or emotionally unavailable?' Tim offered through the steam.

'Yeah, maybe she's not my type. It's been good, but I don't trust it yet.'

'How come?

'A year ago she was dancing in a Melbourne strip club and dating a currency trader. She's getting into climbing, and talks about writing as a career, and we've chatted about living back here, but I don't know how serious she is. It feels like she's always out to reinvent herself, and maybe she's just decided my life looks interesting right now. I dunno.'

'Well, you seem happy.'

I frowned. 'Really?'

'Yeah.'

We lapsed into silence. I leaned back on my elbows, and watched the serrations atop Mt Glorious slowly turn pink above the darkening forest.

'This'd be the way to end the trip, not kick it off,' Tim said finally. He looked as cooked as I felt.

'We should get out soon,' I said, 'or there's no way we're climbing tomorrow.'

We pulled ourselves up from the reddish mineral water, dressed fast and wandered back to the hut. The three Frenchmen we'd met earlier were standing on the porch.

'How'd you go finding beds?' I asked.

'There are no beds,' the leader said. 'And anyway we have no money. So we have to go back.'

'You're going back *now*?'

The man shrugged.

'Do you have torches?'

'No. But it is a good track. See you later.'

We watched them vanish into the inky bush. They wouldn't be back at their car till at least three in the morning, and it was already brutally cold. I didn't have the heart to tell them that a kind woman had offered us the spare bunk beds in her deluxe hundred-dollars-a-night room.

•

At 5.30 a.m. we crept out of the hut in the icy dark while the forty people inside slept on. Lacing up my running shoes on the deck, I saw some kids had left their socks out to dry, and they'd frozen stiff. I could just make out plumes of steam from the springs drifting above the trees. A tiny crescent moon hung high to the north. We clicked on our head torches and sped up the track to Welcome Flat.

I'd assumed that the reward for walking up the Copland Valley was a soak in the hot springs. But the real reward is the flats, just twenty minutes further east up the track. Dense forest gives way to expansive grasslands and a wild mountain grandeur that's hidden from the hut. Waves of jagged stone and hanging glaciers thrust up from nothing to 3,151 metres atop Kakīroa (Mt Sefton). The southerly lifted a plume of ice crystals from the summits into the first rays of sun. The dawn chorus rang out.

'What is that?' I asked Tim.

Away from the roar of the river, a madrigal of unusual birdsong filled the air. Tim paused, listening intently. 'Bellbirds,' he said.

'Are you sure?'

The agile notes and pure tones seemed right for bellbirds, but the sequence was foreign.

'Yeah, but they're speaking a different dialect,' Tim said.

'They have *dialects*?'

'It's different in different parts of the country.'

Tim is a brewer, but he worked as a jazz musician for years. He told me a Ngāi Tahu musician friend of his from Auckland spoke good bellbird. 'Jeremy can sing to them and they'll sing back. But I don't know if he'd be understood down here!'

When Hinetamatea and her whānau came up this way, the

flats would have been swarming with birds. The first European to visit, explorer Charlie Douglas, wrote:

> The kiwis were of larger size than usual, and very light in colour, some being completely white on the belly. Many of the wekas showed the same peculiarity, large sized... The robins ate out of one's hand; the bell-bird sung its chorus in a style only now to be heard south of Jackson's Bay.

(Douglas also wrote that he shot and ate two enormous birds of prey in a nearby valley. These may have been the last remaining pouākai, though he did have a dry sense of humour.)

Tim and I moved steadily up the Copland Valley to where it narrowed above the flats. Among the tatty yellowing ribbonwoods above Douglas Rock Hut, a vast flock of finches flew past, soaring and twisting in a continuous stream, as if they were a single being.

Given that there were so many birds in the Copland Valley, I wondered what had persuaded Hinetamatea to follow a single tui, flitting branch to branch. Perhaps if she saw the same bird again and again, resting just ahead of her, eating pine-scented red tōtara berries, she might have paused to watch. The glossy black bird would have darted away whenever she approached, until she found it waiting in a fine shaft of sunlight. This time it didn't flee. I imagine her with a long grey plait and brown eyes, moko kauae tattooed on her chin, studying the strange markings across the bird's breast, and its piercing pale eyes—he manaia, he atua: a bird-spirit.

The bird rose and flickered through the understorey, then came to rest in another island of light, among thicker forest to the north. Off the trail: towards mountains that were blinding with new snow and rime ice in the morning sun. Hinetamatea waited for her sons and their wives to catch up, one hand outstretched as if to say *hush*, her eyes still on the tui.

'He manaia arataki,' she murmured to Tātāwhaka when he reached her side. *A bird spirit leading us on.*

'Me whai tātou?' he asked. *Should we follow?*

'Āe.' *Yes.*

•

Tim and I left the frozen valley floor and zigzagged up the southern wall of the Aroarokaehe Range, into the sun. We were moving among the big mountains now, approaching Aoraki, where the land became harsh, and the plants tiny and tough, and any indecision in the traveller would be burned away. To our left the black slabs of Mt Unicorn and Dilemma Peak cut the sky like shark fins. The Main Divide ridge leading to Kakīroa reared up in jagged steps.

If you'd followed a bird to the head of the valley, and now wanted to cross the Divide, this was the only route you'd try. The spur we were on led to an easy snow basin, with an inviting dip in the ridge overhead. This was actually the tougher Fitzgerald Pass, whereas the Copland gave easy passage through rocks to the left. It was high, but the travel looked straightforward. If you were here in summer there'd be little snow.

Tim and I camped in the snow basin halfway up, and rose at dawn to lilac light. Sunlight clipped the tips of the peaks. Before we crossed into Canterbury we were keen to climb one of the peaks along the Main Divide. We opted for Du Faur Peak, named for another pioneering woman, the Australian climber Freda Du

Faur. In 1909 and 1910 she bagged numerous first ascents in these ranges. She was the first woman to climb Aoraki, and her ascent was the fastest at that time.

The storm two days earlier had left the upper faces of the mountain armoured with wind-sculpted rime ice. We picked an easy route through the cliffs, plodding up through deep snow, with just one short hand-over-hand scramble to bypass a gully humming with rockfall. The rope stayed in the pack. Up we went, up and up.

The last ten steps to the top of a high ridge are always exquisite. Monotonous hours spent staring at your feet give way to a sensation of taking flight. One step, and the blue-white serrations of the eastern ranges came into view. Two more, and we saw the green lower flanks of the mountains, then the dusty gold of the river flats. The grey-blue ribbon of Te Awa Whakamau (the Tasman River) flowed to Lake Pūkaki and the distant high-country plains. Pōpātea, the mysterious land of plenty in Hinetamatea's story, was somewhere down there.

Another few paces and the wind was full in our faces. We reached the cornice, with its vertiginous drop to Hooker Lake a kilometre below. Standing over everything, finally: Aoraki. The son of the Sky Father, Raki, and his first wife, Poko-hārua-te-pō; conduit between heaven and earth; focus of Ngāi Tahu's mana and power.

'Nothing compares with Aoraki,' Paul Madgwick later told me. 'It's such a dominant force, like an Argus watching over us, whether close at hand at Makaawhio, where it's only forty kilometres from summit to pā, or just about anywhere along the coastline of Te Tai o Poutini.'

Cloud usually cloaked Aoraki's face. Today, in brilliant sunshine, the ancestor mountain and his brothers gleamed with the vivid blue of reflected sky. Tim and I turned in slow circles, drinking it in.

The landscape all around us was sacred and storied for Ngāi Tahu, and the key to unlocking it lay in whakapapa. The three rūnaka (councils) who hold mana whenua (authority and guardianship over the land) in this area on the eastern side, Moeraki, Waihao and Arowhenua, have a genealogy describing much of this view. It shows lines of descent from Aoraki and his brothers to the other major mountains in the area, south to the sacred lakes Pūkaki and Takapō, to the ancestor mountains in Te Manahuna (the Mackenzie Basin), down the generations to the Waitaki Valley to Korotuaheka, an ancient village on the east coast.

The chant links Ngāi Tahu to the landscape through genealogy, and is another oral map listing the key landmarks needed to navigate between high country and coast. Like all whakapapa, it's also a compendium of history: you could write a book about the story behind each line.

Take 'Ki te taha wahine a Aroarokaehe' (And to the female side and the Hooker Valley). Aroarokaehe, the mountain range we'd just climbed, was a crew member of the Araiteuru waka, which reached New Zealand only to run aground on a reef at Matakaea (Shag Point), off the far-south Ōtākou coast. She and the other crew swam ashore, then went exploring inland. They had to be back at the canoe by daylight. But some were still out at dawn, and when the sun struck them they turned to stone, and are now important landmarks spread across Te Waipounamu (including the Christchurch Cathedral). Aroarokaehe became a mountain in the foothills twenty kilometres south of here, until Kirikirikatata (Mt Cook Range) convinced her to leave her lowly station and move up into the high Alps at his side. In this tradition, Kirikirikatata carries his grandson, Aoraki, on his shoulders: the highest mountain is a child, supported by the generations who came before.

You sometimes hear the idea that Araiteuru is a mythical waka, and that when people said 'our tīpuna came here on the Araiteuru', they were talking in vague, mystical terms. But Araiteuru was the waka (conveyance) by which people arrived here: it's the name of a navigational star path used by early Polynesian voyagers to reach Aotearoa. A star path is the memorised sequence of stars that rise or set throughout the night at the point on the horizon where you wish to go. When the first arrivals made landfall, they went exploring, and gave those navigational stars' names to the mountains of their new home, including Aroarokaehe. Recalling the stars as people who crossed the sea, then became mountains when the sun rose (stars not being much use by day), is a damn good way of ensuring that the celestial knowledge was passed on.

All of these ideas unfold from a single line in the chant. And while the chant takes the form of whakapapa, this is not just a metaphorical device. We descend from these mountains because life begins here. As David Higgins, the charismatic Upoko of Moeraki Rūnaka, and a pivotal figure in the tribe's Treaty negotiations, told me: 'Aoraki and his whānau, and Tititea (Mt Aspiring) and his whānau, and Horokōau (Mt Tasman) and his whānau create the environment for life for us. We acknowledge our mauka atua [spirit mountains], our mauka teitei [lofty mountains] as a broad feeder for the sustainability of life. As the tears of Aoraki roll down our valleys into our roto [lakes], into our awa tapu [sacred rivers], their importance becomes real.'

With so many of the places in the chant visible beneath my boots, I wondered how often people had climbed into the ice and snow, and enjoyed the sweeping views. Could I picture Hinetamatea, her sons and their wives standing here, wrapped in dog-skin cloaks, contemplating the new land laid out at their feet?

.

The most obvious argument against early Māori mountain climbing was the need for specialised gear. Tim and I wore mountaineering boots and crampons, Gore-Tex over-trousers, canvas gaiters, polarising sunglasses, and helmets of lightweight ballistic plastic. We carried ice axes, walking poles and an aluminium snow-stake each, plus a water-repelling rope and a small rack of rock-climbing hardware that jingled when we moved.

But Tim and I had only used the boots, and the axes as walking sticks; the ascent was just a hike in the snow. Hundreds of inexperienced nineteenth-century European tourists had done the Copeland in tweed jackets and woollen trousers or skirts. Would an early Māori travelling party have had the gear needed to cross the pass?

For underlayers, they used garments sewn from whītau, finely woven dressed flax with the texture of linen. Cloaks of dog fur, weka or kākāpō skin, or perhaps even moa skin, enabled travellers to layer up for warmth. The traditional thatched flax rain-cape was waterproof. Woven pārekareka (gaiters) were essentially the same as modern designs, with a cinch cord to seal the top and a tongue covering the top of the foot. They were stuffed with grasses for insulation, and would have provided protection against sub-alpine scrub, and snow. We know our ancestors lived for months in the high country during the winter harvest, so this clothing must have worked well in sub-zero temperatures.

Would you venture higher with sandals instead of boots? The only footwear in those days were pāraerae, tough woven-flax sandals. These often had a double-thickness sole, came up around the sides of the foot, and could be insulated with grasses. For rivers and lowland travel they were perfect. Up here, you'd risk frostbite. The soles would provide little traction, and on ice they'd be lethal.

But I also recalled Dad telling us that when hiking around Annapurna, in Nepal, he had been overtaken by two locals off hunting in the snow—barefoot. In soft snow, on relatively low-angle terrain like the Copland, paraerae would have worked. In summer only the top section of the pass would be under snow. A few unpleasant hours was all it required.

As for a hiking pole or ice axe: standard travelling equipment included the tokotoko, a long wooden staff, often with a sharpened tip, or a bone point, called a pīauau—perfect for self-belaying in snow. Travellers also carried adzes, and there are accounts of steps being cut in steep earth banks, so it's conceivable this was done in ice. Māori ropes were made of braided dressed flax. Tests on replicas have shown they were almost as strong as modern climbing ropes, and there are many examples of early Europeans finding fixed lines left to allow easy ascent of cliffs.

In *Foot-Tracks in New Zealand* (2011), Pete McDonald's exhaustive study of the country's foot travel, he observes:

mid-nineteenth-century Pākehā travellers left many...
descriptions of routes up or across steep and exposed
ground, such as sea cliffs and rock barriers on ridges.
Collectively these accounts indicate that Māori were
strong, wiry, agile and that they possessed what a modern rockclimber would recognise as an effective combination of balance, skill and judgment.

So it is possible that early Māori occasionally went up into the
snow and ice. And language also offers clues. Te reo Māori has
words not just for snow, ice and thick ice, but for permanent
snowfields, glaciers, snow sloughs and avalanches. Such specific
vocabulary suggests experiences to match.

Further small clues come from oral histories of alpine disasters.
One describes the death of the warrior Takawa in a blizzard while
crossing Nōti Raureka; another details an avalanche that killed
twenty men. There's the story of the chief Te Kaumira, who died
in a snowstorm on the range known as Te Tari-a-Te-Kaumira,
and whose body was preserved in a nearby cave. And then there's
the tale of Hinetamatea's crossing of the Copland, and her death
beneath Aoraki. Perhaps it's like today, when only mountaineering
accidents make the news, despite thousands of successful climbs
every year. For every disaster story Ngāi Tahu handed down, it
seems fair to assume that there were other alpine expeditions that
ended in success.

The last piece of the puzzle is Hinetamatea's descendants, the
people who related her tale in 1897. Bob McKerrow's 1993 essay
'Māori Mountaineers of South Westland' shows how they and
their descendants were living proof of Ngāi Tahu's connection to

the Alps, forming a small but important dynasty of Māori guides and mountaineers.

One was Ruera Te Naihi. Born Taringaroa ('long ears'), he was a dark-bearded ox of a man, his trunk and shoulders heavily muscled beneath a neat waistcoat and shirt. Aged twelve, Ruera and his father, Wī Te Naihi, walked up the coast to Ōkārito for the novelty of seeing their first white man: Leonard Harper. Later on, he acted as porter and guide to two famous European explorers in the area, Charlie 'Mr Explorer' Douglas, and Arthur P. Harper, Leonard's son (who went bush during the years of his father's trials). Ruera ferried huge loads, caught birds and eels when their stores ran low, and literally handed over his last slice of bread when starvation threatened. Ruera was a fine bushman but terrible on steep ground; he helped keep the Europeans alive on the flat, and they returned the favour when the more serious climbing began.

Rakatira (chief) Kerei Tūtoko was another of the figures sitting at the fire telling Hinetamatea's story in 1897. Kerei had also been on a rite of passage when aged twelve. In 1835 he walked up the West Coast to Māwhera (Greymouth), across the Alps via the Hurunui Saddle, over the plains to Kaiapoi, then all the way home. The round trip was a thousand kilometres. He later befriended and guided Gerhard Mueller, the first government surveyor in the area, who spoke of his abilities with awe.

In 1895 the American climber Edward FitzGerald and his Swiss guide Matthias Zurbriggen became the first white people to cross into the Copland Valley, using a steep route immediately south of Nōti Hinetamatea. They descended to the Karangarua River, where they met an 'immensely powerful [Māori] lad' named Dan. He took them up the coast to Te Moeka-o-Tūawe

(Fox Glacier), then accompanied them into the high mountains via Chancellor Ridge. The conditions were awful, with the men breaking through a thin crust and sinking into deep snow, but Dan was right at home on the glacier. FitzGerald was astonished. 'Certainly, if his physique is a typical instance of that of the Māori race,' he wrote later, 'a fine race of alpine guides might be cultivated from them'.

FitzGerald was right, except that 'Dan' was Tāne Te Koeti, and it was his ancestor Hinetamatea who'd discovered the better pass north of the one the men had just crossed. Tane and his brothers did become alpine guides, at the Hermitage Hotel in Mt Cook Village. One brother, Pahikore, famously did the entire Copland Pass crossing from the Canterbury side to the west, then continued south to Makaawhio (Jacobs River) down the coast—in fifteen hours, without a track. He spent the night with family, then reversed the trip the next day.

Over the years, members of the Kāti Māhaki mountain families—the Te Koetis, Wilsons, Bannisters, Fluertys—cut the Copland Track itself, opening the route to tourists. They built the original Douglas Rock Hut in the upper valley, and bagged local first-ascents. They continued the tradition of taking their kids on epic rites of passage, like twelve-year-old Bob Wilson, who crossed Copland Pass—twice—in under twenty-four hours.

In the old days, travellers clearly preferred lower passes like the Hurunui in the north or Tioripātea (Haast Pass) in the south. No one I read or spoke to was suggesting that high-alpine travel was a regular occurrence. But I could readily believe that, on rare occasions, parties had crossed these alpine passes. Which meant they would have stood, as Tim and I now did, quietly awed by the view.

·

When cold began to outweigh beauty at the top of Du Faur Peak, we plodded off back down towards Copland Pass. We'd had a cruisy morning and a long lunch up top; by early afternoon, sun-warmed rime ice was fast turning the mountainside into an enormous disintegrating chandelier. Falling ice triggered small avalanches, or sent rocks cannoning down the slope. Rather than risk rockfall by zigzagging down lower-angled terrain, we chose to abseil steeper cliffs that were relatively clear of debris.

The minute we were off the abseil, Tim sheltered at the base of another nearby cliff while I stood ready to pull the rope. The thin cord disappeared up and out of sight, taut in my hands. I worked the knots from the ends with sweaty, gloved hands. It was cooler here in this little gully, out of the sun for the first time in hours. The soft snow underfoot was shrapnelled with debris.

'Are you protected there?' I called. 'No evidence of rockfall?'

'None,' Tim called back. 'Go for it.'

The rope came whipping down, and I grabbed it and bolted back to Tim's safe position. He began to flake it out, getting rid of kinks and knots before packing it away. Hours in the sun had made us lethargic. I had a bad feeling in my gut.

'Hurry, bro,' I said, hovering back from the cliff, ready to depart. 'Maybe just stuff it in your pack and we'll sort it when we're down?'

'It's cool,' he said. 'Nearly done.'

I heard a loud crack away to my left.

'Rock!' I called automatically, then looked up. It was about the size of my head, spinning out from the face.

'Fucking big rock!' I screamed. 'Move!'

Tim dived away from me. Straight into its path.

The rock struck with a sickening *thwack*.

Tim lay sprawled in the snow, unmoving, then a second later picked himself up. We stared at each other in disbelief. The boulder had passed between his outstretched, diving arms, and slammed into the snow. I had no fucking idea how it had missed him.

As we plunge-stepped down through soft snow onto safe ground, repacked gear we'd earlier stashed and traipsed on towards the pass, the moment faded; but from time to time I still felt sick. I'd had near misses, but nothing that close. If I got hit, I got hit. But the idea of my brother getting hurt was too much.

We decided to camp just below the pass. All in all, it'd been a glorious day. But, drifting off to sleep, I replayed that hiss and thump over and over, wincing as the rock smashed down.

·

In the grey light of dawn, Nōti Hinetamatea wasn't the obvious dip in the ridge but an uninviting line of rocky serrations a little further north. Tim and I climbed through a freezing mist that coated our faces and clothes with fine layers of ice. A line of dark clouds like war canoes massed along the Divide. The sky was an ominous slate-grey, with just a gold rim glowing at the eastern horizon. South along the ridge, a strange arch of cloud hovered above Kakīroa and The Footstool, like an electric current arcing between the peaks.

We emerged through the broken gap in the ridge's teeth. The view north-east opened onto row upon row of raw stone peaks surrounded by glaciers like smashed jewels. Another strange cloud-arch covered Aoraki's head. Directly across the valley from us lay Ball Pass, a dip in the ridge leading up to Aoraki. That was

our ultimate destination on this trip. First, we had to get down
Copland Ridge. Our route down to the Copland snowfield was
an easy but exposed traverse above a deep 'schrund.

'Look okay?' I asked Tim.

He nodded. 'Want a quick belay, though?'

We were both feeling cautious. 'Sure,' I said, 'why not.'

Off the pass and into Canterbury at last, storm-driven snow
swept in at our backs. We romped down through soft snow
towards the rounded red barrel of Copland Shelter, sitting on the
prow of the ridge below. Icy whirlwinds blasted our backs, and in
the big gusts we had to brace ourselves to stay upright. Here and
there we turned round to front-point down an icy section. I was
glad I wasn't doing it in flax sandals.

At the shelter we slammed the door on the whistling gale and
fired up the stove for coffee. I flopped down on the sleeping platform to wait.

'Let's just have a quick break, then push on,' I said. 'If we get
out to the village today, we can have tomorrow off before Ball
Pass.'

'I think we should stay put,' Tim said. 'The forecast's for things
to get worse. And that wind's already bad.'

Tim was always careful, and I was always pushing us to do
more. As usual, he was right. The descent to the glacier followed
a narrow steep ridge which wouldn't be much fun in a gale. I
grumbled for a while, but once I'd had a coffee and worked off my
frustration, I was glad we'd stayed put.

Plenty of people had got into trouble round here. One guy
went up to the pass without crampons and hit ice. He'd returned
to the shelter, stolen the snow shovel and used it to painstakingly

cut steps all the way to the top. Then there were the two tourists who had accidentally taken the obvious but much steeper Fitzgerald Pass. They didn't have crampons either, or ice axes, or a rope, and had an insane time inching down across sections of bullet ice. Cam Mulvey, the cheerfully morbid warden at Wyn Irwin Hut, had woken in the night to find the pair on his front lawn, totally wrecked, praying and weeping with relief at having made it down alive.

Others haven't been so lucky. Rockfall, a slip, avalanche, hypothermia: for every climber, the possibilities are ever present. Serious mountaineer friends of mine like to joke that, for the media, the only good climber is a dead one. (Six months after this trip, I heard a breaking-news story that a young Australian woman had been killed on The Footstool, along the ridge from Du Faur Peak, and knew instantly that it was my friend Nicola. It was like being punched in the guts.)

The old Ngāi Tahu stories also make the dangers of mountain travel clear. Though we don't know how she died, Hinetamatea was buried somewhere on the eastern side, 'beneath Aoraki'. Afterwards, her two sons Tatawhaka and Kōmarupeka and their wives kept going. But as they travelled they saw a rainbow, sent by the taipō (an evil spirit). They called a halt to consider whether they should turn back.

Today it's hard to imagine a rainbow as an evil omen. But the various Māori words for rainbows all relate to atua. Kahukura was an important god of war and migrating travellers, who separated good weather from bad, and sent his sign in the form of a rainbow, or cloud or mist hovering in the mountains, which was studied for omens. (Paul Madgwick told me that people on the Coast still use

Aoraki to forecast the weather, based on the clouds moving across his face.) Another word for rainbow describes the arch: atua piko (literally, 'curved spirit'). Kakīroa was also known as Mauka-atua, 'peak of spirits', and is often covered by an arch of cloud like the one Tim and I had seen. Had Hinetamatea's whānau seen that, too? The distinctive arch appears today as the logo for the outdoor-equipment brand Macpac, but it has long been famous as a sign that a nor'-west storm is on the way.

> Then at midnight the storm burst on us, with its peals of thunder and its vivid lightning, adding to the noise of the avalanches, and causing an indescribable din... echo[ing] from the surrounding precipices, sounding as if all the demons of ancient and modern times were loose. Poor old Bill 'no likee', and during the hour or two after midnight...I believe he was calling all the gods to witness that he would never come into such a place again! Every now and then with a nervous laugh he would say, 'I me tinkee Taipo (devil) here!'

'Old Bill' is Ruera Te Naihi, Hinetamatea's descendant, and a celebrated ancestor of the Kāti Māhaki people today. The writer is Arthur P. Harper. The two men got caught in a storm in 1895 near the Douglas Neve, off the south-western shoulder of Kakīroa. Harper uses 'old Bill' for comic relief; but during the storm, it reads to me like Ruera was reciting karakia, incantations for protection and solace, and perhaps to drive the taipō away.

Centuries earlier, Hinetamatea's family made a Māori oven. They baked food over hot stones, which symbolically ended tapu, signalling the transition from sacred to profane. There would have been karakia, too. The mountains could be threatening, and death was real, but there were rituals that allowed travellers to proceed unharmed.

·

When Tim and I woke in the morning the wind had vanished, leaving behind the plump, hushed silence of new snow. I opened the hut door to thick mist and cloud, interrupted only by the glowing slit of dawn.

We cruised down the long, steep spine of the ridge, scratching with crampon points to find purchase under the soft carpet of snow. The mist lifted, revealing another hard-shadowed blue day. Travel was exhilarating, with airy views straight down to the milky teal of Hooker Lake. I could see why this had been such a famous trans-alpine route, and why Susan and Paul hoped it'd be viable for Aoraki Bound.

In Hinetamatea's day, once you reached the bottom of the ridge, you stepped onto the white ice of the glacier and followed its gentle ramp down. Even when Dad last did it, in the 1990s, the descent hadn't been too bad. But as Tim and I lost height, the wasteland of the Hooker moraine filled our vision. From the grassy terrace at the ridge's base, we stared off the edge of a cliff. The glacier lay 150 metres below. The changing climate had eviscerated the ice; the total volume of the Southern Alps' glaciers has reduced by more than a third in the last thirty years. Ice holds these mountains together, and as it retreats, the mountains fall apart. A billion tonnes of rubble filled the valley, like the bombed ruins of Europe during the war.

It got ugly from here on down. A German tourist had recently gone for a tumble, and ended up in Copland Gut with a broken leg. By some miracle he'd had phone coverage. A rescue helicopter managed to pull him out, though not his pack full of brand-new gear. How to safely extract it was a favourite topic of conversation among dirtbag climbers at the Chamois pub in Mt Cook Village.

Tim and I had two options for our descent. First, via an ad-hoc steel cable installed by anonymous local climbers. It had been hit repeatedly by rockfall, and its anchors were fast being undercut by the collapsing moraine. Tim and I looked down at the collection of steel pickets, fencing wire and purple slings holding it all together. It didn't look too bad. But it was useless if the whole section of terrace it sat on collapsed.

That left soloing the wall, down-climbing 150 metres without a rope. Moraine walls are made of loose boulders perched in sand, so there was no chance of protecting the route. Anything we could attach the rope to was liable to pull out at the slightest tug.

Cam Mulvey from Wyn Irwin Hut had been adamant that the cable was the only safe way down. But the Department of Conservation people we spoke with had strongly advised us to leave it alone, and were planning to remove it in the coming weeks.

'If you're going to do it,' Cam had told us, 'do it now.'

We opted to go solo, eyeballing a route down through a lower-angled section to the north. My first few steps onto the moraine wall triggered a slew of loose rocks that gathered momentum and plunged into Copland Gut with a dusty roar. 'Jesus, this is going to be fun,' I said.

'Hmph,' Tim replied.

The first seventy or eighty metres were fine. Loose scree is common in the Southern Alps, so descending with boulders rolling underfoot was familiar to us. But as we neared the glacier, the moraine wall steepened. Soon we were down-climbing hand over hand. Time slowed. Each foot and hand hold was merely a rock balanced in sand. We weighted each with infinite care, sensing rather than thinking our way down. In the pause between movements I could hear the gentle hiss of sand, and gravity, and time. One of us moved, then the other. Often we climbed side by side, so that dislodged rocks could fall free to the glacier below. I watched Tim lower himself precisely from one ledge to another and felt a rush of gratitude. There was no one I'd rather be with.

When we stepped off the wall onto the moraine below, we looked back at the jumbled stack of boulders. Some were the size of cars. We exchanged tired smiles.

'Should've used the cable?' I said.

'Yeah,' Tim said. 'Let's not do that again.'

·

As we scrambled around the edge of Hooker Lake, a couple came past in a canoe. They pulled alongside to chat. It was Guy McKinnon and Jane Morris, two of New Zealand's top mountaineers. In the time it'd taken us to descend the moraine wall and walk out, they'd raced up the cable, climbed to Copland Shelter and back, then zipped down again, all for an afternoon jaunt. Except for the foolish like us, or the gifted like Guy and Jane, Hinetamatea's route was largely done.

They paddled serenely on, and we went back to the ankle-twisting moraine. Soon we were out onto the Hooker Valley Track. Then we were dumping our packs outside Wyn Irwin Lodge, and jogging along Hooker Valley Road, heading for the Chamois. We'd made it to the magical land on the other side: the pub. We had the evening to unwind before meeting up with the rest of the Ngāi Tahu crew in the morning.

Over beers, Tim and I mused on the location of Pōpātea, where Hinetamatea's family settled. The root word, Pātea, is an ancient place name found across the Pacific, and was bestowed on various places in Aotearoa. In the south we have Tioripātea (Haast Pass), Parapātea at the head of Lake Wānaka, while Pātea itself was a general term for the West Coast region and is today used for Fiordland's Doubtful Sound. In mythical terms it's a place of abundance on the eastern side of the Alps.

While prospering in Pōpātea, Hinetamatea's descendants must have passed down the knowledge of her alpine route. A few generations later some of them migrated back across the Alps using Hinetamatea's pass. Over the following centuries their descendants continued to cross back and forth as alpine guides, porters, hut-builders and track staff. The history of Māori association with the route was one long, unbroken line.

'But there's no chance the Aoraki Bound crew could use it now,' Tim said.

I nodded. It was sad to think that the route was finished. But Kāti Māhaki were maintaining their connection regardless. Paul told me they were aiming to take over management of the Copland Valley as an enterprise, and a means of reconnection. Young cultural guide Kahurangi Mahuika-Wilson was leading Māhaki youth on mountain missions throughout the area, including up the Copland Valley in the footsteps of Hinetamatea and her whānau. And the wider tribe was engaging with the high Alps in other ways.

·

The next morning, eight of us bounced around in the back of a Troop Carrier, on our way up the Tasman Valley. Lurching into strangers' laps was a good way for us to get acquainted. Kaharoa was a rowdy, hilarious Māori-language teacher who was also being schooled in traditional lore. Donelle, vivacious and mischievous by turns, ran Ngāi Tahu's outdoor-engagement programmes, including Aoraki Bound. These two, and Tim and I, were on a Ngāi Tahu trip to pay our respects to Aoraki. Up front, Elke and Paul were guides with Alpine Recreation. Each year a partnership between the guiding company and the tribe gave four Ngāi Tahu the chance to learn basic alpine skills, then to climb and stand beneath Aoraki and look upon his face.

In the coming days we would climb Kaitiaki Peak on Kirikiri-katata (the Mt Cook Range, and another ancestor from the Araiteuru canoe), cross Ball Pass, and descend the Hooker Glacier, right across from Hinetamatea's route. The journey would take us from te taha tāne (the male side of Aoraki) to te taha wahine (the female side). Donelle and Kaharoa were also on a mission to harvest the leaves of the matua tikumu (mountain daisy) for their aunties to use in weaving a cloak.

First, we had to reach the start of the track. Huge boulders perched above the road. I thought back to our descent off the moraine wall.

'Man,' I said. 'It'd only take one of those to roll down and the road would be blocked.'

'Oi,' Kaharoa said. 'You'll jinx us.'

We rounded the corner. A huge boulder lay in the middle of the road. The truck stopped. Everyone looked at me.

'Hey, I—'

'All right,' Elke called. 'Everybody out!'

Paul saw the look on my face. 'Don't worry. That boulder's been there for years.'

We untied the packs from the roof and grabbed our ice axes. While Paul led a tourist party off ahead of us, we gathered in a circle for karakia, bowing our heads. Kaharoa's deep, rhythmical chant asked blessings for the journey, and acknowledged Aoraki as a chief, as a pillar holding up the tribe, holding up the sky. His voice brought stillness and focus. I thought of Ruera Te Naihi in 1895, chanting in the teeth of a storm. This was the right way to begin.

The first hour was an easy stroll along terraces beside Haupapa (Tasman Glacier). We walked with a clear view of the austere but beautiful valley: the snaking glacier framed by crumbling rock peaks and snow tinged blue with distance and sky. The moraine here was just as bad as the Hooker, with the ice shrinking and the lake growing so fast that the maps are always out of date.

Tim and I had spent all of yesterday gazing across the valley to Aoraki, but now Ball Ridge hid the ancestor-mountain from view. After a couple of hours of climbing, Donelle piped up. She was a tramper, but this was steep. 'Not to sound like a whingey little kid or anything,' she said, 'but is there much further to go?'

Elke, brisk and cheerful, had just recounted a twenty-two-hour climb up Aoraki's Hillary Ridge. She smiled. 'A little further.'

Quite a lot further, as it turned out. Our banter died away. The world shrank to the sound of our breathing, the rocks we were clambering over, the packs on our backs. We forgot where we were. Then we crested the ridge and looked up. The immense blue-white bulk of Aoraki filled the sky, soaring two vertical kilometres from where we stood.

Tim, Donelle, Kaharoa and I looked up in awe. The mountain had gone from an outline seen at a distance to a fully formed self: ice faces, rock ribs, a ridged spine leading to his mighty head. It wasn't just the height, but the mass. A being so vast creates his own gravity, and weather. Clouds shaped like manaia, the bird-spirits of Hinetamatea's tale, drifted over the ridge. A westerly was blowing, but here in his shadow the air was perfectly still.

'Tēnā koe e te rakatira!'

We shouted out to him, greeting him in Māori, telling him who we were, and our voices echoed back. We'd just started walking again when a booming roar stopped us in our tracks. A torrent of ice and rock avalanched off the Caroline Face.

'Hey,' Kaharoa said with a half-grin, eyes wide. 'He's mihi-ing back!'

The others turned and headed along the ridge towards Caroline Hut. There, we'd trade stories of the mountain with the alpine guides, and gear up to climb Kaitiaki Peak the following day.

Many Ngāi Tahu introduce themselves by naming Aoraki as their ancestor-mountain, making him central to their identity. The Alpine Recreation partnership was important because many Ngāi Tahu have never had the chance to visit Aoraki, let alone see him from this close. But we were still pretty far away.

I found myself lingering, gazing up at the top of the ancestor's head. Two Ngāi Tahu guides, descendants of Hinetamatea, had set out to climb Aoraki in the early twentieth century. One summited; the other chose to turn back. Could I? Should I? One day?

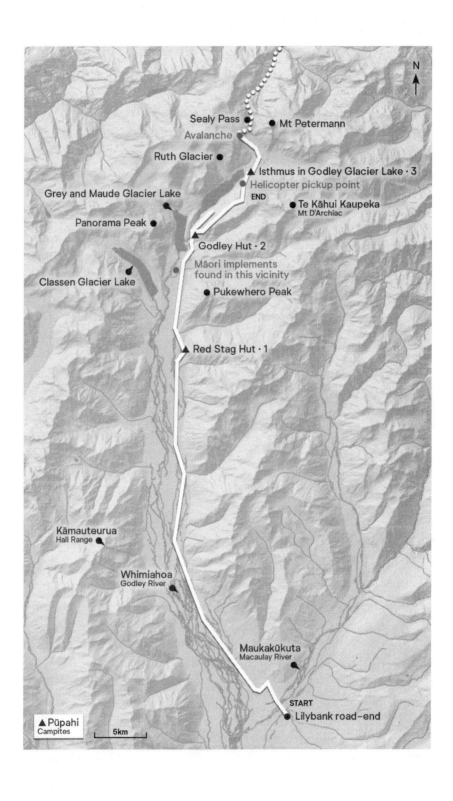

N

Sealy Pass ● ● Mt Petermann
Avalanche ●
Ruth Glacier ● ▲ Isthmus in Godley Glacier Lake · 3
● Helicopter pickup point
Grey and Maude Glacier Lake ● END
Panorama Peak ● ● Te Kāhui Kaupeka
Mt D'Archiac
▲ Godley Hut · 2
Māori implements
found in this vicinity
Classen Glacier Lake ●
● Pukewhero Peak

▲ Red Stag Hut · 1

Kāmauteurua
Hall Range ●

Whimiahoa
Godley River ●

Maukakūkuta
Macaulay River ●

START
▲ Pūpahi   ● Lilybank road–end
Campites   5km

6

Sealy Pass

E Ruaimoko puritia tawhia kia i ta i ta i ta e!
E Ruaimoko, hold fast amid the thundering,
   thundering, thundering!

*—old Ngāi Tahu war chant, calling on the
god of earthquakes, thunder and lightning
to restrain the fury of a storm*

PART I: LILYBANK STATION, HEAD OF TAKAPŌ (LAKE TEKAPO), CANTERBURY ALPS. MIDWINTER.

Winter came on hard that year. Heavy snowfalls closed the passes. Any thoughts of an Aoraki expedition had to be shelved.

But after a decade of longing and intermittent visiting, I couldn't ignore the jagged white line on the horizon. In Christchurch I pored over maps and researched and wrote, but I was restless. And there was another pass, immediately behind Aoraki, which had drawn my curiosity. Deep in the high Alps, Sealy Pass was another route over heavily glaciated terrain. I was heading back to Melbourne for the rest of winter and spring—to write, find work, see Leigh—and I was dying to check it out before I left.

•

On a serene July evening I carved an arc in the snow with my car at the end of Lilybank Road. A rabbit twitched away into half-shadow. I killed the engine and the lights, and all thought. The immense snow-covered land gleamed with the indigo and pink of the sky. Cloud rose off the peaks like spume from a breaking wave. The dark giants of Maukakūkuta (Two Thumb Range)—Cerberus, Myrmidon, Ajax—stood a way up the Maukakūkuta (Macaulay River), haloed by a dying sun. To my left the Godley Valley curved away out of sight. That was my pathway to the sky.

I'd barely glanced at the route, because I wasn't going to attempt it. The trail went up Whimiahoa (the Godley River) to the foot of the Main Divide, then up the glacier to the Neish Plateau, and across the Divide at Sealy Pass. From there the trail went down Scone Creek to the rough-as-guts Perth River, and a slog out to Whataroa on the West Coast.

All that was six months away: a trip for summer, with friends. Here, in winter's grip, all I would do was ski up the valley and wander across the frozen glacier lake. I'd gaze up at Sealy Pass and fix it in my mind, then trudge back out. I was willing to go all that way, just for a look, because there had long been speculation that it was a Ngāi Tahu route.

On this side of the mountains, settlements, mahika kai and wāhi tapu (sacred places) studded the vicinity of Takapō (Lake

Tekapo). On the other side, there were settlements at Ōkārito. The mountains separating the two rarely dip below two thousand metres. At 1,722 metres, Sealy was perhaps the most viable link. What's more, old Māori implements had been found high up the valley, right at the snout of the glacier. There wasn't much to hunt or gather in that blasted rubble, so the finds could suggest travellers heading west through the mountains. A scrap of oral history about the area tells the traveller to be alert to omens: 'You watched a peak and went by its signs. Fog on one side meant you could get through; fog on the other side warned you not to attempt to cross the pass.'

I pitched my tent beneath a series of the silky, bulbous nor'-west clouds, watching them dim from pink to slate grey as night came on. Though they appeared stationary, they were standing waves, their edges blurred with speed. Snow and high winds were on the way. Good thing I was staying down in the valley. I fell into an easy sleep.

•

'Whoa! Heeeee!' I hooted with shock as I plunged into the ice-fringed Maukakūkuta river in my boxer shorts, with just a pair of Crocs on my feet. After a few steps my legs went pleasantly numb. I paused midstream to marvel at the vast wheeling blue overhead, the warm sun on my face. Those same clouds hung overhead, exquisite as stealth bombers. Black cliffs ran along the western wall of the Godley Valley. Snow gleamed bronze on the crown of another ancestor from the Araiteuru canoe, Kāmauteurua (Hall Range). Aoraki was beyond that range, thirty-five kilometres away.

On the far bank I stuffed my numb feet into dry socks and boots, and set off on skis across the snow-covered runway of

Lilybank Station. The station was once owned by Tommy Suharto, son of the Indonesian dictator. At the pub in Takapō they say he built the runway so he could fly in and out in his private jet. They also say there are tunnels beneath the luxury lodge so he could flee in the case of an assassination attempt.

Takapō means 'to roll up bundles at night'. An exploring party had once camped a few kilometres south of where I had, at the head of the lake. Something spooked them in the night. They packed up fast and bolted, leaving the name behind. It's not clear what spooked them, but another translation sometimes given is 'a fall in the night'. Its waters were famously home to a tipua (spirit creature) in the form of a giant fish. The tipua controlled the winds, and caused the lake's colour to change abruptly to an iridescent green-blue if storms or enemy warriors approached. People feared the tipua and avoided the shores after dark.

At the end of the runway, my right ski-binding broke with a metallic ping. I looked down in disbelief. Sure, I was using an improvised system of stuffing mountaineering boots into telemark skis, but it'd worked in the past. I dumped my pack, hauled out my repair kit and fiddled around for half an hour. Short of lashing my boots to the skis with a mess of zip ties, nothing doing. Walking would be fine.

I ditched the skis in a copse of trees near the station's outbuildings and continued on foot. The snow cover was patchy anyway, and the slower pace would give me time to quiet my impatient mind. Except that I was going straight into Te Mauru, the howling, gritty nor'-west wind. It's also called 'te hau kai takata' (the wind that devours people). I dropped my head and forged on. Each step felt like two. Iced-over puddles cracked underfoot.

Relax, I told myself. Focus on the sound of the wind.

I reached into my pocket for my new beanie, to reduce the noise in my ears, and found nothing. I grimaced. It must have fallen out. That was okay: I had another hat.

After eight months of doing these long walks, I was starting to get an intuitive feeling about the landscapes I'd taken to calling 'ancestor country'. I'd visited enough known settlement sites with Ngāi Tahu experts now to have hunches about where others might be: around lakes, in the lee of prevailing winds, beside springs or streams. I also knew when I was leaving those hospitable places behind.

Down here in the Godley Valley, snow-flecked black cliffs created a long, barren corridor leading towards the Divide. These east-coast river valleys now had their own feel, too: fast routes to the other side of the island. Crossing the Alps had once seemed a big deal, but with familiarity the journey now felt matter-of-fact. I was starting to grasp how our ancestors had done it all the time. The West Coast was just over that range.

But when I rounded Kea Point, the end of the valley had been erased. I stared into a void. Pure whiteout, from the earth to the sky. I exhaled, breath whistling. Here comes the storm.

Twisting wraiths of ice high on the ridge to the west caught in the dying sun. I'd hoped to make it further up the valley, but without skis the going was slow. I'd be content to sit out the worst of the weather and read my notes on the area. I turned towards the safety of Red Stag Hut.

Inside the tiny four-bunk hunters' hut I unpacked and cooked. I'd prepared extensive research notes for the trip but I'd some-how left them all behind. I was forced to read dog-eared hunting magazines by candlelight while squalls buffeted the thin walls.

In my peripheral vision, someone stole past the window outside. I looked up sharply, listening for the crunch of boots. Who the hell would be out there, now?

Dead silence. I realised that the storm had passed without my noticing. I opened the door and stared into the blackness outside.

'Hello? Who's there?'

As my eyes adjusted, a soft grey nothingness emerged, broken only by a subtle line at the horizon: darker below, lighter above. That was the earth; that was the sky—Papa and Raki, pressed together in a suffocating embrace. The air glowed with a persistent light that had no source. I thought of the old chants about Te Kore, the void from which life began.

Faint sounds reached my ears now. The river shuffled away to my right. Still no reply to my calls, but to be sure I clicked on my head torch. In a flash a thousand moths swarmed my face. I cried out and reeled backwards, hands raised to fend them off.

My torch beam had conjured a million fat flakes of snow. They spun lazily, settling without a sound. I laughed, killed my light and turned to go back inside, when the whole sky twitched.

Strange.

Stillness, and quiet.

Then the sky rippled again, to the north, somewhere up towards the pass, an electrical shimmer too fast and diffuse to really see, or even name. A storm was happening somewhere out there, but gently.

I went to bed. Cocooned and warm, I gazed out the window at the intermittent shimmer.

•

That night, threat filled my dreams. Walking the streets of my old neighbourhood in Melbourne, I passed a policeman sheltering behind a house with his gun drawn. At home I found an old friend waiting for me inside: a tough, aloof man I hadn't seen in years. He had something important he needed me to hide. I realised he was the one the police were hunting. Then in slow motion the police raided the house, bursting through the door and sweeping through each room the way a wave washes up a beach. I felt afraid, but they were gentle and calm. One of the cops had strangely fused teeth, just a long white ridge of bone in the top of his mouth, and another below. I woke thinking of te kauae ruka and te kauae raro, the upper and lower jawbone, the two types of knowledge in the old world: the sacred and the profane.

Come morning, snow had transfigured the valley into a smooth white ocean. South towards the plains, powdery blue sky arched overhead, while up-valley the whiteout blizzard remained. Towering walls of cloud billowed up as if from unseen fires beneath Mt Acland and Panorama Peak. The storm seemed local, seemingly issuing from the mountains themselves. I could see a hint of blue sky above, and sun at the shoulder of Pukewhero Peak. It didn't look too bad. I'd gear up, and go on.

As I cleaned my contact lenses, one tore in my hand. Standing at the outside sink, I scowled and flicked the tiny filament of vision away into the snow. Good thing I always carried glasses. Then I lost twenty infuriating minutes trying to find my gaiters. I thought I'd left them inside the back door with my boots, but they were gone. Perhaps they'd blown away. Annoyed, I cut the tops off a pair of socks and pulled them over my boots to keep out the snow. They looked like something Hillary would have worn in the 1950s, but they'd do.

The wind rose to meet me as I set off towards the snowstorm. Ahead, in a stray shaft of sunlight, the entire surface of the valley, more than a kilometre across, lifted off in one great swarm of ice and raced towards me. Exhilarated, I counted the seconds till impact. 'Three, two, one, here we go!' I hollered, turning away as ice blasted my back with a scouring hiss. The gust faded and the wraiths settled back to earth.

Soon I entered the whiteout, and visibility dropped to twenty metres. With my compass around my neck, reciting times and bearings as an incantation against getting lost, I advanced up the valley, moving among strangely sculpted moraines. In the past, three glaciers had met at this point—the Maud, Grey and Godley—forming one enormous tongue of ice. The historian Johannes C. Andersen says that Māori implements were found near the glacier's face. Today all that remained of the ice was a little green-grey lake. I stood listening to wavelets lap the shore. Wai para hōaka, it's called: cloudy water from the grindstone. The name likens glaciers slicing through rock to hōaka (grindstone) cutting through pounamu. Above me I could see the raw, scraped faces of the glacier's old tracks, then the mountains vanishing upwards on all sides. The broken black triangle of Gordon Peak's lower face emerged from mist like the hollow nose of an enormous skull.

After a scramble over large boulders joined by snow bridges that tended to collapse under my weight, I reached my destination, the antique green Godley Hut. I still wanted to visit the glacier's terminal lake and catch a glimpse of Sealy Pass, but cloud and mist had reduced the world to a glowing haze. I'd take a look tomorrow. I shot the bolt and creaked open the door.

Godley Hut was a long, narrow time capsule built from beautiful dark wood. Paned windows at the far end threw dim light
across bunks, benches and tables, and an assortment of battered
tins and trunks. Apart from some newer bandages in the first-aid
kit dating from World War 2, everything else was from 1934,
when the hut was built. Under one bunk I found a pair of hand-
stitched leather ice-skating boots with blades of Sheffield steel.
The pots and pans and enamel basins were all stamped *Made in
England*. It felt like a party of pre-war climbers had gone out in
their hobnail boots and never come back. I melted snow for a cup
of tea, wrapped myself in my sleeping bag and sat down to read.

As night came on, the mountains beyond the window grew
ghostly. Again, a faint pale light trembled across the landscape,
so fast I could never catch its source. The nor'-wester whistled in
the hut's guywires. I went and stood outside the door. Cloud still
hung about the Divide, and every so often the sky rippled with
subtle fire. They called that kapo, lightning that played about the
horizon over and over. It was considered an omen in the old days,
but I couldn't remember if it was good or bad. On reflection, it
was probably bad.

But it looked to me like the weather would improve. Stars
pricked through gaps in the cloud. If it cleared properly, tomorrow
I'd take my crampons and ice axe out for an explore.

•

Dawn revealed absolute blue sky, marked only by the morning star
and a high late moon. I set off to the glacier lake. There wasn't a
whisper of wind. Snow smoothed the Main Divide peaks above
me into a mass of silky domes. My eye followed the ridge from

Gordon Peak to Mt Wolseley and down to an unmistakable low dip. There it was: Sealy Pass, offering a passage west via the gentle ramp of the Neish Glacier. Given my musings about Hinetamatea and early Māori travel on snow and ice, it looked possible from here—in summer, of course. Still, with the forecast set to improve, how great would it be to cross the lake and bivvy on the glacier, to get a feel for the terrain? I'd brought all my gear with me, just in case.

I'd banked on walking straight across the frozen lake. But as I approached the edge I saw a four-kilometre-long reach of gleaming water striped with intermittent bands of ice, bounded by crumbling cliffs.

I knew I should turn back. But perhaps there was a way around the edge of the lake. I made a foray on the eastern side, climbing through the snow and traversing until I reached a gully littered with fresh rockfall. I halted and watched boulder after boulder spinning down from the unstable cliffs above. They punched through the snowy crust of the lake with dull splashes. This was as far as I would get. I wandered back down and ate lunch sprawled in the snow in full sun. Not quite camping on the glacier, but sweet enough.

After another hour's exploring, as I headed reluctantly back to the hut, a ridge leading up onto the range east of the lake caught my eye. I hadn't considered climbing anything, because the avalanche danger would be too high after the storm. But this ridge faced north-west, directly into the wind, and would have been scoured clean of new snow. The map suggested good travel north at about seventeen hundred metres. I wasn't beaten yet.

As the shadows lengthened in the valley, I climbed fast in

perfect firm conditions. In an hour I was high above the valley, watching the milky-grey river winding out towards the plains. In another hour I was following the tracks of Himalayan tahr—a goat-like animal introduced here for sport—along a wide bench at exactly the same altitude as Sealy Pass.

I paused, raised my camera and snapped the pass with the sun striking a single ripple of cloud above Mt Petermann. I wished the oral history about the route was more specific: *You watched a peak and went by its signs. Fog on one side meant you could get through; fog on the other side warned you not to attempt to cross the pass.*

'Don't even think about it,' I said aloud. 'That's the lee side of the nor'-wester. That'll be massively loaded with new snow.'

By dusk, I'd reached a broad chute that dropped half a kilometre straight down to the glacier. I looked at it long and hard. Camp here, return to the hut, or camp at the head of the lake? I had a clear view all the way down. The angle looked fine, and it wasn't too loaded with snow. The map showed another chute further north, and two ridges which would give me options for climbing back out. There wasn't a breath of wind, and the forecast for tomorrow was good.

Bugger it, I thought. I've come this far.

·

I sat on my pack on a small tongue of ice extending out into the middle of the lake. The air was so still that I lit a candle and ate dinner by its unwavering light. I imagined the tiny flame seen from high above: a solitary point of life in a vast silence.

After dinner I lay in my bivvy bag, surrounded by shimmering black water. The sky above was huge and clear, Te Ika-whenua-o-te-raki (the Milky Way) a great pale net. The cold rasped in my lungs. If I rose early and the conditions were good, could I go for the pass? Be up there for sunrise?

No. I wasn't equipped or prepared; regardless, right now this whole area was avalanche terrain. I could go up the glacier to the foot of the pass, just to have a look, and that was all. I planned my exit route back onto the ridge, set my alarm for five and went to sleep.

·

In the small hours the wind woke me, snapping at my bivvy bag like a hungry mouth. I unzipped and looked out. A gale-force southerly was howling up the valley. The ice and black rock hanging above me roared with malevolent life. Cloud whipped over the sheer wall of the Divide in fast-forward. Tiny and exposed, I double-checked my gear so it couldn't blow into the lake, then tried and failed to get back to sleep. The encircling peaks were frightening to behold. In the end I zipped back up and lay in darkness with my eyes turned away.

·

At some point I must have drifted off, because seemingly a moment later I woke to the alarm, feeling somehow warm and relaxed. The wind was still stiff, but not as bad, and by first light I was plugging steps up the Godley Glacier through deep, soft snow. It was only a kilometre and a half to the foot of the pass. I might as well take a look before heading out.

I moved slowly, probing for crevasses around likely contours. I was taking a risk travelling solo and unroped, but with this much snow the slots were well filled. I turned towards the Neish Plateau. Cold cloud billowed overhead, but directly over Sealy Pass I could see blue sky and golden light. A rough southerly here meant fine and settled weather on the other side. I was nearly at the base of the pass.

The higher I went, the deeper the snow. My progress slowed to a trudge. I was drenched with sweat despite the cold. Oh, for my skis, or some snowshoes. I grew tired and hungry and more determined with each step. A little further, a little higher. There was a gully above me to the left of the icefall, between the seracs and the sheer cliffs coming off unnamed peak 1925. The standard route was on the other side of the glacier, but this gully was low-angle, and looked okay from its base. I might as well take a look. Up I went.

At some point I looked across the broken blue face of the icefall and found myself gazing right at the pass. It was less than a kilometre away. I still had to top out of the icefall and cross the Neish, but it was close. I gritted my teeth. A little further: see how it goes.

Each step became a struggle. I fought my way up through waist-deep powder that refused to provide a firm footing. The wind blasted ice into my skin like hail. One more step. Another. The angle in the gully wasn't bad at all, and then it was awful. I looked up towards the lip of the icefall: way too steep to go on. That was the killer angle above, where loose snow sat poised and ready to go. Time to get out of this gully. I only had one ice axe, but it would do the trick. I swung the pick into the solid blue serac next to me, kicked in my crampons and front-pointed on up. Solid purchase underfoot. I was moving again.

The steeper seracs were marginally safer, having already shed their loose snow, but I was sweating so much my glasses had fogged. Cursing my torn contact lens, I hung off my axe and with my free hand zipped my glasses into the pocket of my shell. I only needed to see as far as the next swing of the pick. The wind rang maddeningly in my ears. Spindrift stung my face. I was so close.

Right near the top of the icefall, the angle on the ice finally lessened. Snow once again dusted the glacier underfoot. No longer front-pointing, I booted a crampon in and got ten points into solid ice. Good. I felt myself relax. I would make the pass. Two more solid steps. *Come on.* Another step and the points of my crampons meet no resistance. My boot sank all the way in. It was just snow. Resting on ice.

'Oh fuck,' I said aloud.

A crack formed beneath my boot, and raced away across the pristine white surface. Just a hairline a metre or so long, irrelevant among five hundred kilometres of storm-bound Alps. I was the only living soul who knew of its existence. I had time to watch it form. I had time to think: *slab avalanche.* I had time to dive left, because time had stopped. And then I was gone.

PART II: NEISH ICEFALL, GODLEY VALLEY, CANTERBURY ALPS. MIDWINTER.

Over the previous days, I'd seen lightning playing about the pass. I've never believed in omens, but I've always believed in stories. The old Ngāi Tahu stories hold clues about how our ancestors navigated the mountains, and the gods and spirits that inhabit them.

When you see lightning, and hear thunder crack and roll across the peaks, that's Tāwhaki and Whaitiri. The chiefly Tāwhaki is lightning and his cannibal grandmother Whaitiri is thunder. Their story is a riddle about gaining ancestral knowledge and the pathway to the heavens. In parts it's humorous, in parts baffling; but pay attention to that feeling of bafflement. Unfamiliar ideas and strange logics can be a sign that you're reading the real thing—as in the following, from a version of the story recorded on Ruapuke Island, off the southern tip of Te Waipounamu, in the 1840s.

.

Whaitiri was an old cannibal goddess who lived in the sky. She'd been blinded for transgressing tapu, and spent her days sitting among the reeds, counting out items of food, flailing about with a club trying to kill anyone who approached. She was constantly rumbling away, rumbling away, breaking wind—which is where thunder comes from.

Whaitiri's husband was a mortal, Kaitangata, and down on earth she had a son, Hema, and three grandchildren. Her granddaughter Pupumainono was skilled in karakia. Tāwhaki, the youngest grandson, was noble and brave. Karihi was the eldest grandson, and nothing more.

One day Hema was murdered. Armed with their sister Pupumainono's advice, Tāwhaki and Karihi went looking for their grandmother, hoping to climb to the higher realms of heaven to learn how to avenge their father's death.

They found Whaitiri sitting in the sky with her club, listening intently and lashing out at anyone who came close. The brothers managed to restore her eyesight, and in return she welcomed them into her home. But Tāwhaki and Karihi were wary: her house was littered with human bones. Before bed, they collected cat's-eye shells from the beach, and slept with them over their eyes. Whaitiri came for them in the night. Looking into their room, in the firelight she saw the gleam of eyes gazing back, and was scared to attack.

In the days that followed, the brothers questioned their grandmother about the correct way to reach the upper heavens. 'Where's the path?' they asked.

'It's right here,' the old woman said.

They searched the paths to the urinal, the stream, the latrine, the place for gathering firewood, the place for performing kūmara rites. They couldn't find the way. The brothers persisted in their questioning, and the old woman finally gave in.

'Well, if you are determined, I hold the road to that part of the sky you want to reach.'

'Then where is the road?' they asked.

'The road is on my neck,' she replied. 'Loose this cord.'

Whaitiri had a cord around her neck which stretched up into

the heavens, which the brothers needed to climb. Before they set off, she warned that they would be attacked by the winds of the western sky.

Tāwhaki, the youngest son, began to climb hand over hand towards the heavens. He'd learned the correct chants from their sister Pupumainono, and recited them as he ascended. He climbed the aka matua (parent vine) and safely made his way into the sky. After many adventures, Tāwhaki became lightning, and is the one seen flickering on the horizon or flashing overhead. He's chiefly and noble, and often seen clothed in fire.

But what about the older brother, Karihi? He forgot the karakia his sister had taught him, and he chose the wrong path. As he struggled his way up the cord, the winds of heaven grew stronger. They gusted and battered at him until he couldn't hold on. Karihi fell to his death.

.

The slope liquefied and dropped me into darkness and a chaotic cartwheeling, over and over beneath a wall of snow, buried with no light or direction beyond the dread pressure of my jacket hood against my face, and the sudden violence of the mountain hurling me away. I felt my body grow weightless as I entered freefall off the front of the seracs, then I hit the snow again, the mountain swarming into my mouth, thumbing my eye sockets and stopping my ears. My ice axe disappeared from my hands, and I tumbled again and again, with a dull sense of disappointment that this was it—death was real, and this was how it arrived, without warning or reason beyond my own stupidity, a long way from home—before daylight flashed, then heels over head into night, and another flaring hope like the world turning faster and the days and nights accelerating until the world exploded into being, and I thudded to a halt in warm sun.

I lay on my back, staring at the sky. I could breathe.

·

The avalanche had spat me out the bottom. I felt cold fire all through my clothes, down my back and legs and wadded into my boots, but no pressing weight on my chest. I hauled myself up and marched away down the slope like a wind-up toy.

I must have been in shock, because I'd taken a good twenty paces before I stopped and looked back at the trail of debris marking my fall, fanning out from a single point high above. I hadn't hit anything on the way down. I'd come to the surface. Somehow I'd survived.

But I'd lost my ice axe, and my ski poles had been torn off my pack. I spent the next hour walking a grid through the debris, like a search party hunting for a body. I saw the neon-yellow tip of one pole, then the other, but no trace of my axe. Eventually I gave up and retreated down the glacier. I could always buy another axe.

Down I went, following the faint traces of my powder-filled footprints. I wove between hummocks of ice that glowed underfoot with a weird opalescence in the afternoon light. Fatigue set in. I hunkered down out of the wind and made lunch while the mountain piled itself against my back. I put my knife point-down in the snow, looked up at the craggy spire of Te Kahui Kaupeka (Mt D'Archiac) to the south-east, then looked down again and the knife was gone. Another futile search. The longer I stayed, the more the glacier would take.

When I made it safely off the ice, I stopped to drink cup after cup of melt-water out of the lake, taking a little back from the glacier. My brain re-engaged. *Fuck.* How am I going to get out of this valley without an axe?

The next three hours were a slow pacing up and down the base of the eastern ridge through howling wind-blown powder, checking map and photos against the terrain. The southerly had loaded powder into the chute I'd come down, and the one I'd earmarked further north as well. That one had already avalanched, with a fan of debris out the bottom big enough to destroy a city block. I'd anticipated this, and planned two separate routes out via steeper ridges, but they'd be impossible without an ice axe. And I already knew there was no way around the side of the lake.

Either I risked going up the gully I'd originally come down, wading uphill into loose powder for the second time that day, or I could hunker down for the night and try again tomorrow with a clear head. But by then there'd be more snow, and I still wouldn't have an axe. Whichever way I looked at it, I was in trouble. They say lightning never strikes twice, but each time I considered going back into marginal terrain, all I could think of was being buried alive.

For years I'd carried a personal locator beacon in the backcountry. It got thrown in the top of the pack, carried in a chest pocket on risky ground, lent out to friends. I'd never really considered the circumstances in which I'd actually use it. I took out the small white and yellow brick. I felt sick at the idea of my family fearing the worst, at the waste of resources and risk to a rescue team. I was warm and dry, with several days of food and fuel. I should give it a go. I could figure something out. I always figured something out.

I spent another hour out in the snow trying to identify a safe route. Perhaps there was a way round the other side of the lake, but when I got closer, it was all exposed to steep snow slopes above. Each time I considered another option, I relived the plunge. Knowing I'd lost my nerve made it worse. The sky was a shape-shifting snarl of clouds. Down-valley a localised front darkened the lake with fresh falling snow. Running out of daylight. Time to decide.

I took the beacon from its pouch and stared at it for a while. Then I flipped up the aerial and set it off. I wept briefly and angrily for having given in.

•

In the story of Whaitiri and Tāwhaki, Karihi is the character who interests me. He isn't noble or chiefly and has no spiritual powers. He isn't thunder or lightning, or a tohuka. He doesn't know the right karakia, and he chooses the wrong path. Māori stories are full of characters like Karihi, who fail to observe omens or protocols and come to a bad end. If my story was an old Māori tale, it's pretty obvious which character I'd be.

Speaking to the historian James Herries Beattie in the 1920s, the great Ngāi Tahu tohuka Teone Taare Tikao talked movingly about how omens and storms were understood in the old days. He drifted from one story to the next, in and out of ideas, pausing here and there to smoke his pipe or eat before moving on. Most often he stopped to lament that his memory wasn't so good, that he'd forgotten the answers to Beattie's questions. It was a shame, he said, that the old knowledge was being lost.

What he did remember about lightning was that there were three types: uira, striking down; kohara, zigzagging all over; and kapo, flashing here and there around the horizon until it grew strongest at one point. That was where the storm would ultimately come from: kapo was a battle between lightning, with the weaker ones eventually giving way, leaving the strongest to take possession of the wind and hurl it against the earth. 'This victorious kapo is mana,' Tikao said. 'It is a fire.'

So lightning was spiritual power, and also an omen. 'Tohu nō te ora, tohu nō te mate,' Tikao said. An omen of life or an omen of death.

Kapo flickering around the horizon over and over was a sign that a rakatira (chief) would die. Lightning showing time and again at a specific place, a mountain or a river or an alpine pass, meant death at a distance. People needed to pay attention to where it fell.

It could be a bad omen, bringing news that a person would be killed. But it could also be a sign that there would be an accident, Tikao said. The person might be lucky enough to escape.

•

Hunched under an overhanging rock to escape the wind, I listened to the creaking music of the lake icing over. Somewhere nearby, a small stream whispered beneath the snow. Every thirty seconds, the modern world punctured the air. *Beep, beep.*

I'd left the beacon on a rock in the middle of the ice to converse with its satellite brethren. The yellow plastic housing was the only colour in the valley. I snapped a photograph: *Landscape with Locator Beacon.*

'I live in the first world, in the twenty-first century,' I said aloud. The beacon was my karakia, the helicopter my god.

Snow swirled overhead. I levelled a campsite under an overhang in case no help came. The slightest shift in the wind sent me out into the open to scan the sky. I dreaded and hoped that someone would show up. I had a long time to think.

•

A couple of hours later a helicopter emerged from the gathering dusk, a tiny insect approaching against the ice, making the peaks loom larger than ever. As it clattered overhead I stood waving my pack liner like a drunk at a parade. The pilot swung west and began scouring the godforsaken maw of the Ruth Glacier, on the far side of the lake. The beacon's signal must have been out by about five hundred metres.

I stood listening to the distant racket, hoping they'd come back. They turned and made one last sweep, all the way up to the top of Godley Glacier, then suddenly banked and dropped towards me.

'You hurt? What happened?' yelled one of the searchers, climbing out and crouching low in the blizzard of the rotors.

'I'm fine,' I yelled back. 'Avalanche. No ice tools. Couldn't get out.'

The rescue team were grizzled veterans from Aoraki / Mt Cook Village. The cockpit was pungent with rollie-tobacco smoke. I looked around at a ring of friendly, chapped faces with etched smile lines and hard eyes. Wedged between real climbers, it became clear to me that I was play-acting at mountaineering. A little knowledge was a dangerous thing.

We lifted away from the glacier, and the brute reality of that wind and ice receded to a view. The pilot radioed ahead to let my family know I was unharmed, and one of the knots in my heart released. As we thudded south I looked down at the long white ribbon of the valley below, criss-crossed by the Godley River's azure braids.

When we came clear of the mountains, white shaded to gold

where the tussock showed through. Lake Takapō was deep purple at sundown. Storm cloud and pink haze coloured the inland sky. My camera hung heavy around my neck.

'Where do you wanna be dropped?' the pilot's voice crackled over my headset.

'Um, my car's at the end of the Lilybank Road,' I replied.

We debriefed on the ground, where the cheerful local cop was waiting. We talked through terrain, aspect, conditions and experience, then shook hands, and the team climbed back into the chopper.

'Buy a Lotto ticket, mate,' one of them said.

'And make a donation to LandSAR!' added another, referring to the volunteer rescue service. I did, as soon as I returned home.

The conversation had confirmed that setting off the beacon had been the right decision, and that most other decisions of mine had been wrong.

They lifted off and swung north.

'You right to drive?' the policeman asked through the window of his truck.

'I'm fine.'

He raised a hand in farewell. The dust plume behind his vehicle faded into nothing.

Silence returned. The snow-laden mountains glowed with an intense pale fire.

Takapō, to flee in the night.

I stood beside my car, and looked at my boots.

PART III: CHRISTCHURCH, MIDWINTER.

I called Leigh from the airport a couple of days later, on my way to a writers' festival up north. I'd messaged her briefly about the rescue when I'd got out, but we hadn't spoken.

'Hey,' she said. 'How are you?'

'Good. Just about to board. You?'

'What happened up there?'

'I went up to the head of the Godley Lake, then a bit further to look at the pass. It was stunning up there. Until the avalanche.'

There was a pause: hushed airport conversation and the distant roar of a plane landing crept in.

'What happened?' Leigh repeated.

I sat sprawled across a bench, chatting away about the beauty of the glaciers, the snow, losing all that gear, the stupidity of it all. I laughed. 'I'm just gutted I had to call it in. I talked to Jon and he reckoned the gully that'd already avalanched would have been fine.'

'Are you okay?'

'My neck was a bit sore the next day, but no damage done.'

There was another pause, like she was waiting for me to say more.

'Anyway, how are you?' I said. 'How's the book coming along?'

Her answers were brief. An attendant called my flight to board. I hung up and walked to the gate.

•

In the weeks that followed, the events in the Godley replayed in my mind. I thought about gear and technique and judgement. I'd planned the trip to avoid the high mountains, and left my climbing partners and gear behind. I'd looked at Sealy Pass and concluded numerous times that it was lethal. And yet, through a dreamlike stubbornness, I'd walked myself up to catastrophe, one step at a time. I'd do more avalanche training. Learn about decision psychology and heuristic bias. Make sure I was always with more-experienced climbers. I'd get my technique right.

But there was a feeling I couldn't shake. On that trip everything had gone wrong. I had to ditch my skis, lost numerous items of gear, tore a contact lens, and even ended up climbing without my glasses, reminding me that in the old stories, the punishment for transgression was often being struck blind. I'd dreamed about disaster. I'd repeatedly found my way barred by wind, water, rockfall, snow. I'd left all my notes behind. Instead, I'd been forced to read the signs in the landscape itself, and found myself illiterate.

Plenty of modern climbers are superstitious. And when our European ancestors headed into the mountains, they were all guided by spiritual ideas. In mediaeval Europe, mountains were the abode of the devil. For the Victorians, mountains were Nature's cathedrals in which to worship God. I'd read plenty about how the peaks held spiritual significance for old-time Māori, but I was still unwilling to entertain the idea that it could be meaningful to me.

I was still in contact with the friend in Melbourne who I'd once fallen in love with. We'd been working hard to restore our friendship. She was a historian who worked a lot on prophecy and dreams. She said to me: 'You have to treat old knowledge as if it's alive, and it's trying to tell you something. You can't learn anything if you treat it as dead.'

What to make of the idea that storms and wind could be prophetic, and that the mountains were ancestors with mauri and wairua of their own, and that on my trip up the Godley, the omens were bad?

'You should and go see Maurice,' my mother said on the phone, her tone matter-of-fact.

•

Maurice Manawaroa Gray is a tohuka of the present day, trained as an Anglican minister but also in old Ngāi Tahu lore. I made a time to visit him later in the week. I knew whakapapa was the first thing he'd want to discuss. After the smothering darkness of the avalanche, death felt close, and for the first time, whakapapa felt real. I'd somehow felt the line of ancestry passing through me, stretching from my neck up into the heavens—and that it could so easily be cut.

The night before going to see Maurice, I started reading whakapapa seriously for the first time. Mum and Dad were away. Sitting in their house, with the curtains pulled against the southern winter, I took out the family whakapapa box and laid out the manuscripts. Some were complex charts, others scribbled on Post-it notes. Dad had linked them all into a master document on the back of a roll of ornate old wallpaper.

Late into the night, I worked back through the complex spiderweb of ancestors, amused to think that most people did this only once they'd retired. I reached the point where European names disappeared, then went beyond. The lists were incomplete, and barely meaningful without the stories that went with them, but I could still home in on names from the Ngāi Tahu histories. There were Tānetiki, Moki and Tūrakautahi, who had competed verbally for Kura Tawhiti. There was Te Rakitāmau, who led an early expedition across the Alps after Raureka revealed her route. Through Te Rakitāmau's wife Punahīkoia, the line stretched all the way back to Rākaihatū, captain of the Uruao waka, leader of the first peoples to arrive in the south, the one who'd dug the inland glacier lakes. I could run a finger from myself back to him. My lines were inconsequential, like a peasant tracing his connection to William the Conqueror. But each time I saw a link, the stories grew more real. The past was a continuum.

There had been a break in that continuum, though, and I found it towards the bottom of the box. I lifted a hand-tinted studio portrait of my great-great-grandfather John Hunter to the light. He was a barrel-chested man rendered with pale skin and rouged cheeks. An enormous moustache disguised his mouth. And there, beneath the photo, was a copy of his handwritten memoir, *Adventures in N.Z. and the Islands that Lay to the South*: the one I'd been putting off reading for years.

Around the turn of last century, John Hunter had written about growing up as a white man at the southern edge of the British Empire. As a teenager, Mum had read the original notebooks, but she hadn't seen them for fifty years. When a copy resurfaced, from my aunt, Mum had rung me straight away.

For nine years I'd carried the unopened file with me around the world. I was always working on something else, and I didn't want to read it until I could give it my full attention. More than that, I knew I'd be obsessed. Now, the time had come to sit and read.

.

About the year 1855 my father bought a farm about two hundred acres for something like £40 on the north bank of the west T[a]ieri river. At that time, the whole of the flat was one vast swamp spreading out like a sea to the foot of the mountains; and islands of bush dotted down here and there that looked blue in the distance, and fringed with flax and swamp grass. However a homestead was built on the farm near the river bank, at [the] time being the only suitable place which is now called Hinley, now one of the finest [e]states in New Zealand.

When John Hunter is a little older, he and his wealthy merchant father sail south to Rakiura (Stewart Island), the largest island below the South Island. A boat 'manned with natives' arrives to take him to the smaller Ruapuke Island, where he is to go to school.

When some distance from the cutter I tu[r]ned and looked in that direction and I could just make out the form of my father and the crew standing motionless. I now hid my face in my hands for my feelings at that moment I can never describe; and when I next looked up the cutter was a mere speck in the bay. We now opened out the rough coastline of the island and I took notice of the lofty mountains which loomed against the western sky.

Over the years, Master John attends to his education, and lives and dines with the German Lutheran missionary Reverend Wohlers and his family. Outside the classroom he explores the mainland on a thoroughbred loaned by King Toby, the 'invincible' local chief Topi Pātuki. He regularly meets the dark-skinned natives, observes them at prayer and enjoys an ongoing flirtation with Mary, the gorgeous half-caste maid, who has a tendency to faint into his arms.

On the day John Hunter completes his schooling, he changes into a new outfit and gazes at himself in the mirror. A dashing 'college gentleman' in a black velvet suit gazes back, bringing 'a flash of pride' to his cheeks. He farewells his hosts, resists the urge to press Mary to his breast, and rides out on the road towards the port.

He sees a white man coming the other way, and takes no notice until they are face to face. All of a sudden, John leaps from his horse. 'Well, father, don't you know me?'

The man turns and looks at him. 'Can I believe my eyes? Is that you my boy, Jack?'

Yes, John replies.

His father, 'a European', is shocked at how much he has changed. 'I would have passed you like a stranger, Jack.'

•

I put the manuscript down, electrified. It was 3 a.m., and the temperature in the room had dropped.

John Hunter had changed so much that he'd become white. His mother, Kawiti, was Ngāi Tahu. His father was an American whaler with Sioux blood. The writing was as much fiction as fact. Was it a memoir or a novel? Either way, in writing himself into existence as a white man, he had tried to erase his Māori identity, to cut the cord of whakapapa stretching up to his ancestors. Later, aged fifty-two, in the grip of delusions brought on by influenza, he wrapped a bedsheet around his neck instead. The death certificate was there in the box, too.

I went to bed feeling off-balance from the strangeness of it all, wanting to know more about my ancestor, and flat-out sad. If I ever had kids, I'd want them to be able to grow up proud of who they were. I checked my phone before sleep: 1 a.m. in Australia. Too late to call Leigh.

My walks were steadily taking me further south, towards the Murihiku (Southland) coastline where John Hunter had lived.

·

In the old days, if you had spiritual questions you went to a tohuka. It was said that, through the power of karakia, they could cure sickness, shift the weather, strike an enemy dead. Today, spiritual values persist strongly through all aspects of Ngāi Tahu life, but the tribe's leadership is predominantly secular, and variants of Christianity are the main focus of organised Māori faith.

Tikao, carrier of some of Ngāi Tahu's most sacred knowledge, said in the 1920s that a lot of Māori spiritual power had been destroyed by the coming of the Pākehā. Old beliefs had gone underground, shifted, changed. Some died away. Even Tikao said he'd forgotten so much, and that was generations ago.

'Tikao wasn't forgetful!' said Maurice Manawaroa Gray, a mischievous gleam in his eye.

The next morning, a crisp winter's day, I was seated in Maurice's living room. He was leader of the Ōtautahi Rūnaka, the urban Christchurch branch of Ngāi Tahu. He'd had the grim but loving task of blessing most of the dead after the 2011 earthquakes. Now in his fifties, he was a big man with a gentle face and hearty laugh, his measured cadences interrupted by outbursts of a younger, cheekier self.

He sat forward and placed one hand on the table, drawing me in. 'Tikao wasn't forgetful. He was just providing the shell of

what he knew. The essence? He wasn't going to give that away!
A lot of our people did that. They weren't going to tell historians
everything. But Tikao *did* teach everything to his daughter, and
she wrote it all down. She was my great-grandmother. I've got all
her manuscripts.'

Maurice raised a hand above his head and rolled his eyes. '*This*
much! I haven't read them. It was all taught to me orally.'

The A-B-C of traditional Māori knowledge was chant and
incantation, whakapapa and history, observation and ritual, often
passed down within families. Whare wānaka, schools of esoteric
learning, were dotted around the inland high country. Wānaka,
south of the Godley, got its name from its whare wānaka, and there
was another at Manuhaea, at the head of Lake Hāwea. The wānaka
pūrākau recently started by Tā Tipene and Maurice Manawatu
was a revival of this tradition, and Maurice Gray still took students
out to the foot of Aoraki.

Before we met, he'd asked me for a list of all the books and
manuscripts I'd read. Now he listened intently as I told him about
the journeys I'd undertaken so far. I related my story about travelling up the Godley to the point of the avalanche. He nodded
without interrupting, then finally asked: 'And what is it you want
to know?'

'I've been learning about the routes people took and the gear
they used, and the histories,' I said, 'but it feels...technical. So
I guess I want to talk about the spiritual aspect. When people
looked at the peaks, what did they really see?'

•

Over a long conversation, punctuated by three phone calls from
people seeking his advice, Maurice told me there were different

ways of seeing the mountains, one for each successive wave of migration to the south. The earliest went back to the Waitaha days, to the first arrivals.

'What was the name of the first Waitaha canoe?' he asked.

'Uruao?'

'And what does Uruao mean? Uru, to enter. Ao, the world. To enter the world. This was the celestial waka that entered the world, and there was another that returned to the sky, Ururaki. Some of the mountains are doorways, the places where the spirit canoes entered the world.'

As Maurice spoke, he rested his eyes to one side of my face, his gaze distant but his bearing alert. He spoke of the second way of seeing the mountains: how the canoe of the ancestor Aoraki overturned, and how he and his brothers Rakiroa, Rakirua and Rārakiroa turned to stone to form the Southern Alps.

'But what people don't realise is that Aoraki and his brothers are doorways, at the north, south, east and west. They're the gateways between heaven and earth. Aoraki, of course, means just that—world of the heavens—and his brothers, through their positioning, become the doorways to another realm.

'And coming from the brothers, you have the glaciers that forge the areas that you were travelling through.'

Maurice looked up and away, mentally tracing the landscape as he talked.

'So you're moving to the back of Takapō, up to Sealy Pass... You're talking about the four brothers, the glacial gorges that have been carved out, then the waters, the wai-puri, that come out and form these sacred streams that we use for rituals.'

Maurice looked directly at me for the first time. 'What that's

telling me is that you need to be initiated. You need to undergo a
tuhi and a tua ritual to mark you and, more importantly, to give
you a name that allows you to follow in the sacred footsteps of
your ancestors, without fear—'

'Without avalanches!' Maurice's wife, Kay, chimed in from the
kitchen. 'Did that happen because of the work Nic's doing?'

'What he is to do,' Maurice said with a laugh. 'What he is *to* do.'

'Oh, okay.' Kay grinned at me. 'No pressure.'

'There is a bigger purpose to crossing the passes than just taking pounamu or harvesting food,' Maurice continued. 'There is a
lot more to it. Now, if you didn't have your mother's whakapapa
then you'd probably get away with thinking about the avalanche
as wrong place, wrong time. But when you carry a bloodline, then
that creates a different balance in life.'

Before going any further, Maurice said, I needed to properly
learn my whakapapa. I needed to learn karakia, and undergo rituals at the foot of Aoraki. That was just the beginning. Then he
started talking about an ancient prophecy, and tasks to be fulfilled.

As he spoke, I was gripped by an uncertainty I couldn't quite
keep from my face. I wasn't sure what I'd expected, but not this.
Without deep grounding in tribal lore, I had no way of knowing
how to react. I'd read allusions to prophecy in several manuscripts,
including Tikao's—and in Barry Brailsford's work. I wasn't about
to take them literally, or believe they had anything to do with me.

The conversation moved on. Maurice started talking about
fabricated traditions: supposedly old stories and beliefs that were
actually made up.

'You have people giving stuff out to dumb people,' Kay said
with a smile, 'and the real stuff stays secret.'

Maurice nodded and grinned his cheekier grin, and I felt myself relax. They were messing with me. He knew my family, but much of what he was willing to say off the cuff was intended to put me off the scent, to see how gullible I was.

We have a tradition of doing that. James Herries Beattie, the diligent recorder of Ngāi Tahu traditions in the 1920s, and the man who'd interviewed Tikao, was the butt of an affectionate joke within the tribe. The old people would groan when they saw Beattie pedalling up the road on his bicycle. His list of questions could sometimes take a fortnight to get through. When the sessions were finished Beattie would pedal off to the railway station, and the old people would cry with laughter at some of the things they'd made up.

Blinking in the sunlight on the way back to my car, I smiled ruefully to think how Maurice and Kay had been gently teasing me in the same way. I felt a glimmer of excitement, too: people were still thinking and talking about mountains as spiritual entities. Old Tikao had hidden 'the essence' from the outside world, but passed it on within the tribe. I would keep learning whakapapa, keep talking to people about mauri and wairua, keep studying the manuscripts. But I wouldn't be going on any quests to fulfil ancient prophecies any time soon.

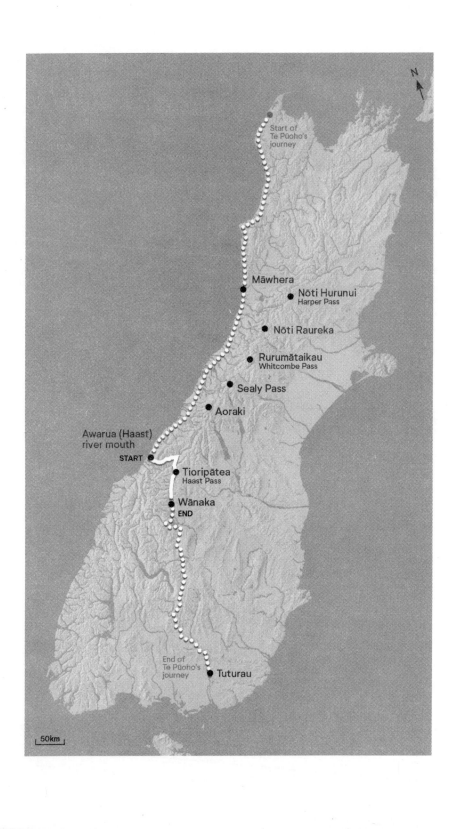

7

Tioripātea
(Haast Pass)

AWARUA (HAAST RIVER) MOUTH,
SOUTH WESTLAND. SUMMER.

For the rest of that winter and all of spring, I kept my distance from the mountains, and instead spent time with the tohuka of the present day.

At my first wānaka pūrākau (traditional-history workshop), in the cosy meeting house at Wairewa (Little River), I sat spellbound and intimidated by discussions between the tribe's historians, whakapapa experts, archaeologists and educators. Led by Tā Tipene O'Regan, twenty of us studied creation chants, some so old that lines defied modern translation; applied Cicero's rhetoric to Māori oratory; and pondered the darkness before the creation of the world, when some of the kore, the voids, were placed forever in maunganui-a-te-whenua, the 'huge mountain of the land'. Using the tribe's Cultural Map, we tracked the journey of ancestors via satellite map. All the while, kids flitted in and out, chatting in te reo, playing together or on their phones, absorbing knowledge by osmosis. I left that weekend hungry for the next, and confirmed in my ignorance, and reconciled to the fact that this was many lifetimes' work.

In spring, when snowmelt flooded the rivers, I flew to Melbourne. I wandered through the arrivals lounge scanning people's faces, until I spotted Leigh. She walked towards me with a strange mix of shyness and certainty, her face aglow. We sat kissing in her car for so long we fogged the windows, then drove north, heading for the small mudbrick cottage I rented in the hills.

For six weeks we returned to our idyllic writing life: day after day seated at our desks looking out over the bush, huddled in puffer jackets against the spring chill; breaking off from writing to go climbing on the granite slabs in the nearby hills. We were both living off savings. It felt like we were on some delicious holiday from real life. Her declaration of love, and my reticence, hovered over us the whole time. And at a party in Melbourne, the old friend I'd once fallen in love with pulled me into her bedroom and told me that she'd come to believe we were soulmates, and should have kids—except that she could never see it working out.

Back in New Zealand, the rivers subsided and the passes reopened. The dry shrill of cicadas on nor'-west nights announced summer's return. I walked the length of the Waitaki River with the descendants of Hipa Te Maiharoa, the prophet who'd marched into the high country with his followers in 1877 to peacefully reoccupy ancestral land. I climbed Te Ruataniwha (Ben Ōhau) to

stand where he'd had his vision of a promised land. I swam Lake
Māhinapua (freezing, tannin-black, the mountains a pale smear
above the trees), where Hikatūtae had swum with the heads of
slain chiefs carried by the topknot in his mouth. I explored the
ranges around Maruia and Lewis Pass, where several Ngāi Tahu
routes converged. And in January, Leigh joined me for a journey
that was personal to my whānau: to retrace the footsteps of my
great-great-great-grandmother Kawiti, John Hunter's mother,
across Tioripātea (Haast Pass).

●

When I began reading whakapapa in earnest, Kawiti's name stood
out. The story of how she crossed the mountains and travelled to
the south coast, where she met her future husband, wasn't your
usual romance. In 1836, she was captured from Ōkahu (Jackson Bay) on the West Coast by a band of a hundred Ngāti Tama
guerrilla fighters. Having already walked most of the West Coast,
they marched her across the Alps at Tioripātea, then down into
Murihiku (Southland), intent on launching a surprise attack on
the main settlements along the coast.

After six months on the trail, having walked more than a
thousand kilometres, the raiders surrendered without a fight.
Ngāi Tahu forces surrounded them at Tuturau. The young Ngāi
Tahu chief Topi Pātuki (the 'invincible' King Toby in John Hunter's memoir) shot their leader Te Pūoho through the heart with
a lump of scrap iron. Kawiti and the other prisoners went free.
Later, she married John Hunter's father, the whaler. I'd known
about Te Pūoho's raid for a while. Learning that it was pivotal in
our whakapapa made it real.

●

Leigh and I set off from the mouth of the Awarua (Haast River), north of Ōkahu, in the aftermath of a week of storms. Rocks and branches littered the road. Tioripātea was once a key track through the southern part of the Alps, and is now traversed by State Highway 6.

At dusk on the second night, we pitched camp in a tiny cove at the edge of the Awarua. The water was unusual, the current divided in two. Closest to us the river ran clear, while the far side was milky blue with glacial meltwater from the Ōtoatahi (Landsborough) just upstream. I pitched the tent while Leigh lit a driftwood cooking fire. She was subdued. Her feet were a mess of blisters. We'd spent much of the day musing about Kawiti's life.

'Can you imagine a hundred armed men materialising from the bush right now?' I asked.

'Not really,' Leigh said. 'I had a few tense moments cycling through southern Pakistan, but nothing like that. You'd never think your enemies would walk this far.'

'That whole period must have been nuts, with the arrival of Europeans, and guns. Change happened so fast back then.'

'I don't think that's changed,' Leigh said. 'Who knows what's around the corner for us?'

I dipped the billy into the river, feeling the fluttering of the current like a fish on a line, and wondered whether she meant for our society, or the two of us. I perched the billy over the fire. 'What gets me is that if the raiding party hadn't set out to attack Ngāi Tahu, I wouldn't exist.'

'What do you mean?'

'If they hadn't captured Kawiti and marched her over to

Murihiku, she'd never have met my great-great-great-grandfather. It's like the minute the raiders descended on Ōkahu, the Hunter line popped into existence.'

Leigh's eyes creased in amusement. 'Tell me you don't believe in fate.'

'I believe in—probability,' I said. 'And randomness.'

Leigh scoffed. 'You're such a romantic.'

'What, you do?'

'Well, yeah. Your walks kept bringing you to the mouth of the Taramakau, right where I was staying.'

'So what, our great-great-great-grandchildren popped into existence because I went for a walk?'

'Ha ha,' Leigh said, looking at me intently. 'I thought you didn't want kids.'

'Hypothetical grandkids. I'm joking.'

'Huh.' She nodded, and I thought she would say more. Then she turned and ducked into the tent. I could hear her laying out her sleeping bag and mattress. I made dinner while the river and the traffic rushed past.

A while later, Leigh came back out. 'It's my birthday,' she said quietly.

I wrapped my arms around her. 'What? Happy birthday! Why didn't you say?'

'I don't know. Because you've been grumpy all day.'

She was right. I hated walking on the highway. 'I'm sorry. Forty-one?'

'Forty-one.'

'And your birthday dinner is freeze-dried peas.'

'I've got whisky.'

'Then we should celebrate.'

We ate dinner while sipping whisky from tin mugs and fighting off swarms of sandflies. Our small plume of smoke mirrored the mist drifting up from the valleys across the river.

Leigh's face was pink from sunburn, but she still looked in her early thirties. 'How does it feel to be over the hill?' I joked.

She shrugged. 'I do wonder what's around the corner.'

'Your book's out in a few months.'

'I've wanted to write a book since I was a kid.'

'Not nervous?'

'Mostly excited. Why?'

'It's pretty...exposing?'

'Ha ha.'

'You're not worried about what your family will think?'

'Not really. Why? What do *you* think?'

I hesitated. I'd only known Leigh as a writer, not a dancer, but since reading her manuscript, I found a lot about her former life didn't sit well with me, not least the syrupy persona she'd had to adopt. 'There's heaps about it that I don't get,' I said.

'Like what?'

'We were raised not to stare at women. It's weird to think that being stared at was your job.'

She grimaced. 'It was a *job*. I played a role, and I got paid well to play it. I had the power.'

'Maybe you did. It just fries my brain that you could be empowered by that.'

'By what?'

'By looking hot and...playing dumb? You've got three degrees. Wouldn't you rather get paid for your ideas?'

'Yeah, *writing*. It's what I've always wanted to do, and it's what I'm doing now.'

'Yes,' I said. 'Yes you are.'

We looked at each other in the flickering light of the fire. There was so much more to unpack, but I could feel something shift, some relief in confrontation, however unresolved. I didn't want to look away.

'What I want is pretty simple,' Leigh said. 'A little house in the hills, with a desk and a bookcase, and time to write. The odd trip overseas to somewhere warm.'

'We could do that. We already do.'

'Yeah, but—' Leigh tailed off, looking miserable again.

'What?'

'Well, what if you want kids? I'm *forty-one*.'

'That's what's on your mind?'

She nodded.

'I'm sorry,' I said. 'I was just tossing around ideas. But yeah... the idea's there.'

Neither of us had wanted kids when we'd met. We'd bonded over being child-free as friends coupled up and disappeared off to breed. But since I'd started to study the branching maps of whaka-papa, since coming home to all the aunties and my Māori friends with their badgering about having kids, since drifting towards death at the foot of Sealy Pass, I wasn't so ready to rule out the idea.

We finished dinner, and Leigh topped up her whisky and went back into the tent. I doused the fire and stood over the hissing coals. Overhead, a flight of ducks arrowed across the darkening sky. Leigh's manner was increasingly abrupt, and I couldn't blame her. I'd invited her into my life, into this landscape and this history, but I hadn't invited her into my future.

I climbed into the tent and lay down next to her. 'Hey,' I said. 'I'm sorry it's been a shit birthday. But I am happy we're doing this together.'

She turned in her sleeping bag to face me. 'Thanks.' After a pause, she said, 'I haven't been sure you've actually wanted me here. I feel like you'd rather be walking with someone from the tribe.'

'I love exploring with you,' I said. 'You've dragged me into the weird world of stripping, and I've dragged you into this, and I'm glad. And you know what you said about the house in the hills, and a desk to write?'

'Yes?'

'Would it be here, in NZ?'

'I've always imagined living back here on the Coast,' she said.

'Do you think—we could actually make a life together, like that?'

'Maybe?' Leigh was trying to compose her face. She looked a little bit hopeful, and mostly scared.

I forged on. 'I've been holding back for so many reasons. I kept expecting you to turn around and tell me that I've read the signals all wrong. And there's all the stuff about your old life I'm trying to get my head around; and I know how much you're into new things, so I worry that you'll get bored. Most of the time I'm not here in the mountains. I'm at a desk writing...I'm rambling.' I took a breath. 'What I'm trying to say is that I'm sorry I've been holding back, and I love you, and I'm willing to try. Kids or no kids.'

Leigh nodded slowly, her lips pressed together, but she was suppressing a smile. Her eyes were clear. 'Then let's,' she said.

The possibility of another tiny thread of whakapapa, of the future, flickered into life.

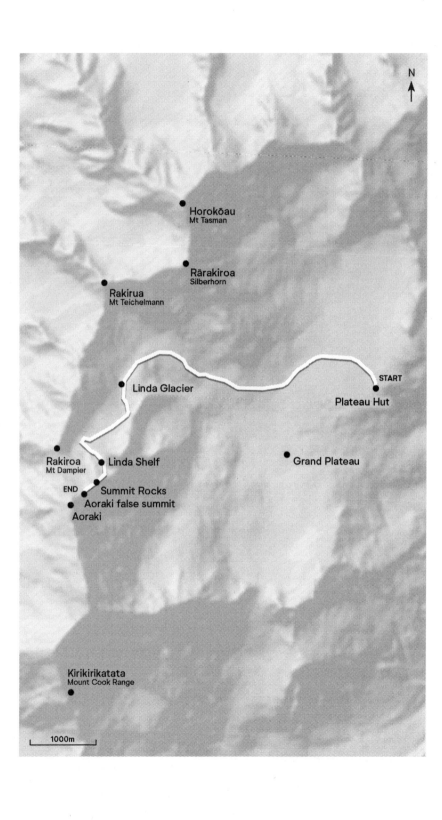

N

Horokōau
Mt Tasman

Rārakiroa
Silberhorn

Rakirua
Mt Teichelmann

Linda Glacier

START

Plateau Hut

Rakiroa
Mt Dampier

Linda Shelf

Grand Plateau

END

Summit Rocks

Aoraki false summit

Aoraki

Kirikirikatata
Mount Cook Range

1000m

8

Aoraki

Ki te tuohu koe, me he mauka teitei,
ko Aoraki anake.

If you must bow down, only bow to
a great mountain, Aoraki.

**PART I: ANAKIWA, MARLBOROUGH SOUNDS.
SUMMER.**

Peep, peep, peep, peep! We woke to a demented dawn chorus of
digital watches. It was 4.45. I opened my eyes to total darkness.
An older man's voice began to chant. As usual, Koro was already
wide awake.

Ka haea te ata—*Dawn opens*
Ka hāpara te ata—*Dawn slices apart*
Ka korokī te manu—*The birds begin to call*

Birdsong filtered in. A dozen more voices joined the chant.

Ka taki te umere—*The cacophony rings out*
He pō, he pō—*Night and darkness*
He ao—*Light*
Ka awatea!—*Dawn!*

The harsh eyes of the fluorescent lights blinked open and the dormitory exploded into action—bodies throwing on clothes, lacing shoes, numbering off—then we pushed out into the dawn, running with lungs on fire as mist rose off the sea. The green hills steepened and we turned for home, stretching out for the finish, heads down, legs done in, stumbling over the line and into the sea with a slap. I tasted brine, heard muffled shouts, and we surfaced, gasping and grinning at each other, feeling half-dead and utterly alive. Next came press-ups and squats, cold showers, breakfast, scrubbing out the ablution blocks, and then, finally, the day began.

For three weeks this would be our life. We were Aoraki-bound.

•

Aoraki Bound is Ngāi Tahu's flagship leadership programme. For a hundred and fifty years, fighting for justice over land sales consumed the tribe. I've heard it said that Te Kerēme (the land claim) *was* our culture. Since settlement at the end of the last century, for the first time in seven generations, the iwi can look forward. That means investing in culture, environment, land and people. These things all come together in Aoraki Bound.

Each year the programme takes two groups of thirteen; most are tribal members, the rest Pākehā allies keen to learn. Each rōpū (party) starts at the top of the South Island near where Rākai-hautū first landed, then comes south. On top of a boot-camp exercise regime, we would explore tribal histories and values, hunt for pounamu, and walk Raureka's trail through the Alps. We'd be forced into leadership roles in performance, ceremony, diplomacy and language. If we survived all that, we'd paddle across Lake Pūkaki, then run a half-marathon to finish at the ancestor-mountain's feet.

·

The van looked like a garden shed on wheels, and after the long drive from Anakiwa, it felt like we'd been trapped inside it for days. When we finally arrived at Arahura marae, just north of Hokitika on the West Coast, we let out a cheer.

Thirteen of us stumbled out. Most of us were Ngāi Tahu; some deep in the culture; some, like me, who had been away from it for years; others reconnecting after generations of dislocation and stigma. Our crew included a renowned singer, a fire chief, a teacher, several professional managers, and a young negotiator working for the tribe.

Ahead of me, Koro Graeme Pepper swivelled his hips, then lowered himself gingerly to the ground. At sixty-seven, Koro was the oldest person to have attempted Aoraki Bound. His home marae was Puketeraki, on the Otago coast. Tall, olive-skinned, with a handsome square jaw and salt-and-pepper hair, he looked like your friendly local publican—which he'd once been. Days earlier, a mountain-biker had run him off a steep track, sending him sprawling down a bank. We panicked. He just picked himself up and yelled, 'Why didn't you ring your fucking bell!' But since then, his leg had been giving him grief.

'How are you doing?' I asked.

'I'm going to do that marathon,' he said, reading my thoughts. He was always up for a laugh, but he also had a quiet, fierce mana that impressed us all.

I watched him walk stiffly towards the marae entrance, wishing I could be as cool and calm; in fifteen minutes I had to speak for our group at the welcome. Public speaking never fazed me, but this was in Māori; I'd only spoken publicly in te reo once before.

After eight days in and around Anakiwa, we'd come to Tuhuru, named for Ihaia Tainui's grandfather, and home base of the Kāti Waewae hapū, to learn more about pounamu. After the karaka (calls of welcome), we moved through into the striking black whare. The pillars of the house were all ancestors, holding up the roof over the head of the living. Ihaia's carved form stood on our left, a greenstone mere in his hand. Raureka was represented on the wall above our heads. Below the carved figures were the smiling faces of their descendants, sitting in rows.

Somehow I made it through my whaikōrero (speech), and if I stuffed it up, the uncles and aunties were generous enough to hide their smiles. After the feast we returned to the whare with our bellies full of kaimoana (seafood) fresh from Poutini's coast. Taua Horiana Tootell, a youthful elder who was by turns playful and utterly direct, had us haul pounamu boulders into the room. We sat at her feet as she talked us through the stories and qualities of the numerous shades of green. Along with the Kāti Māhaki hapū, further south along the coast, Kāti Waewae hold deep knowledge of the stone. Taua Horiana recounted Raureka's story for the group.

'There's a song that Raureka gave us when she arrived on the other side of the mountains.' She nodded at Tiaki Coates, one of the Ngāi Tahu facilitators. 'Here, you help me sing it. And don't go too fast, like you usually do!' He hauled himself to his feet, grinning sheepishly. The two of them began to sing, slow and rhythmical and deep, two notes rising and falling to the stroke of an imaginary axe.

> Whakaatu rā e tāku toki—*I stretch forth my axe*
> Ki te kāuru—*To the head of the tree*
> Koia pānukunuku—*How it moves, how it resounds*
> . . .

I listened, transfixed. I'd read the words in an account from the 1930s, but had no idea it was still sung. The words were far older than Raureka, and they'd come down to us from her mouth. We would learn her song and cross her pass.

•

The next day, we set off up the Arahura River in steady West Coast drizzle. It was energising to return to the valley with a big group under the mantle of Kāti Waewae. Armed with walking poles, Koro moved at a slow but determined pace, chatting away with Arama, the youngest in our rōpū. By the time we reached the swing bridge across The Cesspool, rain was clattering hard against our hoods. Some of the group cruised across, comfortable with the flooded grey Arahura boiling beneath their boots. Others took tentative steps. For them, walking with a pack in the mountains was new.

Though there hasn't been a widespread walking culture within Ngāi Tahu since the late nineteenth century, many individual whānau have maintained their connections with the high country. One person who championed Ngāi Tahu's ongoing relationship with the mountains was the late Uncle Kelly Davis, from Waihao in South Canterbury. He loved encouraging people to get out into the landscape. When he heard two young tribal members, Iaean Cranwell and Craig Pauling, stand up and name Aoraki as their ancestral mountain in their pepeha (introductory speech), he challenged them: 'If you haven't seen your tupuna maunga [ancestor mountain], then who are you? How can you stand up and do your pepeha?'

He took them to see Aoraki. Later, the pair did Outward Bound. They were blown away by the experience, but came back wishing the programme had addressed Māori ideas. With the backing of leaders like Kelly Davis, Tā Tipene O'Regan, Joe Waaka and Maika Mason, and the first dividends from the Treaty settlement starting to become available, the tribe found itself in a position to act. The partnership with Outward Bound was born. It was only natural that Aoraki became the focus for a new push to get Ngāi Tahu people back out into the hills.

·

After dining on dogfood dressed as corned beef, and a sodden night under tarps, we pushed on up the valley once the flooded side creeks finally subsided. From Lower Arahura Hut, we went on to Waitaiki (Olderog Creek), with Koro setting the pace.

Last time I'd been here I was a long way up the valley, above where pounamu is found, and without any right to take the stone. This time we were passing through the heart of pounamu country with permission from Kāti Waewae to fossick along the way. The mood was reverential. People moved quietly, dipping their hands into the same waters as their ancestors had done. Koro stood with his hands on his knees, peering into the shallows, looking for a flash of green.

We took our treasures to Tiaki.

'That's leaverite,' he said.

'What's that?'

'Leave 'er right there!'

At Waitaiki, we stopped in brilliant sunshine to watch the famous side creek tumble into the Arahura. Waitaiki is the waterway, but also the mother, and the motherlode, of pounamu. In the creation story of pounamu, the taniwha Poutini brought the kidnapped Waitaiki up into the mountains. Realising he couldn't keep her for himself, he turned her to greenstone and laid her to rest beneath the water, right here. We gathered among waterworn boulders at the river's edge and greeted Waitaiki aloud with speech and song. Many in the group wore Arahura pounamu around their necks. One by one we loosened the cords, lifted the carvings over our heads, and dipped the stone into the river where its life began.

·

In some versions of Raureka's story, she ended up at Arowhenua, just out of Timaru on the east coast, and so did we. But we'd already lost days to rain, and Koro and another teammate, Chris, were moving slowly with injuries, so we were never going to make it over the pass on foot. We went the long way: by bus.

·

Ka haea te ata
Ka hāpara te ata

Twenty to five. As usual, Koro kicked off the dawn chant. The old bugger had the infuriating quality of seeming to need zero sleep, and delighted in waking us all slightly before the alarm.

I opened my eyes onto an echoing hall. Bare white walls, polished floorboards, four or five glowing exit signs. The meeting house had just had a million-dollar upgrade. The inside was new, though the red and white facade looked the same as ever, like a wooden church, with the striking name of the house written across the front: Te Hapa o Niu Tireni.

'Some say it means "The Mistake of New Zealand",' Tewera King said, once the day was underway. The Upoko of the Arowhenuau Rūnaka smiled wolfishly, gold glinting in his mouth. He wore his hair pulled back in a ponytail and watched us from behind small, dark gold-rimmed glasses.

'But it really means "the Broken Promise of New Zealand". This isn't a whare tipuna named after an ancestor. It was named for the promises made to Ngāi Tahu by the government, and the struggle to have those promises honoured. This house is in the centre of the island, so for generations this is where our leaders met to plan the fight against the Crown.'

Growing up, I'd heard dozens of stories about Te Kerēme, the delegations and litigations, the long nights spent hammering out strategies ever since Kemp's land purchase a century and a half ago. I'd been here several times before, but had never quite made the connection that this was where it all took place.

'We've got this flash new wharekai [kitchen], the new amenities block; we've even got *heating*!' said Karl Russell, gesturing round the hall with eyes wide. In jandals and shorts, with his enormous beard, he looked like the frontman for a reggae band. He was a passionate advocate for mahika kai. He sat forward in his chair, looking each of us in the eye. 'But it hasn't always been like this.'

Over the next hour they told stories of the watercress years, the years without boots. While they pursued the claim, the people at Arowhenua lived off potatoes, and kai harvested from the now-poisoned rivers beside the pā. There were stories of people pawning their cufflinks to pay the train fares to meet government officials in Wellington. It was the same across the island. My cousins Auntie Jane and Bill Davis had mortgaged their house and pub to raise funds. People had been feeding the beast since 1849.

It began with Matiaha Tiramōrehu, chief at Moeraki, an authority on tribal history and whakapapa, and a direct descendant of Tūrakautahi, the founder of Kaiapoi Pā. A year after Ngāi Tahu sold twenty million acres under Kemp's Deed in 1848, Tiramōrehu picked up a pen and laid out his case to Lieutenant-Governor Edward Eyre: Walter Mantell, when marking out the reserves, had ignored his instructions. In each area, the multitude of the tribe was confined to an area of land suitable for one white man. The people wanted to grow wheat and potatoes, and needed land to run pigs, cattle and sheep. Tiramōrehu finished his letter with a promise: 'This is the commencement of our speaking to you, Governor Eyre; and although you should return to England, we shall never cease complaining to the white people who may hereafter come here.'

He wasn't kidding. Decades of advocacy and pressure led to the Smith-Nairn Commission in 1879, which found that promises of large permanent reserves, and of schools and hospitals, hadn't been kept. When its interim report came out, the commission had its funding cut and was shut down. An 1886 Royal

Commission reached similar conclusions, but its recommendation of two hundred thousand acres in compensation was ignored. A further report by the judge and commissioner Alexander Mackay documented the abject poverty of the tribe; nothing was done. In 1891 the villages again welcomed Mackay and again people gave evidence. In his second report, Mackay noted the irony that by welcoming and facilitating European settlement, Ngāi Tahu were now kept 'in a chronic state of poverty'. Nothing was done.

By then it seemed nothing *could* be done, because the South Island was almost all privately owned. Settlers would be unfairly punished if the government forcibly acquired their farms to compensate Ngāi Tahu. Yet almost immediately, between 1893 and 1905, the government forcibly acquired ninety-one enormous estates, all of them former Ngāi Tahu territory. The land was subdivided into small farms for 'the common man'. Cheap loans helped settlers buy and improve their farms. It was a wonderful scheme. My English great-great-grandparents Benjamin and Sabine Low were allocated rich alluvial farmland at Willowbridge, just down the road from where we now sat at Arowhenua.

But the scheme was closed to Māori. Instead, in 1906, the South Island Landless Natives Act (SILNA) allocated fifty-seven thousand acres in recognition of the tribe's dispossession and poverty. My grandfather owns lots of SILNA land, scattered across the map. Finally, something was being done—except that SILNA land was koraha (wilderness), the dregs of Crown blocks in the far reaches of Southland and Stewart Island. Most of it was dense bush on inaccessible ground, uninhabitable and economically ruinous. There were no roads in or out, and no loans to build them. Europeans got a *minimum* of thirty hectares of rich farmland. Ngāi Tahu people got a *maximum* of twenty hectares of steep scrub. The Waitangi Tribunal later called it 'a cruel hoax'.

And still men and women kept coming back to Arowhenua and the other marae to plan their fight. While our European ancestors worked hard to build their farms and hand down their wealth, our Ngāi Tahu ancestors poured everything into the claim. What did they get? The 1921 Native-Land Claims Commission: nothing. The 1944 Ngāi Tahu Claim Settlement Act: ten thousand pounds per year for thirty years, for the whole tribe, awarded without consultation—a drop in the bucket compared to what was owed. The 1950s and 1960s: nothing at all.

One of our sayings about the claim is 'He mahi kai takata, he mahi kai hōaka': *It is work that devours people, as greenstone devours sandstone.* There's a grim elegance to this, because the image comes from the art of carving. It implies that you'll be left with a treasure in the end.

The work wasn't wasted. In the 1970s it started to pay off. A nationwide cultural renaissance brought Māori ideas, arts and politics into the mainstream. The Black Power movement in the US emboldened younger activists here. Huge land marches snaked their way across the country, heading for Parliament chanting 'Not one more acre!' The public mood shifted, and the Treaty of Waitangi, the 1840 agreement between Māori and the Crown, came to be seen as the nation's founding document. Most important of all, the Waitangi Tribunal, set up in 1975 to investigate contemporary breaches of the Treaty, in 1985 had its remit extended to include historical breaches going back to 1840.

Ngāi Tahu was ready to go. The legendary Uncle Rik, Henare Rakiihia Tau, filed the tribe's formal claim in 1986.

In a strange echo of Walter Mantell's 1848 walk through Ngāi Tahu territory to allocate reserves, the tribunal members also toured the South Island visiting Ngāi Tahu marae. Half the members were Māori, half Pākehā, backed by an army of lawyers and historians. It was to be the largest claim the tribunal heard. Covering not just Kemp's Deed but all land sold, Ngāi Tahu's evidence ran to fifty volumes, literally tonnes of material, and its impact was profound:

> The Tribunal cannot avoid the conclusion that in acquiring from Ngāi Tahu 34.5 million acres, more than half the land mass of New Zealand, for £14,850, and leaving them with only 35,757 acres, the Crown acted unconscionably and in repeated breach of the Treaty of Waitangi. As a consequence, Ngāi Tahu has suffered grave injustices over more than 140 years. The tribe is clearly entitled to very substantial redress from the Crown.

It took nearly another decade to hammer out that redress, but the essentials were this. First, a public apology from the Prime Minister of New Zealand, on behalf of the Crown. Then NZ$170 million in cash. Also vital was the return of some land, and the right to buy more Crown land as it came up for sale: Ngāi Tahu is now the largest landowner in the South Island, after the Crown. Ownership of pounamu returned to Ngāi Tahu. Then there were the seventy-two nohoaka sites approximating mahika kai camps, and a degree of joint management of certain conservation lands. Key places would have their original Māori names added to official maps. While all of this amounted to less than one cent of every dollar owed under the deeds of sale, it provided the tribe with an economic base.

The spiritual heart of the redress was our oldest ancestor, Aoraki. We wanted the mountain renamed and ownership returned. But Mt Cook was a mecca for climbers and tourists alike, and on banknotes and in tourism campaigns: it was easy for opponents, including sections of the conservation lobby, to stoke fears that Ngāi Tahu wanted to make the peak off-limits. In the end a compromise was reached. The Crown agreed to return the mountain to Ngāi Tahu. In turn, Ngāi Tahu would gift the mountain to the nation. The name was officially changed to Aoraki / Mt Cook. The tribe asked that no climber set foot on the very top of Aoraki's head.

At the end of the session, Karl Russell looked around the room again. 'Aoraki Bound is an awesome opportunity to go see the mauka [mountain] and learn about your history,' he said. 'But people had to fight for the pūtea [funds] to pay for it. So my wero, my challenge, to you is this: what are you going to do in return?'

.

> Ka haea te ata
> Ka hāpara te ata
> Ka korokī te manu

I opened my eyes to a starry sky. Down the hill at our feet was Pūkaki, with Aoraki ghostly white at its head. A dozen warm bodies stirred along the line of sleeping bags. It was 4.24 a.m.

'Koro!' someone groaned affectionately as the chanting continued. He seemed to be starting earlier by the day.

'Come on! Time to get up!' he chirped. I could hear the mirth in his voice.

By first light we were at the water's edge launching outrigger canoes. By the time the sun went down again we were camped north of Pūkaki, with creaking shoulders and blistered hands, and newfound respect for the ancestors who'd paddled these windswept inland lakes. Pūkaki boasts eight mahika kai on its western shore alone, and archaeologists have found intact earth ovens, rock shelters, a carved adze and a midden full of moa bones.

Tomorrow, after three weeks of intense challenge and friendship, we would go home to our families. Leigh was in Melbourne, but I couldn't wait to hear her voice. For now, though, the half-marathon was only hours away. The organisers explained the rules. If you didn't finish within a certain time, you'd be picked up and driven to the finish line. Koro listened, tight-lipped.

It's fun running in the rain, if it's downhill with a tail wind. But when the out-and-back course along the Tasman Valley swung uphill and into the wind, the pack slowed. Koro and Chris walked at the rear, cheered on by the runners heading for home. Aoraki's flanks stood off in the distance, his head concealed behind a korowai of cloud.

Each time someone crossed the line, those already finished greeted them with a haka. Thirty of us rang out the welcome to the third-to-last competitor as she gasped her way home. But there was no sign of the final two. The rain grew heavier. We huddled under a tarp, scanning the Hooker Valley road.

'There's no way I was ever going to manage a run,' Chris later said. 'But Koro said, "Bugger this, I'm going to see if I can get up a bit of steam!"'

When Koro came round the corner at a shuffling run, knees bandaged, his smile a grimace just short of pain, we raised a roar that would have been audible from Aoraki's crown. No one was ever going to pick Koro up and drive him to the finish line.

Afterwards, at the farewell feast, high on endorphins and real food and the joy of seeing loved ones, we said our goodbyes and made promises to return to finish Raureka's route.

And when the day came to begin that walk, we were all together again—for Koro's taki (funeral). He died suddenly, almost a year on. Haere atu rā e hoa, moe mai rā, okioki mai rā. Rest in peace, friend.

As we formed ranks in the street to send Koro off with the same haka that had welcomed him over the finish line, another twenty-six people were setting off into the bush on that year's Aoraki Bound. The programme has generated struggle and pride, doubt and confidence, and love.

'Loving is above all a matter of knowing,' says Tā Tipene O'Regan. 'To know someone and to know a place and to know things is a form of loving. And I think that's what people yearn for. It's that sense of belonging, that sense of being Ngāi Tahu.'

The programme has brought several hundred of us to Aoraki's feet. But every time I visited that place, I found myself gazing up at the top of Aoraki's head.

PART II: GRAND PLATEAU, AORAKI,
AORAKI / MT COOK NATIONAL PARK. SUMMER.

Nine months later, midnight came too soon. Alarms cut us from sleep. We rolled from our bunks straight into our boots, and drank brutal coffee by head torch, with adrenaline fizzing in our guts. Half an hour after opening our eyes, the four of us stood ready outside Plateau Hut beneath a wild blaze of stars.

South towards the pole a vast emptiness blotted the Milky Way. I looked up at that pyramid of darkness, blacker than night, and quietly greeted the mountain. Two shooting stars, one after the other, zipped towards the horizon, only to be extinguished by its bulk. Aoraki was a mass of rock and ice; an ancestor, and a god.

'Guys, can we take a moment?' I asked, feeling a little self-conscious: mountaineers aren't a particularly spiritual lot.

The others gathered round and switched off their lights. There was an old Ngāi Tahu chant about Aoraki that I wanted to share, with them and with the mountain. In Māori I told Aoraki who we were and why we'd come. Then the old chant rang softly in the emptiness of the Grand Plateau.

> Nā te ao
> Ko te ao tūroa
> Tāna ko te ao mārama...

The chant comes from Matiaha Tiramōrehu, the chief who wrote the 1849 letter of protest to Lieutenant-Governor Eyre that began

Te Kerēme, and it contains our creation story. It begins in pure blackness, with the many voids, with a womb of darkness. From the voids emerges Mākū (moisture), who couples with the long, unbroken horizon to give birth to Raki, the Sky Father. Raki couples with his first wife, Poko-hārua-te-pō, who is the breath of life from the womb of darkness. She gives birth to Aoraki.

So the highest peak in New Zealand is the firstborn son of the sky. Life and weather and land flow from his shoulders. He is our oldest and most sacred ancestor, and the symbol of the tribe. Over the century-and-a-half fight for justice, the return and renaming of Aoraki became central to the restoration of the tribe's mana. Ngāi Tahu's best known proverb says that we will bow our heads only to Aoraki. The most sacred part of Aoraki is his head. No one should stand on the head of a chief.

But on this crisp mid-December night we were setting out in the footsteps of our European forebears. They climbed Mt Cook with axe and rope, intent on planting their boots on top.

Aoraki was renamed Mt Cook after Captain James Cook, spearhead of British exploration and later colonisation in the South Pacific. The peak's mile-long summit ridge and tremendous pyramidal form have drawn generations of climbers. From the 1880s, dozens of attempts saw parties get within a few hundred metres of the summit, only to be forced back by darkness or storms. Now, around a hundred and fifty people climb the mountain each year.

Aoraki / Mt Cook: an ancestor to bow your head to, a peak to climb. Both impulses were in my blood.

Ko Aoraki me Rakamaomao, tāna a Tāwhirimatea

Ko Tū-te-raki-whānoa
Uira ki te Mahaanui a Māui
Ko te ao takata
Tihei mauriora!

At the end of the chant, we stood focused and quiet in the dark.
It was the last time we would be still for the next eighteen or so
hours. The others were gunning for the climbers' summit, a few
steps short of the highest point. This is where Ngāi Tahu asks
mountaineers to stop.

I wanted to attempt a different type of mountaineering. My
plan was to go most of the way up, but at some point, deliberately
and perhaps perversely, to turn back. I wanted to pay my respects
to the ancestor, to speak aloud some of our Aoraki traditions, and
also to honour my Pākehā climbing family, who love the mountain
as well. I wasn't sure where I'd force myself to turn around.

I felt the usual thrill of anticipation at setting out on a climb,
and underneath it, a thin, bright shaft of fear. Since the Godley
avalanche I'd become mildly paranoid in loose snow conditions
on exposed ground. I wasn't looking forward to descending the
Linda Shelf. And I still didn't know what to believe about signs
and omens, and Aoraki as a centre of spiritual power. Should I be
here at all? Some elders had said yes; some had said no. I wasn't
sure where I stood—or, rather, where I should stand.

The four of us nodded to each other. Time to go.

•

Eighteen of us set out from the hut that night. As we contoured
around Aoraki's lap, beyond the small lit sphere of my boots and
the rope extending into gloom, all I could see were hovering lights

in twos and fours. No one talked. Apart from the rhythmic crunch of crampons, there was no sound. These early starts, so close to sleep, often feel dreamlike, as if we were a caravan train crossing a desert at night.

A string of brutally hot nor'-westers, early for the season, had cracked open the crevasses on the Linda Glacier. Some were big enough to swallow a building. The previous week, descending climbers had had to jump slots after the snow bridges melted out. There was a good chance we would be back in the hut before breakfast, our climb merely a visit to gaze into a huge hole.

Smaller crevasses emerged then vanished. We increased our pace across avalanche debris off the Silberhorn arete, then turned and began to climb in zigzagging steps. We were moving fast, but all sense of space and time was gone. Somewhere far up to our right, the boom and roar of falling ice broke the stillness.

I'd come with a friend, Dan, a barrister from Sydney. Because our more experienced friends were away on other trips, with the help of Alpine Recreation we'd enlisted guides for the first time. I was sharing a rope with Lewis, a stocky Kiwi in his early thirties with sandy hair and a broad, shy grin. An intelligent adventure-seeker, he'd come south from Auckland as a young man with a degree in politics and history, and a propensity for getting involved in 'stupid shit'. 'If I hadn't come to Mt Cook and become a guide,' he joked, 'I'd have ended up in jail.'

Lewis was also unusual among guides because he'd grown up speaking fluent Māori at a bilingual school. When we'd chatted about the significance of the mountain to Ngāi Tahu, he'd become quite still, his head half-turned away, listening intently, worry lines creasing his brow. As the only white kid in his bilingual class, he'd been bullied, so he'd had nothing to do with the culture since. But when I'd spoken Māori at the start of the climb, I could tell he'd understood much of what I'd said.

Out on the mountain, Lewis was in his element. We wound through the frozen folds of Aoraki's cloak. Our torches flashed across seracs rearing overhead like the prows of beached ships. Huge crevasses swallowed all light. Above us, the two climbers in the lead turned around.

'No good this way,' one of them shouted down to us. 'Try further west.'

We backtracked in swinging arcs to keep the rope tight. A huge crevasse forced us underneath ice cliffs off the Silberhorn arete. In the pitch dark we couldn't see the danger, but from the tonnes of ice strewn across the glacier we knew it hung above our heads, an enormous sword of Damocles.

'In Europe, this would not be a route,' muttered Dan's French guide.

There wasn't much point in thinking about it. Better to put your head down and keep moving.

Back out in the middle of the glacier, we reached one last slot. Lewis placed an ice screw and led up a short step above a bottomless crevasse. I pulled my second tool off my pack and followed him up on front points. We were through the icefall. So far, so good.

Pausing for water, I checked my watch. Four hours had passed in the space of a breath. I clicked my light off for a moment. A landscape of raw starlight and towering black ridgelines built itself on all sides. There wasn't a spiritual thought in my head.

·

Dawn crept on so slowly. On the rising traverse across the Linda Shelf, the light from our head torches seemed to expand until its faint glow touched the surrounding peaks. What had been indistinct, a rumour of mass, took on form and weight. Silver light brought out the soft detail of the beautiful, monstrous presences of Aoraki's brothers. By the time we reached the 'schrund across the top of the Linda Shelf, they were blue giants pushing up into the heavens.

The climbing started in earnest, with a couple of fast, calf-burning pitches up sixty-degree snow, heading up Aoraki's immense torso. While Lewis led, I swung round in the belay to gaze on the tattooed faces of the brothers, glowing lilac and rose. This was the moment of creation, repeated every day. A thin red slit cut the eastern horizon. I mouthed the words of the chant. The small silver cup of the moon tilted to the north.

The great ancestor's shoulder is also known as the Summit Rocks, a sequence of buttresses at the edge of the East Face. Yesterday's storm had plastered them with ice. The exposure was superb, and the climbing looked even better. We were approaching Aoraki's head with every step, but there was no way I was turning back. Not yet. The rope came tight.

'On belay!' Lewis yelled.

My first axe went in with a solid thunk, and again my mind dissolved. I fitted my body to the corners, cracks and vertical steps in sequences dictated entirely by Aoraki himself. The ice and névé took each tool placement first go. I arrived at each belay grinning, and Lewis grinned back. There was no need to talk. One of the other guides, a powerful man named Alex, appeared over a lip below us and whooped with pleasure. Below him, the long silver ridge leading from Aoraki to Mt Tasman, New Zealand's next-highest peak, turned to fire with the first direct rays of sun. The white sweep of the Tasman Glacier glowed with a deep inner light.

At eight, seven hours after we'd left the hut, Lewis and I reached the false summit, a small patch of flat ground above the Summit Rocks. We were the first ones there. Untracked snow swooped up to Aoraki's head. A final 'schrund divided us from the upper ice cap. At 3,660 metres, this was the famous point of failure for climbers forced to turn back. The top was in reach.

We unroped and sat down, and I bowed my head.

·

In 1882, the Reverend William Spotswood Green was advised by his doctors to spend the winter in a mild climate. He closed up his small church in Ireland, said goodbye to his wife, Linda, and boarded a ship for New Zealand. After seventy days at sea he stepped ashore in Dunedin's Port Chalmers, with a plan to rest and recover—by being the first person to climb Aoraki.

His Swiss guides waited for him at the port. The whole country followed the progress of 'the Alpine Tourists' as they headed inland. 'There is something bold and attractive,' ran one newspaper article, 'about an expedition such as that undertaken by the Rev. W. S. Green and party. Mount Cook is the highest peak in Australasia, and hitherto untrodden by the foot of man.'

In those days, reaching the base of the peak took five jolting weeks in horse-drawn wagons. Though they didn't know it, the party were following a Ngāi Tahu route over Te Kopi-o-Ōpihi (Burke's Pass) into the Mackenzie Country. From there they tracked the eastern edge of Pūkaki, then crossed Te Awa Whaka-mau, the icy Tasman River, and its gravel plains. Already it was late February. They pushed up the Hooker Valley, then launched their first attempt at the summit via the South Ridge. The cheerful reverend wrote in his diary: 'We had failed! We might fail again!'

And again, and again. It took five further attempts before they discovered a viable route. They ferried supplies up Haupapa (the Tasman Glacier), forced their way up through dense scrub and moraine to what is now the Grand Plateau, then bivvied under a waterproof sheet. At six in the morning, Green and his Swiss guides woke and prepared to climb. I wonder what prayers Green said to the dawn.

The men moved up the wreckage of the glacier that Green named, perhaps unkindly, after his wife. Negotiating the deep slots and picking a route clear of the ice cliffs took an age: 'masses of ice were almost continuously falling, and the smaller pieces were rushing down the steep mountain sides with a whiz like a bullet, and the larger ones with a roar like thunder.' They climbed steeply towards a saddle on the North Ridge. The hands of the lead guide, Ulrich Kaufmann, grew black with blisters from cutting so many steps.

At four in the afternoon, still a way off the top, they huddled together to confer. The air was thickening about them, the wind rising. If they kept going, they'd be spending the night out in the open, and probably in a storm. After some debate they decided to press on.

At twenty past six, with the weather deteriorating fast, they reached the main peak. Through the cloud they could see a small hump above them, cut off by a 'schrund that would take too long to cross. Green had come seventy days across the world by ship, thirty-five days across the plains, then spent weeks climbing, only to turn back an estimated ten metres from the top.

The arrival of darkness and the storm found them chopping out a small ledge beneath a rock face, wrapped in yellow oilskins while rain whipped into their faces. The ledge sloped downward, so they had to hang on all night. The ice sheet spread at their feet, thousands of feet below, then vanished into the dark. Thick cloud obscured the full moon. For dinner they sucked Brand's Meat Lozenges and imagined having a smoke. Through the night they told stories, discussed politics and sang songs. How close to their god did they feel, so far from home?

•

Green and his guides weren't the first to be stranded in this place. The first man here had shifted his weight, trying and failing to get comfortable on his narrow ledge. His feet were numb and his lower back an agony, his whole body a dead weight. He pulled the wind-tattered blanket up around his face as tightly as his waxy blue fingers would permit.

He no longer knew how long he'd been sitting there; it had been days, but it felt like years. The gale went through him to the bone. Ice clung to his beard. Rivulets of powder streamed down his shoulders. Each time he breathed, ice crept into his lungs. He grew colder. His blood was a slow river. Rescue would never come.

No one had spoken in a long time. He knew the others were there behind him, but he no longer had the strength to turn around. Strangely, he felt some peace. Dawn was coming, and occasionally a lull in the storm revealed a distant sea, glittering to the west. Consciousness came and went. He huddled in on himself in an effort to avoid the wind, but it was pointless for such a big man. He towered above his brothers. The crown of his head was two kilometres long.

The god who became a mountain was Aoraki, son of the Sky Father's first marriage. His brothers were Rakiroa, Rakirua and Rārakiroa. They descended from the heavens to meet their father's new wife: Papatūānuku, the Earth Mother. They sailed their canoe across the vast expanse of Te Moananui-a-Kiwa, the Pacific Ocean, looking for her, but found no trace of land. Eventually they gave up, and decided to return to their home in the heavens.

Aoraki's brothers readied their paddles. Aoraki stood and began to chant. The brothers thrust their paddles into the great ocean in perfect unison and the waka leapt forward. With each stroke it gained speed, and the prow began to rise, the ocean streaming from its sides. But as they ascended, Aoraki's voice faltered. His karakia was wrong. The spell broke. The huge vessel slammed into a hidden reef and the men plunged into the sea.

When Aoraki and his brothers surfaced, they hauled themselves onto the overturned hull of the wrecked canoe. They sat there shivering, hour after hour, day after day, waiting for rescue. No rescue came. They waited so long that their hair turned white. They froze, and turned to rock and ice and snow. Their canoe became the South Island, which is why it's sometimes called Te Waka-o-Aoraki. The brothers became New Zealand's first and highest mountains, and still they wait: Aoraki, Rakiroa (Mt Dampier), Rakirua (Mt Teichelmann) and Rārakiroa (Silberhorn). In the whakapapa of creation, they're the generation joining the Sky Father to those who dwell below. They're the physical and spiritual link between the heavens and the earth.

·

At first light, Green and his companions had more luck than Aoraki and his brothers. They returned to their camp thirty-seven hours after they'd set off, then headed out to Christchurch, where a victory dinner awaited. Toasts were raised and tipsy songs composed. The papers all reported their success.

But Green never claimed he'd climbed the mountain. He only ever said that he'd shown it could be done. It turned out he hadn't been ten metres from the top, but more like sixty. The sacred head of Aoraki remained untouched.

Hearing this, New Zealand adventurers pricked up their ears. The wonderfully named Marmaduke Dixon and the younger, locally born George Mannering had zero mountaineering experience, had done no training and had no specialised equipment. They beat old metal reaper blades into approach skis, strapped them to their boots, and turned up to try their luck.

Time after time they tried and failed to climb the giant. On one attempt, which took twenty-three hours, they got close but turned back—once again, sixty metres short of the summit. They descended by the thin light of a candle, shadows dancing beneath their boots. Where other parties forded the Tasman and headed out by horse and cart, this bold pair did it the Ngāi Tahu way, paddling down Te Awa Whakamau and the Waitaki River to the coast.

Undeterred, Dixon found new local climbing partners in the Ross brothers and Tom Fyfe. In 1894, climbing via the Linda Glacier route, they were overtaken by a ferocious nor'-west storm. The wind screamed around them and it snowed so heavily that they collapsed the tent to prevent it from being plucked off the mountain. Even when they were wrapped in their sleeping bags with faces down and eyes closed, the 'steel-blue flashes' of lightning still were visible behind their eyelids. Malcolm Ross accompanied the insane din of the storm on his bagpipes. (It's a shame that bagpipes are no longer a standard part of the mountaineer's kit.)

When the storm cleared, down they went. After hundreds of hours of dangerous slog, still no one had stood on the summit. Those final metres could still contain spirits or gods.

Then, in late November 1894, word spread that the famous American mountaineer Edward FitzGerald was en route to New Zealand. He and the legendary guide Mattias Zurbriggen had their sights set on a first ascent. Members of the New Zealand Alpine Club, founded by Arthur P. Harper, 'made hurried though careful plans, and [were] now on the way to Mount Cook, anxious that the honour of the first complete ascent of Aorangi [sic] should not be wrested from New Zealand and New Zealanders'.

To settler society, the mountain was already becoming more than ice and rock. Climbing it was a matter of national pride. 'If Mr. Fitzgerald should fail, as the others have done, we may be sure that the attack will be renewed again and again until the topmost crest of Aorangi "lies under the proud foot of the conqueror".'

·

It's not clear which of the three New Zealanders started running first. It might have been Tom Fyfe, with his wide farmer's face and powerful frame. Or gaunt George Graham, so badly sunburnt that his skin had a mummified sheen. My money is on the youngster, Jack Clarke, just nineteen years old.

I imagine him in slow motion, surging forward with the snow punching out in gleaming sprays from beneath his boots. He would have felt the wind scour his exposed skin, felt the pull of vertigo from the drop on either side, heard his companions' breath at his shoulder. They were exultant to run after a dozen hard vertical hours. Twenty metres to go, hearts light, air burning their lungs; ten metres to go, legs aching, a crow of joy in their throats; till at last there was nowhere higher to go. The top of New Zealand. Christmas Day, 1894. The country laid out at their feet.

Breathing in, breathing out.

Edward FitzGerald was an invisible speck somewhere below them, still making his way across the plains.

If Fyfe, Graham or Clarke found any trace of spirit or god on the summit, they never said a word. And if Aoraki was the symbol of Ngāi Tahu's mana, prestige, authority and power, then the men planting their hobnails on top of his sacred head coincided almost perfectly with the tribe's lowest ebb.

In 1896 the number of indigenous people in New Zealand hit its lowest point ever, giving rise to the widespread colonial belief that Māori were a dying race. There were barely two thousand people left in the South Island willing to declare themselves Māori. Most of those who did lived in poverty. That mountain was climbed.

But not for long.

·

'What do you *mean*, you're not going to the top?' Alex the guide looked at me incredulously.

'Cultural reasons,' my guide Lewis blurted out. He sounded embarrassed, but was also coming to my defence.

'I'm Ngāi Tahu, and—' I started to say.

'I had a guy up here last week who was Māori,' Alex said. 'He didn't give a stuff. But he was only like one-sixty-fourth.'

'Bet he was a North Islander,' I joked. 'They'd stand on top of our mountain in a flash.'

'But we don't *go* right to the top,' Alex said, vexed. 'Like Ngāi Tahu asks. What's wrong with that?'

'Nothing. But I'd get it in the neck if I went that far.'

'How come?'

'Well—'

We were standing on the airy hummock of the false summit, at the edge of the East Face, with just sixty or so metres left to climb. It was round here that Green's party, and Mannering and Dixon, had been forced to turn back. I looked at the handful of climbers in front of me, with the Tasman Sea on one side and the white river of the Tasman Glacier on the other. Was this the time and place to have a philosophical discussion about the mountain's significance? The cultural sensitivities? How Tā Tipene once told the Aoraki Bound cohort that when they looked on Aoraki, they were looking on their own face?

Why the hell not?

There on Aoraki's shoulder, I recounted the story of how my ancestors saw the mountain as the firstborn son of the sky, and the spiritual link between heaven and earth. We talked about the mountain being not just the symbol of the tribe, but one and the same—a huge metaphor that was also real. We'd just started in on the significance of tapu, and how you don't touch the sacred top of anyone's head, when Alex butted in.

'I thought Aoraki just meant "cloud-piercer",' he said, looking put out.

'Māori's a poetic language,' Lewis said, his face carefully neutral behind mirrored sunglasses. 'There's lots of different ways of translating stuff.'

'Literally, ao, world, and raki, sky or the Sky Father,' I said. 'But you can combine them to mean different things.'

'Okay,' Alex said. 'Sure.' He took off his orange helmet and parked it in the snow. 'That's not going to do much if I fall here. See you guys back at the hut.'

He and his client started up the final stretch of the ice cap, and I watched them go.

Did I think they could diminish the mountain by standing a few steps short of the top and brandishing their axes above their heads? Could they affect Aoraki's mana? Seeing their two small figures slowly ascending against the enormousness of the peak, I thought not.

A number of my Pākehā family had climbed the mountain, and while I felt conflicted about it, I was proud of them and their achievement. Climbers and guides respected this mountain: no one stood on the actual summit, and there was no rubbish, no oxygen cannisters, no bodies. There'd also been Ngāi Tahu people up here long before me. Hohepa Fluerty, another descendant of Hinetamatea, and a senior guide in the 1930s, had turned back near the top. He considered Aoraki tapu. Whereas Fluerty's relation George Bannister, also a guide, had gone all the way in 1912. His client recorded the moment:

> It was a glorious day and a more glorious view. It pleased
> Bannister so much that he could not attempt a description.
> It was the first time a Māori had reached the summit

of Aorangi, Cloudpiercer, or the long white cloud, as his
forefathers called it, and afterwards called Mount Cook;
but although most of New Zealand is now owned by
white men, some of whom do not know the consider-
ation due to the native race, nevertheless the mountains
were never bought from the Māoris, and must belong to
that race still.

Bannister's direct descendants are proud of his climb, while others
in the tribe wish he'd turned back. 'This remains a mamae [injury
or wound] with Ngāti Māhaki,' Paul Madgwick said. There are
well over sixty thousand Ngāi Tahu alive, so consensus is rare. But
I knew what I was going to do. Despite some frustrating trips over
the years where I'd turned back against my will, this time it felt
right to leave the mountain unclimbed.

What I did want, though, was to do a haka here, at 3,660
metres: to roar out a Ngāi Tahu war chant into the void. It's a
mark of pride and respect, and I was pretty sure no one would have
haka'd to Aoraki from this close.

By now other climbers were streaming past, grinning as the
final ridge came in sight. I saw myself in their eyes, a skinny pale
dude with his shirt off, slapping his chest and raising his hands to
the sky and shouting in a strange tongue. I wished I was staunch
enough to do it alone. Next time, I thought, I'd come back with
Ngāi Tahu climbers.

But as we turned to descend I thought about Nepal, where
Western climbers visit Buddhist temples for a blessing before
setting out. And about rugby in New Zealand, where everyone
from school teams to the All Blacks performs the haka at the start

of every match. That part of Māori culture is now mainstream and world-renowned. Imagine if Kiwi climbers did it too. It'd be tough performing on steep ground in crampons, but I loved the thought of us all on the false summit, spreading out in formation across the snow.

Kia mau!

Dropping into position to face the mountain in silence, then the kaitaki tāne, the leader's shout.

Ta-hu-pō-ti-ki!

Our voices roaring out as one, the stomp and slap raising the heavens, the chant echoing across the plains, telling our ancestors, all of our ancestors, that we had arrived.

Aoraki Matatū!

Aoraki of the uplifted face!

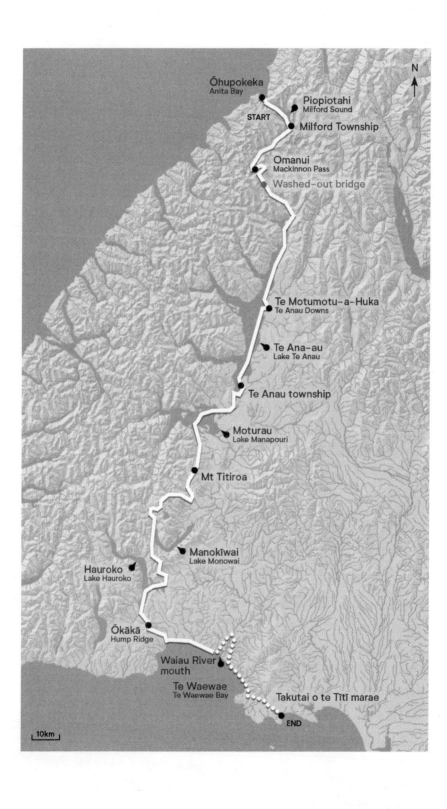

9

Te Rua–o–te–moko Ki Murihiku
(Fiordland to Southland)

I sat forward in the small speeding inflatable as the rocky arc of Te Tauraka-o-Hupokeka (Anita Bay) swung into view. The sea gleamed beneath my fingertips. Briny wind from the Tasman Sea buffeted my face.

'Hope they're still here!' I shouted over the outboard's roar.

Lounging behind me, my friend Bridget Reweti just smiled and looked at me from behind her sunglasses. An artist from Ngāi Te Rangi and Ngāti Ranginui in the North Island, she was tall, wiry, warm, and endlessly amused by the world. Nothing fazed her.

'There they are!' I called.

Five small figures, wrapped head to foot like Bedouins, combed the boulders on the shore, looking for pounamu. One raised a hand in greeting. They were elders from the Ōraka-Aparima Rūnaka, our southernmost tribal region. I grinned at the sight of their helicopter parked on the beach: this was old indigenous business carried out in a modern way. Across the bay, a traditional sailing ship sat at anchor, full of tourists on a luxury cruise: modern business carried out in a nostalgic way. Authenticity, I thought, was a mug's game.

Rosco, the friendly, bearded, piratical owner of Rosco's Sea Kayaks, nosed the inflatable into shore. We hauled out our packs and dumped them beyond the reaching surf. Clouds of biting sandflies enveloped us.

'See you in a couple of days,' Rosco called. 'Good luck!'

Aunties Jane Davis, Betty Rickus, Vera Gleeson and Rangi-maria Suddaby welcomed us with kisses and hugs. They'd come to help us gather pounamu and bless the journey ahead. Behind, a familiar white-bearded figure emerged from the bush and strolled down to the water's edge.

'The places you kids take us,' Dad said, beaming with pleasure. 'The flight in was spectacular!'

Fiordland is easily the wildest corner of an already wild land. The pilot had taken them low across granite peaks, glaciers and oceanic fjords.

'Have a look at this,' Rangimaria said. She held out a flat stone shaped like a heart. It was a warm green, like sunlight through seawater: takiwai.

Takiwai is a rare, translucent member of the pounamu family, ranging from deep green to a smoky teal. Too soft for weapons or tools, it is prized for its beauty, and easy to work. This remote bay is the country's primary source. For centuries our ancestors braved the surf to collect stone for ear and neck pendants. These days all pounamu, including takiwai, belongs to Ngāi Tahu. We'd come with a Customary Authorisation Permit, granted by Ngāi Tahu's several southern rūnaka, giving us permission to gather a small new collection for our home marae, Takutai o te Tītī.

Over the next three weeks, thirty relations and friends would work together to carry the pounamu across Fiordland and Southland, following old greenstone trails. We'd kayak Milford Sound, walk the world-famous Milford Track in reverse, paddle lakes Te Ana-au (Te Anau) and Moturau (Manapōuri) in waka ama (outrigger canoes), then cut through the bush to reach our marae in Ōraka, three hundred kilometres to the south. There'd be feasting along the way, and a formal welcome at the end.

Beyond that journey, our destination was my family's tūrakawaewae, the place where ancestral connections give us the right to stand. Many of my closest Ngāi Tahu and Kāti Māmoe ancestors had lived, and were buried, along that southern coast. It's also where they first married my Pākehā ancestors, and raised children who spanned the old and new worlds. One of those children was my great-great-grandfather John Hunter. Our journey would finish at the Waiau River mouth, right where he'd lived and worked.

·

At eighty, and with a long history of working on behalf of the tribe, Auntie Jane Davis, or Auntie Janie to us, is perhaps the most senior Ngāi Tahu woman alive today. John Hunter's granddaughter, she has a kind and open face framed by short white hair, and the clarity and gentle strength of a lifelong leader. Before taking up the challenge of representing southern interests in the fight for the Treaty claim, she'd fished all through Fiordland with her husband Bill, and had been travelling out to the offshore tītī islands for the annual muttonbird harvest since birth. This ocean and these shores were in her blood.

We stood on the shingle, talking about the history of the bay. 'Is that Hupokeka's famous rock?' I asked her, pointing to a large boulder at the water's edge.

In the 1820s, a party under chief Hupokeka had been gathering takiwai here when European sealers rowed into the bay. Hupokeka had climbed onto the rock to welcome them in. Fresh from a skirmish with a different Ngāi Tahu party further up the coast, the sealers shot him where he stood, then gunned down the rest of the party on the beach. They towed the survivors and the dead out to sea in a burning canoe to hide the massacre. Fifty years later, another sealing party found 'the blackened end of a canoe which still had human remains in it'.

In an oral society, history is written through place names. Te Tauraka-o-Hupokeka is Hupokeka's anchorage. The creek where the burned canoe washed ashore is Te Ahirakatira, the fire of chiefs. Another nearby creek is Te Umumata, the oven of uncooked food, named for sealers who opened an oven to take the seals inside and shot the Māori who resisted. Yet another place name in that bay is Te Tara-o-te-puhi-tuia, commemorating a high-born woman whom sealers attempted to rape.

'Full on what they did back then,' I said.

'It's a dark history,' Auntie Janie said, 'but back then, our people did some terrible things as well. And don't forget, some of your ancestors were sealers and whalers too. Now, look after each other and come back safe.'

'Thanks,' I said. 'We will.'

'And if you starve,' she joked, 'I hear that kererū make for good eating.'

I raised my eyebrows. Wood pigeons are protected.

She smiled. 'That's what your ancestors said.'

By mid-afternoon it was time for the kaumātua to take their treasures home. They glowed with excitement from visiting the bay to gather takiwai.

'See you in a few weeks!' Janie said as the pilot closed the door.

Their chopper lifted with a roar and vanished over the tree-tops. I rose from a crouch, and stood in a cloud of sandflies with a light heart. I realised we hadn't had a formal blessing for the journey before they left. In fact, there hadn't been much Māori spoken at all, and in fact many of our kaumātua didn't have the language. It didn't matter, because our elders' presence and their spirit was blessing enough. But it raised a question. How come, even though their own parents had spoken fluent Māori, and inherited all the old traditions and ceremonies, many had chosen not to pass them on?

Bridget and I returned to combing the shingle for takiwai, with a beautiful yet foul-smelling tawaki penguin watching curiously from metres away. I reached into a cleft between two boulders and drew out a long pendant, naturally shaped and polished by the waves.

'My god, look at this,' I called, holding it to the light.

The internal grain looked like ocean waves seen from the air. Some of the oldest adornments found in New Zealand were made from this stone, including rei niho pendants in an East Polynesian style, shaped like sperm whale teeth. It felt miraculous to find a similar treasure lying fully formed on a beach.

As we fossicked along the shoreline, a small tender from the tourist ship approached the bay. I sat back on my haunches and watched the passengers studying us, the natives on the shore. They were reliving European colonial life, as we were reliving old Māori life. Bridget filmed me climbing onto Hupokeka's boulder as if to welcome them in. I wondered if his story was part of their tour.

•

We went to sleep that night with the sound of music and laughter drifting across from the ship, but at dawn I woke to a loud pattering sound instead. Bridget was already awake.

'Is that rain?' I asked.

'Not exactly.'

My eyes adjusted. 'Holy shit!'

Hundreds of sandflies swarmed against the tent inner. I watched the tiny black predators boil against the netting. I'd seen bad sandflies before, but this was savage. Bridget and I wrapped ourselves up like demented beekeepers and burst out into a cold, damp day. The bay was a dirty teal, desolate and empty. Cloud hung low across the hills. Past the headland named Te Wharekohu (literally, the house of mist), a heavy swell pushed in from the Tasman.

Not long after breakfast, the radio crackled to life. It was Rosco's sea-kayaking crew.

'We've got a serious storm coming in, guys,' the skipper said. 'If I can't get you off the beach in the next couple of hours, you could be there a week. This one's a monster.'

We'd intended to spend a few days exploring the bay before kayaking back to Milford. Instead we broke camp, then laid out the takiwai we'd gathered. We had to choose carefully, and fast.

'This one?' Bridget joked, hefting a boulder the size of a pumpkin.

'Long as you carry it.'

We selected a few modest treasures that showed how the ocean turns raw stone into polished jewels. First was a small cobble studded with barnacles, then a chunk of raw takiwai that looked like a wave breaking in a storm. Then came several natural pendants, each smaller and more polished than the last. Last of all we took a handful of increasingly tiny translucent emerald slivers, like fossilised tears.

Taki-wai. The name translates to tears-of-water, or water of weeping. One of our creation stories relates how Tama-āhua's wives left him in Hawaiki, the Pacific homeland and abode of the dead, and fled to Aotearoa aboard the Tairea canoe. These women were Hinekawakawa, Hinekahuraki, Hineauhuka and Hinetakiwai—all types of pounamu. Tama-āhua pursued them across the sea, searching the coastline of Aotearoa with the help of his slave Tumuaki, and a magic tekateka (dart) that pointed the way. When he finally tracked them here, he found his wife Hinetakiwai turned to stone. He wept over her body and his tears entered the rock. It's said you can see tear-like flecks when you hold takiwai to the light.

So far we hadn't seen anything in the stone that resembled tears, just the teardrop-shaped slivers themselves. We'd found so many on the beach I wondered if they might have played a part in the name as well.

Once we'd chosen our gifts to the marae I loaded them up and hefted my pack onto my back with a grunt. We also had wetsuits and lifejackets weighing us down.

'You know that old tramper's trick where you fill your mate's pack with rocks when they're not looking?' I said.

'Yeah?'

'Funny to be doing it to ourselves!'

Before scrambling west around the rocks to the pick-up point, we carried the remaining treasures down to Hupokeka's rock and threw them back. Fish for another generation to catch.

•

Rosco and his crew had been running sea-kayaking trips in these waters for twenty-five years, and they'd offered to show us the way. We loaded the takiwai into a double-hulled kayak, hauled on wetsuits, and pushed ourselves out into a strong following sea. A lively, fresh-faced guide named Adam led the way through the gunmetal water with sure strokes.

As we paddled south, the windswept bush at the water's edge gave way to sheer rock walls. We found our rhythm, and the boat glided forward. The land on either side was indistinct, seemingly made from shifting heaps of mist. From time to time the mist would solidify into a gleaming silver cliff soaring fifteen hundred metres straight up from the waves. We'd dislocate our necks staring up, before the whole landscape dissolved and blew away.

Te Wharekohu, I kept thinking. The house of mist.

Piopiotahi (Milford Sound) invites superlatives. Its fifteen-kilometre-long reach has been voted the world's top tourist destination, and it sees more than one million visitors a year (which, in a country of under five million people, is quite a lot).

Kipling called it 'the Eighth Wonder of the World'.

When the view finally opened up, we were looking down the sound at a series of headlands receding from slate to silver to gauzy white. I could imagine Aoraki's nephew Tū-te-raki-whānoa standing astride the valley like a colossus, hacking out the fjord with his giant axe; the tourists would gasp as they passed underneath his rāpaki (flax kilt). I could also picture the crew of Māui's canoe, Mahaanui, paddling through this mist, staring up in awe as they competed to add their names to the land.

At Whakamoe-a-tau (Seal Rock), I looked up from the young seal pups playing in the deep to watch an enormous cruise ship ghost down the centre of the fjord.

'How close have you got to one of those things?' I asked Adam.

'They threw us a bottle of champagne once,' he said drily.

Further along the sound, darkness gathered overhead. Cloud formed out of nothing above Copper Point and whipped away east at warp speed. I didn't know much about ocean weather, but in the mountains I'd have been concerned.

'Hey, check that out,' I called to Adam.

He was instantly on the radio. 'You see that above Copper Point?'

'I'm watching it too,' crackled the reply. 'Any minute now.'

Adam flashed us the smile of a man who enjoys wild weather. 'Storm's properly coming in. Let's go!'

We paddled hard, pushed along by the stiffening wind. For the next few hours, passing squalls buffeted our faces and left teardrops shimmering on the ocean's surface. Left stroke, right stroke, left, chopping our way through the sea, with a snarl of clouds overhead.

Off to our left Hine-te-awa (Bowen Falls) plunged 162 metres
into the waves in a curving white plume, while on the right the
iconic granite horn of Rāhotu (Mitre Peak) shot skywards to
ten times that height. Here, I thought, was the Sublime that our
nineteenth-century ancestors craved.

Beauty strengthened our arms. Poporua slid by, then
Tauhokihoki—Bridget Point and Sinbad Gully. The density of
place names down here was astonishing, echoing layers of history
from Waitaha to Kāti Māmoe to Ngāi Tahu, and on into the
colonial age.

At last, in the shelter of Deepwater Basin, just a couple of
hundred metres from the fishing docks, we could relax. The old
landing place for canoes was just up the river, where the overland
pounamu trail began. Adam pulled us into a raft with another
kayak guide and his tourist group.

'So, Nic, do you want to tell us the myths and legends of Milford Sound?' he said.

'Okay, sure,' I said, not feeling so sure. There was something
uncomfortable about distributing cultural knowledge like it was
a packet of biscuits. How much could be made intelligible in five
minutes? When the stories were part of a complex knowledge
system stretching back to old Polynesia? When I was hardly the
most qualified person to tell the tale?

I looked at the other kayakers waiting expectantly: flushed
cheeks, hair plastered, eyes bright from hours of hard paddling.
I thought about conversations I'd had with Auntie Janie when
planning this trip. While some elders were understandably pos-
sessive of our stories, she'd always encouraged me to share. The
whole point was to take Ngāi Tahu knowledge back out into

the landscape. And it was worth honouring people's desire to know.

'Back in the beginning, there was no Aotearoa,' I said. 'Just empty ocean...'

·

Aoraki and his brothers came down from the heavens to meet their new stepmother, Papatūānuku, the Earth Mother. After a long and fruitless search, they decided to return home. But as they rose into the sky, Aoraki made a mistake in his karakia. Their canoe was wrecked. He and his brothers climbed onto its upturned hull, and waited so long for rescue that their hair turned white, their bodies turned to stone. They became Kā Tiritiri-o-te-moana, the Southern Alps.

Years later, the rescue party arrived. Sailing down Te Tai-o-Poutini, Aoraki's nephew Tū-te-raki-whānoa and his people saw the mountains, and figured out what had happened. They grieved for Aoraki and his brothers.

Then, with his axe named Te Hamo, Tū-te-raki-whānoa set about cleaning up the wreckage. He worked his way around the canoe-island, cutting harbours into the coastlines to provide shelter for canoes. At Māwhera, where water was trapped inside the upturned canoe, he forced open a passage to the sea with his massive thighs, creating Te Māwheranui-o-kā-kūhā-o-Tū-te-raki-whānoa (the Grey River Gorge), and the second-longest place name in the world. Tū also brought in the gods Kahukura, Marokura and Roko-nui-a-tau as subcontractors, to help lift up the hills and clothe the land with useful plants. Finally, he made it down to Fiordland, where the real work began.

Here in Piopiotahi, he found a rock wall running from Milford

Sound all the way to Puysegur Point, and decided to hack his way through to let in the sea. Chanting the karakia Tauraparapa to make his feet hold fast, he took up Te Hamo and chopped away at the great mountain wall. Now he chanted Tapahia-te-tapahi, and the stone crumbled under his blows. The sea burst through, filling the valleys in an almighty flood.

Then, thinking there still wasn't enough space, Tū pushed hard against the inland mountains to extend the fjords south. He strained so hard that the place where he stood split in two, forming Kā Tū-waewae-o-Tū (Secretary Island) and Mauīkatau (Resolution Island). He also strained so hard that he shat himself, and his faeces formed another island—though we don't usually mention that to tourists.

The immense depth of Piopiotahi tells you that this was his toughest job. He left the work rough—you can still see his axe strokes in the cliffs—but the effect was awesome in the true sense: a landscape on a godlike scale.

•

Our raft of kayakers sat rocking gently on the swell. I pointed to the mountain above. That was Te Nohoaka-a-Tū. Tū was sitting there resting when Papatūānuku came to ask if he could create somewhere a bit less steep. So he chopped out the only flat land in the whole area, Te Wāhi-o-Papatūānuku. Then and now, it's a sacred place for tourists to park their campervans.

Last of all, Tū was visited by the goddess of death, Hine-nui-te-pō. She worried that the place was so beautiful that humans would never leave. So, just round the corner at Te Namu-a-Hine-nui-te-pō (Sandfly Point), she released the first ever namunamu. The vicious biting sandfly guaranteed that no one could stay here forever.

'And on that note,' Adam said cheerfully, 'let's go home!'

•

That night the storm came in with a fury. We lay awake in our bunks in a Department of Conservation staff house in Milford, listening to the deafening hammer of rain on the roof. The air turned to liquid, continuous as a waterfall. When we woke the next morning it was still going, and all of that day, and the next, until it became a numbing constant. We'd hoped to paddle across Te Awa-o-Hine (the Arthur River) and start on the Milford Track straight away. But each time we wandered down to check, we found the river boiling three metres above its banks.

Word reached us that the Milford Track had flooded and a bridge had washed away. They were helicoptering all the walkers out. Always the dirtbag, I wondered if we could get a back-flight: pilots will often take climbers at a heavy discount if they have an empty chopper on a return trip. If we could get dropped across the river, we'd be ready as soon as the waters went down.

I went down early to the local helicopter company and waited around in a little prefab office for one of the pilots. A short man with a weathered and friendly face greeted me.

'Gidday. What can I do for you?'

I explained that we were a group of Ngāi Tahu retracing the old pounamu route. We'd be happy to pay if they had empty seats going across the river. As I talked the man's face hardened into suspicion, then hostility.

'So you want the ol' sky waka?' he said. 'That's not very *authentic.*'

'I take it that's a no?'

He sniffed and turned away.

•

What the hell was authentic, anyway? Later that day, Bridget and I went for a sodden hike to Gertrude Saddle, at the head of the valley, to pass the time. The smooth, fast waters of Whakatipu-ka-tuka (the Hollyford River) were running thigh-deep above its bridge, and as we waded across we chatted about the pilot's response. In a literal sense he was right—obviously our Māori ancestors hadn't used helicopters—but his tone suggested more than that. I'd heard plenty of people argue that it was hypocritical to advocate for indigenous practices if you used Western technology and ideas. And if you had European ancestry you weren't really indigenous either, except when it suited. It was a binary proposition: either you were authentic, or you were full of shit.

'But photography's an authentic Māori practice,' Bridget said with a sly smile. She often used photography in her art. 'We've been using cameras since the eighteen hundreds. They're an essential part of our culture.'

Halfway up the huge granite cirque beneath Barrier Knob, Bridget posed as if trying to push a truck-sized boulder off a ledge. I lifted my camera. *Click.* A traditional image of a traditional Māori woman moving a mountain, dressed in gaiters, Gore-Tex and boots.

•

Back at the Department of Conservation house that evening, one of Rosco's guides stopped by to invite us to a party. Dad had driven up to Milford with more supplies just before slips had closed the road. We'd all been cooped up for days and felt like blowing off some steam.

At the wharf, he, Bridget and I clambered aboard a crayfishing boat full of friendly blokes with chiselled faces and crushing hand-shakes. They'd been stuck in port for days, watching the clock run down on their fishing quota. Blue tarpaulins across the back deck kept out the worst of the deluge. The sizzle of barbecued chicken drifted across the boat. Rosco's crew were all there, young white-water kayakers and mountain bikers with the attitude and energy of young hunting dogs. I liked them immensely. We drank steadily, shouting over the rain, dressed entirely in Gore-Tex against the constant spray.

A few beers in, our kayaking guide, Adam, and his manager, Abi, took me aside.

'You know, we were nervous before we met you guys,' Adam said.

'How come?' I asked, confused.

'We had another Māori group come through last year, and they were full-on,' Abi said. 'We asked them to teach us stories about the area and they refused. They were pretty hostile.'

I remembered that Adam had pumped us for stories within thirty seconds of meeting us. He'd been overly friendly, bordering on pushy. Now I realised it was just nerves.

'Where were they from?' I asked. 'Which tribe?'

They shook their heads. 'Dunno.'

As far as I knew, there hadn't been other big Ngāi Tahu groups here recently. 'They might have been from somewhere else,' I said. 'So they wouldn't know the stories from round here. And it wouldn't be their place to share them if they did.' I didn't mention that some people guarded stories closely, or got defensive if asked about things they didn't know, but felt they should.

Adam and Abi nodded. 'Well, okay,' Adam said. 'It's just been great that you're so approachable.'

As I moved away through the party, I turned this over in my mind. I was approachable because hostile reactions like the helicopter pilot's were rare in my life. I looked white. Plus, I explicitly wanted more people to know and value our stories, as Auntie Janie had advised. And my Pākehā family were storytellers too. Inside the ship's bridge I could see Dad deep in conversation with one of the crew, who later gave him a thousand bucks' worth of crayfish for our upcoming feast. Things like that happened to Dad all the time.

As the party thinned, I went and talked to one of the crew who'd remained aloof for most of the evening. He was a heavyset man from the North Island's East Coast, dressed in a Swanndri jacket, fleece pants and white gumboots. He looked classically Māori, with a broad, flared nose and wide smile. We were both half-soaked from windblown rain, and thoroughly drunk.

I told him about our greenstone journey and he looked at me strangely. He told me he missed his family. 'I shouldn't be here,' he said.

'Where should you be?'

'None of your business.'

We traded stories of our fishing ancestors. He grew serious when I mentioned Auntie Janie and Bill and their son 'Trapper' Davis, and how they'd run cray boats in these waters.

'I got a lot of respect for those guys,' he slurred. 'They're the real deal. What about *you*? You're city, aren't you?'

He looked at me hard, his eyes rheumy in the dim light. I knew a challenge when I saw one. I looked Pākehā, I sounded Pākehā, so who the fuck was I to be talking about fishing and greenstone routes? I bristled. Who the fuck was he to say I couldn't, here in Ngāi Tahu territory? But also: I didn't feel like I was the real deal myself. And: it's his boat, and he could snap me in half with one hand.

We stared at each other. The deck shifted underfoot with the tide. I dropped my gaze.

I don't remember who said what after that, but I do remember him placing his hands on the stainless-steel gutting table between us. He let his head hang down between his arms, then turned his palms upwards, fingers splayed, as if to say *peace*, or maybe *whatever*.

Time to call it a night.

.

Two days later the rain stopped and the leaden sky lifted. Patches of blue broke through, and the peaks towered on all sides. Bridget and I packed the takiwai and farewelled Dad, and Rosco's crew, who'd been a godsend over the last week: generous, curious, and good company as well. Then Rosco's launch dropped us across the still-flooded river to Te Namu-a-Hine-nui-te-pō.

We stepped ashore into dripping bush, with roiroiwhenua (heat mist) rising through the trees. The modern jetty was right on the old canoe landing point, marking the start of the takiwai trail that was now the Milford Track. We shouldered our packs and set off into the forest. I felt myself relax and my spirits lift to finally be on the move.

The Milford Track is the jewel in New Zealand's nature crown: huge waterfalls, steep mountains, bush spilling into black canyons and long, misty lakes. The entire season's eight thousand walking tickets sell out in under five minutes. Close to three hundred people are on the track on any given day. Supply helicopters buzz overhead.

Ten minutes in, with early-morning light filtering through the canopy, Bridget and I looked at each other in delighted disbelief. Everyone else had been helicoptered out. We had one of the most popular hiking tracks in the world to ourselves: perfect for visualising its history as a quiet, remote greenstone route.

For the first day, we cruised. The track was so wide and smooth we packed away our boots and walked in rubber Crocs. Side streams thundered away just centimetres below the bridges. After being stuck indoors for so long, even wading thigh-deep through sections of still-flooded track was a blast.

Heading south, we navigated using an old oral map passed down through the generations in the form of a song. James Herries Beattie recorded it from an old Ngāi Tahu woman close to a century ago, then extracted the place names from each line. We splashed up the valley to reach the wide, dark mirror of Te Moana-o-Nohorua (Lake Ada), then hiked on to Nukutauroa (Giants Gate Creek and Falls) and the creamy foam of Te Huka-a-Tawhi (McKay Falls).

At sunset, eating dinner on the steps of Pillans Workcamp, we watched Te Tautea (Sutherland Falls) plunge 580 metres from the ramparts beneath Lake Quill. The line from the old song has a playful reversal common to Māori verse, here describing falling water as standing up: 'Ko te tau-tea ka tū,' *there stands the white thread*. Archaeological finds in the valley, including a pounamu adze unearthed near the base of Te Tau-tea, confirm that this was a Ngāi Tahu route. But it's the names that keep the memory of the track alive.

•

The high point where the Milford Track crosses the Main Divide is Omanui (Mackinnon Pass). Approaching it the next morning, we encountered the first walkers coming the other way. Most were middle-aged tourists.

'Um, aren't you going the wrong way?' a woman asked.

Bridget and I looked at each other in mock horror.

'Oh no!' Bridget said.

'Shit,' I said. 'I was sure we were meant to go left—' And we both cracked up.

'We're walking the greenstone route, not the Milford Track,' Bridget explained.

The rest of the woman's party gathered. We passed round pieces of takiwai, and pointed out the Māori names for landmarks nearby. They enthused about our journey and wished us well. Over the next hour the same conversation played out again and again. As yet another group moved off, one woman hung back.

'Are you on a…spiritual journey?' she asked with quiet intensity.

Before we could reply, she addressed Bridget with a tremor in her voice: 'I just want to ask—I have a very old greenstone pendant I bought for my son. Do you think I should get it blessed before I pass it on to him? I've already lost one son. I don't want anything to happen to the other.'

Bridget was measured and polite. She advised the woman to contact her local iwi and ask their elders for advice. Thirty metres on down the track she shot me a wry smile. 'All Māori are spiritual, right?' she said.

More people streamed past. I noticed a Māori woman at the back of a long line. Her face was red, her gait uneven. Like

many of the others, she seemed stuffed after the sharp climb to
the pass.

'How are you going?' I called.

'I've lost the will to live!' she cried theatrically, and everyone
burst out laughing, except her.

From Nuku (Roaring Burn) we climbed into the rocky basin
at the valley's head. A freezing southerly sent tentacles of cloud
over the ridge. By the time we reached Omanui itself, at 1,154
metres, visibility had dropped to ten metres and we were battling
horizontal rain. Our plan to climb Mt Hart went out the window.
But there was one thing we had to do before heading down the
other side.

Whenever we reached a landmark with an old name, we'd
been pausing to build a cairn from the takiwai we carried. Here
it took concentration to stack the green jewels, like playing Jenga
in a gale-force wind. But the process was satisfying, each cairn
a tiny monument to the greenstone trail we followed, and to
the hiking and cairn-building traditions of our European forebears. When each was compete, we photographed it, then packed
the stones away. We were racing with the cairn at the pass: somewhere between here and our beds for the night was an unbridged
stream. Rain this heavy would make it impassable in a couple of
hours.

We plunged off the southern side of the pass and down the
Clinton Canyon at a near-run, drenched but ecstatic to be out
amid such beauty and power. Perpendicular cliffs rose more than
a kilometre above us on either side. The entire valley was curtained
with white water pouring down black rock. I wanted to shout with
pleasure—until we ran out of track.

Beneath Pariroa (Castle Mount) we scanned a boulder field cut in two by the dirty torrent of Marlenes Creek.

'Can you see a bridge?' I called through the rain.

'Yup, there,' Bridget said, pointing to a tangle of steel half-buried in mud. 'This must be where everyone else got helicoptered out.'

The floodwaters twisted and flexed between boulders like a giant eel. It looked lethal, but orange flags led to a marginally better pool. More markers on the far bank beckoned. Maybe it was okay. We listened for the sound of boulders rolling along the bottom, then linked arms.

I shuffled in calf-deep and the current nearly ripped off my leg. I stumbled back. It was like the creek had teeth.

'Shit, no way,' I yelled. 'I can't stand up in that!'

Bridget and I looked at each other. What the hell were we thinking?

We pulled out the map. Soon we found better contours where the creek braided out into smaller streams, and splashed easily across.

Later, warm and dry in the hut, we realised we'd been on autopilot. After two days of cruising along a perfectly marked track with every stream bridged, we'd delegated our critical decision-making to scraps of orange tape. You couldn't afford to switch off in the Clinton Canyon. There's one old tale of an elderly couple who disappeared near here, at a place called Te Rekorare. Apparently the pōua and tāua were eaten by giant eels.

·

The next day we came to a halt at the start of the Milford Track. The misty waters of Te Ana-au (Lake Te Anau) stretched south

between high, forested hills. From here the pounamu route took
to the water in canoes.

We'd planned to kayak the top of the lake, but with five days
lost to rain, and a twenty-strong party of friends and relations
waiting for us at Te Motumotu-a-Huka(Te Anau Downs), we
elected to thumb a ride. Authenticity didn't rate a mention with
the captain of the Real Journeys ferry, who radioed his boss.

'No problem,' he told us. 'Jump in.'

PART II: TE ANA–AU (LAKE TE ANAU), MURIHIKU (SOUTHLAND). AUTUMN.

We motored into Te Motumotu-a-huka to find twenty barrel-chested paddlers and their families launching a twin-hulled waka ama canoe. Half were our relations from Ōraka-Aparima marae, the rest a local paddling team made up of our tribal cousins from Ngāti Kahungunu.

'All right, cuz—ready to go?' said my cousin Karina Davis. She gave me a huge hug, then shoved a paddle into my hands. Karina has her mother Janie's beaming round face, and the same wild frizzy hair as my mum. As well as working, raising kids and doing a master's, she'd found time to organise the crews to transport the stone across lakes Te Ana-au and Moturau (Manapōuri).

Bridget and I carefully unfolded the greenstone from its bag and passed the pieces round. The circle fell quiet. The men and women warmed the taoka (treasures) in their hands and raised them to the light, and I felt a faint ripple of the old world. Collecting and transporting pounamu had been a key reason for journeys into the mountains. It had also been done in extended family groups like this. According to James Herries Beattie, the last time it'd been done here in the south was 1838.

Tane Davis, Karina's brother, bowed his head and chanted out a karakia for the journey ahead. Another brother, Trapper, the man who the cray-fisherman at Milford had called 'the real deal', waited to accompany us in his huge black speedboat with a skull-and-crossbones painted on the front. We launched the fibreglass waka ama boats, took up our laminated wooden paddles, slipped on life vests crammed with lollies and sports drink, and climbed in.

Karina's voice rang out across the silver water. 'Set it up!'

We reached forward, paddles fully extended.

'Hoe ki te wai!'

A dozen paddles slipped softly into the water. We tensed like sprinters on the starting blocks.

'Hoea!'

A dozen blades dug into the lake and the boat leapt forward. Stroke, stroke, stroke, and we slid out into the day. Paddling feels miraculous when you pull down and feel the boat move with the power of a dozen pairs of arms. Left, left, left, then 'Hup!': the kaea shouted the change. We swung our blades overhead, reaching for the opposite side.

'Gah! It's raining!' shouted Will Payne, as I lost rhythm and sent water flying.

'Sorry,' I said. 'I can paddle or talk, but not both.'

'You just talk then. Faster for—'

'Hup!' Karina called.

'Faster—'

'Hup!' Karina yelled again, after only two strokes. 'Shut up and paddle, you lot!'

Soon the shore fell away. Our breath synchronised, our shoulders torquing and reaching as one. Sunlight sparkled off our wake, and I felt a strange hypnotic calm descend. Mist wreathed the thick bush rising on all sides. We knew our tīpuna travelled on water whenever possible. After our lugging the takiwai on foot, the graceful, silent speed of the boat made perfect sense.

•

The shores of Te Ana-au are packed with old camping places, pā sites, histories and traditions, but my favourite is its creation story, from the Waitaha tribes.

In those days, instead of a lake, there was a magical bottomless spring hidden by a thick grove of trees. If you lowered a net into the waters, you'd pull it up squirming with enough fish to feed the whole village. To protect those powers, only the tohuka, Te Horo, and his wife were allowed to look upon the spring.

One day Te Horo heard rumours of wars to the north-east, in Ōtākou. The tohuka resolved to go to help mediate peace, leaving his wife at home to fish for the village. Before he left, Te Horo warned her not to let anyone else gaze into the sacred pool.

But his wife had a lover, Te Marino. Once Te Horo left, he convinced her to let him look at the spring. He gazed into its deep clear waters and, wanting a better view of the swarming fish, he leaned forward. Instead of the fish, he saw his own face mirrored in the pool. In a flash the spring erupted, flooding the village, drowning the people and filling the valleys—until it became the mighty lake Te Ana-au.

With its fertile pool surrounded by a tangle of undergrowth, the story's message about sexual fidelity is pretty clear. Mokopuna (grandchild) is literally moko, a facial tattoo, and puna, a spring: a grandparent looking at their grandchild sees their own face, as if reflected in a spring. Disaster came from someone else's face being reflected in the pool.

All these old stories encode values. Marriage was formal and strategic. Whakapapa and who married whom was of major importance to the tribe, especially when it came to inherited rights to resources and land. Which is interesting, because Ngāi Tahu women in the south intermarried with Pākehā from the start for a range of reasons: as a way of building relationships and trade, to improve their lot, as a matter of love. Each new generation of faces reflected in the spring looked different from the last.

Today, some Native American tribes determine membership according to strict blood percentages. For Ngāi Tahu, people need only show descent from one ancestor. You are free to fall in love with whomever you choose, safe in the knowledge that your mokopuna will still belong to the tribe.

As we paddled south the kilometres dropped away, and some of the grandchildren jumped into the waka to take a turn. Some were pink-skinned with blond hair; some were coffee-skinned with black hair and dark eyes. They all paddled hard.

·

At Te Anau township, Tane Davis stood and called in Māori to the supporters on the shore. A baying call from Dad's pūkāea (long wooden trumpet), and a woman's voice raised in karaka welcomed us in. We flopped over the side into the freezing water, whooping, and waded up through the shallows to kisses and hongis.

'That was awesome, cuz!' Karina said, giving me a big soaking hug.

True to the ancient Māori tradition of photography, a camera crew had tailed us down the lake in a speedboat, shooting footage for the Ngāi Tahu communications team. Now they pounced to conduct interviews. Auntie Janie spoke first, in a sunhat with a radiant smile. Then it was Karina's turn.

'I wanted to follow in the footsteps of our ancestors,' she said.

'We're out training on the rivers every week, but we've never paddled here on the inland lakes before. It's just awesome to see the
natural environment where our tīpuna lived.'

I was next. 'Hang on a minute,' I said. 'Let me get into some
dry clothes.'

Bridget and I bolted up the hill to a tourist gift shop. We'd
been carrying the takiwai in a white calico bag that was now filthy.
I wanted something more presentable for the cameras.

'How 'bout this?' Bridget said, holding up a simple black cloth
bag.

'Umm...' I hesitated.

She smirked. 'What, it's not *Māori* enough for you?'

I blushed. She was right. I'd hoped to find a woven flax basket
that'd look authentic on film.

'You got me.' I laughed. 'That'll do fine.'

·

The Tākitimu mountains stand visible for miles at the head of
the Southland Plains. They're an essential landmark for southern
Ngāi Tahu, formed when the Tākitimu canoe was washed inland
by three massive waves.

That night our crew feasted at the base of the mountains, at
Te Kōawa Tūroa o Tākitimu lodge. When the plates were cleared
Auntie Janie stood, barely taller than the seated paddlers, and
told us the story of the place. After more than a century of being
alienated from this land, the tribe's recent economic success had
allowed our rūnaka to buy the lodge. Now Te Koawa hosted people
relearning mahika kai practices. Sitting listening to these success
stories, I shared the pride in what Janie's generation had achieved.

Before bed, she placed a small pebble of our takiwai in each paddler's calloused hands, as a thank-you for the day's effort, and a bribe for the next.

The lodge was just one building, and our journey was brief, and each pebble was tiny. But there's a saying for those things: Ahakoa he iti, he pounamu. *Although it is small, it is precious.*

·

Late that night my brother Tim arrived. We hugged in the foyer, and grinned at each other. It was wonderful to see him looking fit and strong. He looked more like our Māori grandfather's mokopuna, with wiry, tight-curled hair and the same hooked nose. (I had recently spoken at a writers' festival about Māori history, and afterwards a florid-faced elderly man had approached me. 'Good speech. But you're more Scottish than anything, aren't you?' he said, the note of accusation unmistakable in his voice.)

From Te Ana-au, the pounamu trail went down the Waiau River via mōkihi to Moturau. Early the next morning Tim and I ran a section of the Kepler Track linking the two lakes, pacing beside the wide, clear river in the cool dawn air. On the northern shore of Moturau, Karina, Bridget and the others picked us up in the waka and we paddled out into another sparkling day. There was a history of battles around Moturau, and we decided to power up to attack speed, just for fun. On Karina's command we doubled our stroke time.

'Hoea!'

The canoe seemed to lift from the water and skim clean across the top of the lake, surging forward with each stroke. Our muscles screamed. The kaumātua, kids and dogs cheered from the support boat. The small forested islands of Puhiruru (Rona), Uenuku (Isolde) and Nihorere (Holmwood) slid by, until we collapsed, laughing and gasping. Niho-rere was named for a woman who visited the island not by canoe, nor by swimming: the tradition says she flew.

In the sheltered crook of Hope Arm we picnicked on the beach. The takiwai was unloaded, along with our packs. There were yet more hugs and hongis.

'See you on the other side!' Tim and I stood waving as Bridget, Dad, Karina, Janie and the rest of the whānau paddled off up the lake. I would miss Bridget. She'd been the perfect travelling companion: energetic, curious and thoughtful, up for whatever challenge the land threw our way. I also loved the way she expressed being Māori, with self-possession and wry humour. I felt like I could learn a lot from that.

•

That night Tim and I camped in a mossy hollow on the side of Mt Titiroa. Thick mist swallowed the surrounding forest. After the warmth and rowdy camaraderie of collective travel, it felt unnaturally quiet to be on our own. We cooked and chatted about the next six days.

From Moturau, the old greenstone trail went down the Waiau to the coast on rafts. We could have walked it, but like so many Māori tracks it was now the main road. We had opted to go off-track instead. Our plan was to visit two significant lakes further south, Manokīwai (Monowai) and Hauroko, and pay homage to the hiking tradition, both Māori and Pākehā, of the good old-fashioned slog through the bush.

One morning we were climbing Mt Titiroa, the pale fin of rock visible for miles across the Southland Plains. The next we were crawling around the steep sides of Manokīwai, through scrub so dense that progress was a blind man's buff. On the Kaherekōau tops we slept beside mirrored tarns reflecting the gleam of the Milky Way, and woke to rain squalls strafing the surrounding hills.

For these last few days we had picked up a new travelling companion, another member of the Ōraka-Aparima Rūnaka. Dave Taylor is a fit, friendly, kind-hearted man in his fifties. He once headed the Department of Conservation in Southland, and had been a huge help in organising this trip. Dave was raised Pākehā, and came to his Māori side later in life through doing Aoraki Bound. As we walked, he told us that the experience of reconnecting to the culture had been profound, but not always what he'd expected.

'People spend a lot of time drinking tea and gossiping and scheming about politics,' he said one morning, looking down on Manokīwai's silver expanse.

I had to laugh, because gossiping and scheming about politics was about as Māori as you could get.

Towards the end of a glorious day spent rambling along the tops, I talked us into taking a short-cut. Standing above Lake Hauroko with the blue sweep of the ocean ahead of us, we discussed our planned descent.

'Those contours look pretty tight,' Dave said, indicating the south face of Oblong Hill on the map. None of us relished the idea of navigating bluffs in fading light.

'What about dropping off the saddle to the east?' I said. 'Contours look better. We can just follow the river out. It'll be fun.'

Famous last words. After an hour we were climbing down a steep and active landslide, one at a time to avoid rockfall. Two hours on we were slithering and tripping over fallen trees in a gorge. I was down to my last, ancient, sloppy pair of socks, making every foothold feel insecure. Then rain blew in and the light failed completely, and we slogged back up into the bush to scratch out a camp. There was no flat ground. Dinner was tuna but I'd somehow bought cans without ring-pull tabs. As I sat in the dark in steady drizzle, trying to open a tin of fish with a rock, tiredness hit me hard.

Clunk. The rock bounced off the tin.

Normally I lived for these off-track missions. But I'd been on the go for a couple of weeks now.

Clunk.

For a couple of years, even: it felt like I was permanently walking in the mountains, recovering from a trip, writing about a trip, or researching and planning the next one.

Clunk.

I wondered what my city friends were doing. I wondered what Leigh was doing, and how good it would feel to be together in one place. I wondered what it would be like to sleep in my own bed. To eat food that wasn't freeze-dried. The coast was only a few days away now. Soon we'd be at the marae handing over the pounamu, having a hot shower, going home.

Clunk.

'It'll be fun,' I muttered.

Crack.

Once we'd liberated the tuna and cooked it up with spaghetti and capers, it was. We sat round a fire telling stories, bellies full, smoke drifting into my beard, while not far down the slope, stags roared in the mist. We lapsed into silence and I looked down at the ring of stones around the blaze, and wondered how long it would remain there after we'd left, and how many millions of other such rings remained around here from nights like these.

·

The final step in our short-cut took us out to Hauroko the next day, through a swamp. We scraped through tātarāmoa vines that ripped at our skin, and waded through mud, until Hauroko emerged through the trees like a mirage. Low cloud sat just above the lake. The place had a stillness to it, a sense of a landscape waiting with breath held. Few people visit today, and even in the old days Hauroko had been a place of quiet repose. Some translated the name as 'the listening wind'. There were burial caves hidden all around here, too.

Tim and I had just plunged into the lake to wash off the mud and blood when a jetboat roared up.

'Where are you guys off to?' the driver asked once his passengers had left, and we'd been reunited with our clothes.

'Teal Bay Hut,' Tim said. 'The guide says nine hours, so we thought seven. What do you reckon?'

He laughed. A recent storm had toppled dozens of trees. 'Two guys went through a few weeks back. Took them fourteen. Want a lift?'

'How long by boat?'

'Nine minutes!'

Tim, Dave and I conferred, but not for long. I had wanted to walk in order to feel landscape and history underfoot, but if I'd learned one thing about Māori mountain travel it was that you went by water whenever you could. And right from the start, our Māori ancestors traded waka for whaleboats for schooners. Helicopters and jetboats were next. There was none of the through-hiker's aim to walk every last step, the romantic's desire for purity. And whatever the abstract arguments, right now I was dog-tired.

We roared off across the lake.

·

Our first proper glimpse of Te Waewae Bay came from the top of Ōkākā (Hump Ridge) the following morning. There was the pale blue expanse of Te Ara-a-Kiwa (Foveaux Strait), coming ashore in a rim of white breakers against the half-moon bay. The distant Waiau snaked out to the coast through a wedge of green farmland. A gap in the surf marked where it poured into the ocean. That was where a mōkihi, laden with pounamu, would have finished up. That gap was also the ferryman's domain.

Though I'd grown up in Christchurch, and though Melbourne had been home for more than a decade, this would also be a homecoming of sorts. Down at the Waiau mouth, where we would finish this walk, John Hunter had plied his trade: a Māori ferryman who reinvented himself as a white man.

Seeing the river now, I realised the entire river system and trail we'd been following had led us here. The minute we'd crossed Omanui, Mackinnon Pass, the greenstone route took us down the Clinton River into Te Ana-au, through Te Ana-au into Moturau, and then along the Waiau River to Te Waewae Bay. Where the river flowed out into the ocean was where our great-great-grandfather had lived. My brother and I were seeing the landscape that formed him for the first time.

We dropped from the ridge and descended sharply through beech forest dripping with lichens and moss. Mist blurred and swallowed the land. Our overgrown and muddy track gave way to a forestry road through clear-felled ground that was fast being reclaimed by scrub. This was land granted to our great-grandparents under the South Island Landless Natives Act, the scheme the Waitangi Tribunal had described as 'a cruel hoax'. Our grandfather had shares in these blocks. I stepped off the road to piss, and it occurred to me that one day I might inherit the square metre of dirt under my feet. I might clear the scrub, and ring it with a miniature white picket fence.

As I returned to the road, a stag roared.

Dave froze. 'I don't think that was a stag.'

'Huh?'

'Sounded like a hunter,' he said, then shouted: 'Hello! Anybody there?'

We heard an engine start, and soon after a quad bike pulled up, driven by a thickset Māori guy with a rifle slung over his shoulder. He looked disappointed that we only had two legs.

'Where've you guys come from?' he asked.

'Milford Sound,' I said.

He squinted. 'For real?'

I showed him the takiwai, explained our trip.

He looked intrigued, and suspicious. 'Cool,' he said, in a voice that meant *you're nuts.*

We plodded off, tall and pale. He roared away on his quad bike, stocky and dark. He was living off the land, thanks to fossil fuels. We were chasing the mythical past on foot.

The scent of brine grew stronger, and finally in the late afternoon we passed through a break in the trees to reach the shore. After so long enclosed in dense bush, the wide ocean vista was a startling relief. We hugged and splashed saltwater on our chapped faces, and built another takiwai cairn.

Then we meandered east in bare feet, boots slung over our shoulders, following the curve of the bay towards the river mouth. Sea-haze softened the edges of the land. The swept-back bush and low hills followed wind-sculpted curves. Drowned trees stood in black silhouette, and we passed great piles of their ossified root balls like anti-ship mines. The sand and waves felt incredible between my toes.

I saw a small figure in the distance, walking towards us.

•

At the turn of the last century, John Hunter worked here beneath the gunmetal Murihiku skies. He never came down the Waiau by mokihi, carrying pounamu as his ancestors had, but he'd paddled it daily, so he knew every eddy and tide. He was a big man, powerfully built. His main work was taking fishermen up, down or across the river. The newspapers of the day were full of glowing accounts: 'Anglers from other parts of the Dominion or from abroad never refer to their Waiau experiences without mentioning Hunter's name. His amiability, his cheerful response to midnight calls upon his services, and his excellent boatmanship, impressed every fisherman who visited.'

I imagine him seated in the back of his boat in clear sunlight, shirt open at the neck, his calloused hands resting on the oars as passengers stepped aboard. He'd written about himself as white, but he was also Māori. Did he think and dream in English or in Māori? What did it mean, for him, to belong to this land?

In writing his memoir, *Adventures in N.Z. and the Islands that Lay to the South*, Captain John Hunter worked so hard to appear Pākehā that he might have wanted to be remembered as an immigrant. In the notebooks there's no mention of his Ngāi Tahu mother, Kawiti, nor his father's Sioux blood. He fudges his origins so it appears his family are wealthy settlers. In one scene, even though he's standing on ancestral Māori land, he sings that great old sentimental colonial song 'Home, Sweet Home': 'An exile from home, splendor dazzles in vain / O, give me my lowly thatched cottage again!'

When his father sends him away to Ruapuke for an education, there's no mention that the island was a Ngāi Tahu stronghold, nor that the missionary school there was for Māori kids. 'Young master John' lives with the only Europeans on the island, the Reverend Wohlers and his family. He eats at their table, plays with their daughter, sleeps under their roof. At times he's almost absurdly English, relishing sacred music and the hymns and prayers. His bedroom is 'sufficiently furnished for any gentleman in the land'. There are natives in the school, natives on the mainland, natives on the ships, but John is not one of them.

He studies hard. On the day he finishes his schooling, his transformation is complete. 'I dressed myself in a beautiful black velvet suit and a light pair of patent leather shoes...and as I gazed at the mirror I could hardly believe my eyes for I now produced the appearance of a college gentleman...a flash of pride came to my cheeks.'

Mokopuna: the face reflected in the spring.

Free to seek his fortune, he leaves the school and sets out for the port. Like Oedipus, he meets a man on the road. They pass with no more than a 'Good day'. Suddenly John leaps from his horse to greet his astonished father.

'Can I believe my eyes, is that you, my boy,' his father, 'a

European', says. 'I would have passed you like a stranger, Jack.'

I would have passed you like a stranger. That line had stayed with me. John Hunter's education had transformed him beyond recognition. Through writing, he'd gained the power to create a new identity, and erase the old.

In 1910, after decades as a boatbuilder, a ship's owner and captain, a ferryman, and a father to a large family, John Hunter contracted influenza. It was said to have 'developed into insanity'. The police were called, and the magistrates at Aparima (Riverton) directed that he be sent to Seacliff Mental Hospital near Dunedin for treatment. His daughter Ruby, Auntie Janie's mother, accompanied him to Invercargill. He was quiet on the train, yet so distant that he didn't recognise her.

When they stopped overnight at Invercargill Hospital, John was calm. The last person to see him alive was the nurse who checked on him in the padded cell at midnight. She found him out of bed, standing quietly at the door. He might have been waiting for someone to arrive, or perhaps to leave. He was clearly very unwell. He left behind a large family, and his memoir for his descendants to read.

Before catching influenza John Hunter had been perfectly sane; I don't think he chose to take his own life. And there was no real relationship between his revisionist memoir and his death. But they *felt* connected. Back then people expected that Māori would assimilate, or die.

·

John Hunter's widow was Jane Newton. She raised Auntie Janie, who remembered her as a woman with a funny accent who barely spoke English. At Te Kōawa, Janie had told me about a vivid memory from when she was a young girl. She'd arrived at their house in Riverton to find it full of people. Her grandmother began to make a terrible noise.

'I remember this strange sound started coming out of her mouth. I was so scared I hid under her big hoop skirt! When I asked what she was doing, she said, "Don't you worry yourself. You be a Pākehā, girl. It'll be better for you."'

The event would have been a taki, with the body kept at home for several days. The strange noise Janie heard would have been a karaka, the ritual calling between women to negotiate entry when visitors arrived. Jane Newton and her generation were fluent in te reo Māori and the traditions. Some chose not to pass them on to their grandchildren. In that era Māori was a common synonym for 'dirty'. Murder was known colloquially as 'Māori killing'. Missionaries had waged war against Māori customs for close to a century, and it was widely believed that the race was dying out. So it makes sense that some people wanted their mokopuna to pass as Pākehā.

With her white hair and rosy pink cheeks, Auntie Janie doesn't look remotely Māori. Like most of her generation, she speaks only a little of the language. She's also one of our most revered and loved elders. She absorbed all of the mana of her ancestors, and stepped up to play a major role in the Ngāi Tahu claim. Though long retired, she still acts as an informal adviser to senior leaders, and sits on the tribal scholars' council and the board of Ngāi Tahu's philanthropic fund. Now that we've reached a settlement, like other elders, she has counselled me to remember the past but without indignation; to be inclusive, to look forward.

Even John Hunter's efforts to write himself into existence as a white man show how much he was part of the Māori world.

He commends Reverend Wohlers' ability to speak Māori, as only a native speaker would. He's at pains to point out the natives' cleanliness and godliness. And everywhere he goes, the natives turn out. They line the shore where he arrives on Ruapuke, they're there when he goes to church, and they send him off with a hurrah. Their chief, King Toby, entertains him at his table and lends him his favourite thoroughbred to ride. If he was a European boy, those things wouldn't matter. John Hunter is going out of his way to demonstrate his mana by showing that the people and their chief hold him in high esteem.

King Toby's esteem is especially important because he is the Ngāi Tahu chief Topi Pātuki. As a young man he shot Te Pūoho through the heart at Tuturau, ending the Ngāti Tama guerrilla raid on the south. John Hunter's mother, Kawiti, was among the slaves freed. He owed King Toby his life. So it's a memorable scene on the beach at Ruapuke when John Hunter gets ready to sail away into a new life, leaving the Māori world behind.

The natives are all assembled. King Toby presents John Hunter with 'a valuable native carcahu [kakahu]': a woven mat or cloak, given as a mark of rank and prestige. The chief then turns to John's father and says: '"Pity boy go away, he very good boy" whereupon my father replied "Oh he may come back by and by" and to this the King seemed satisfied and a smile passed over his dusky features.'

John Hunter is about to leave the Māori world.

Pity boy go away.

Oh he may come back by and by.

Walking the beach at Te Waewae Bay where John Hunter spent his days, bound for a marae that would be filled with the warmth and life of his descendants, I felt that he had never really left.

•

'Karaka mai! Karaka mai!'

It was windy and overcast the day thirty of us huddled outside our marae on the foreshore at Ōraka (Colac Bay), waiting to be called on. This bay was home to many of the greenstone parties of the past. Around us were the paddlers from the waka ama, and all the friends and whānau who'd supported the journey along the way. Takaroa, god of the sea, pushed in against the breakwater at our backs. The ancestral dead waited alongside in the grassed urupā to our left.

Our heads were bowed. The bag of takiwai was heavy in my hands. Mum's voice rose, plaintive and strong, making that same 'strange noise' as her great-grandmother Jane Newton once had. 'Karaka mai kā whānau Kāi Tahu o Takutai o te Tītī e! Anei ko mātou te kāhui takiwai e!'

There was movement ahead at the gate, then another woman's voice came to us over the wind. Auntie Janie, making that strange noise as well, calling us in. 'Haere mai, haere mai, haere mai, te whānau takiwai-e! Haere mai...'

We moved slowly forward through the gate, then filed into the whare. A room full of smiling cousins waited for us. I stepped forward and placed the bag of takiwai on the ground in the empty space between our two sides. The stones made a faint musical clatter before settling into the silence. I remembered the first walk I'd done, when I'd made an offering like this, to the sea.

Stewart Bull, chairman of the rūnaka, with his broad frame, huge white beard and kindly face, came forward and picked up the stone. He gave me a subtle nod. Everyone sat.

After the speeches and singing, Stewart and Janie blessed and welcomed the stones. Each piece passed from hand to hand along each row, and I watched them go. Over the weeks dozens of us had handled each piece, polished them with the oils from our fingers, come to know their shape and weight. I didn't know if they'd been sacred before we'd picked them out from the beach, but they were now.

I loved that the whare was the old schoolhouse, which now nurtured rather than attacked the culture. I loved that there had been discussions into the night about how we would run this ceremony, because no one knew the protocols for bringing takiwai back from Milford Sound, because no one had done it like this for a hundred and eighty years.

Using all their favourite elements of custom and ceremony, Janie, Stewart and the other elders had improvised. Normally you only welcome visitors. This was our tūrakawaewae, the harbour for our feet, the place where strong ancestral connections gave us the right to stand. We weren't visitors—so instead of welcoming us, they welcomed the stone.

John Hunter had invented to erase his past. At the start of my first walk on the Hokitika coast, I had invented a ritual because I didn't know that past. It felt tika, right, to finish my journeys among family on ancestral land, improvising together, breathing new life into tradition. And afterwards, at the hākari (feast), when I found myself telling exaggerated stories of our journey to others around the table, I realised that my propensity to talk everything up, to be whakahīhī (a bit uppity and proud), was part of my inheritance from John Hunter. The impulse that made him aggrandise his origins had passed to his outrageous daughter Emerald Anne, with her cigarette holders and furs, to my stubborn, bombastic grandfather Percy, whose stories about himself and those he loved were always larger than life. My mother could be just as whakahīhī, and so could I.

When I sat down to write his story, and our history in the mountains, he'd be there with me in every word.

EPILOGUE

Ko te kāhui mauka, tū tonu, tū tonu;
Ko te kāhui takata, karo noa, karo noa ka haere.

The people will perish, but the mountains
shall remain.

Outside the plane window, the peaks of Kā Tiritiri-o-te-moana surfaced from cloud like the fins of killer whales. I gripped my armrest and craned forward. Through gaps in the cloud cover I could make out the Rakaia river system snaking down past Whaka-matau, and, higher up, the tributary branches coming down from Rurumātaikau, Ōtūtekawa and Nōti Raureka. We droned west past Maukakūkuta, where the names of the mountains are ancient navigational stars, past Te Kahui Kaupeka (Mt D'Archiac) and the Godley Valley, though Sealy Pass remained hidden from sight.

Slowly, majestically, the head of the great ancestor Aoraki came into view through the windows on the other side of the plane. I unlatched my seatbelt, climbed over my neighbour and went to peer through the tiny porthole in the cabin door.

Several years earlier, I'd seen this bird's-eye view of the Alps on a screen in Takerei Norton's office. Since then I'd walked many of those valleys and passes; had started learning their histories with my feet. Kirikirikatata came into view, Aroarokaehe, the notch of Nōti Hinetamatea above the Hooker Glacier's curling tail. I pressed my nose to the glass as we crossed the huge white expanse of the Fox Glacier neve, then turned to watch the giants recede. Beaches and headlands passed beneath us, and then there was nothing but the sea.

I returned to my seat, and settled in for the journey to Melbourne. I'd helped set up a Ngāi Tahu taurahere (expat) group to run language and culture workshops for our 650 relations in Melbourne; I also needed to go back to earn some money, write, see friends. Most of all, I was looking forward to seeing Leigh. Her book was out in the world, clocking up sales, and she was settling into a writer's life of magazine features, radio interviews and figuring out what to work on next. Since I'd stopped doubting, we'd become inseparable. We were moving in together, into the little mudbrick cottage up in the bush.

The first thing we'd do together was build a hearth from local stone, heave a wood stove into place and light our own fire. Two years later our son, Ahi, would be born. Ahi, echoing Ahikāroa, the home fires. We'd continue to cross the sea each year, and one day we'd take him back to Te Waipounamu for good: we belong to that land. But for now I was leaving, and the feeling was bittersweet.

.

On a narrow island, all journeys begin and end with the sea. When I'd first set out across Nōti Raureka from that distant coastline, Leigh had been a stranger, and I'd known little beyond my desire to learn. But over weeks, months and years of my returning to the mountains, certain ideas had started to sink in.

I'd previously done years of casual tramping; now, I'd come to see how rich travelling was when you gave up on wilderness and set out to explore the past, and to puzzle out the logics embedded in the landscape—even when those logics remained largely out of reach. Glimpses were enough, like when I stood atop Christchurch's Port Hills on a nor'-west afternoon, the sky dusty gold and purple, the blue Alps spanning the horizon, and realised that, seen from up here, of course they were a line of paddlers seated in a great canoe.

At times I'd been bored. Often I was impatient. But after I'd spent so long out there, Te Waipounamu had acted upon me in subtle ways. I'd started to intuit the shifts in weather that swirl across the island. When you walk with Te Mauru in your face, week after week, it makes sense that the winds have names and personalities, and are the grandchildren of the sky and peaks. I grew attuned to those sheltered and abundant natural stopping places that so often had old Māori names. I wasn't surviving on mahika kai, so I was never deeply aware of the seasons, or the life of birds. But in remote valleys, or knee-deep in a fast-flowing river, the mauri of the land, its vivid brimming life, called up that same sense in me.

I felt the poisoned rivers of the plains as an ache in the gut, though I never drank from them. The ruined glaciers filled me with grief.

My journeys had connected me with people as much as place. At times I'd dipped into sadness about how much knowledge had been lost, until I realised that sometimes what was missing was my connection to the people who held the knowledge. Everyone I talked to had stories that weren't in books, but were being discussed and debated kanohi-ki-te-kanohi, face to face. Which means that there remain an infinite number of stories to be told about Kā Tiritiri-o-te-moana. Fluent speakers of te reo will see a thousand things I've missed. As will those who have been schooled in traditional history, or global indigenous futures, or whose whānau have always harvested mahika kai. I hadn't walked all of the old trails, and was only writing about some of the ones I had. There wasn't room for even half the stories about each route.

Most of all, I'd started to internalise the knowledge that our ancestors had criss-crossed the entire island on foot, and mapped its entirety in language, through oral maps, whakapapa and history. Stories and genealogies enmeshed the whole country in a vast net.

Walking point to point, I'd started to glimpse this complexity, but also the simplicity: journeys on foot across the Alps could be routine. My body had grown accustomed to the trail, the load, the long day. I walked until I understood on a physical level that our ancestors went over the Divide all the time, because it wasn't that hard to do. That made me hungry for more Ngāi Tahu, for everyone, to pace out our histories in the Alps. We could reinvent tramping to encompass the stories, and mahika kai, and waka and mōkihi (white-water rafts). Let our kids learn from the constellations that rise with the first frosts, from the peaks whose names encode the star paths used by the first arrivals. Let them speak te rco, let them understand the chants and the whakapapa of the land, and the climate science and the GIS data. Let them climb mountains to pay respects, to draw strength. We could expand our modern selves to include the rhythms of the land that formed us as a people. We could sing the old songs, and the new.

Behind me, on the ground, the mountains and their stories were safe in the care of those who maintain ahikāroa. It's the kaumātua, leaders, rūnaka members and tribal staff who live daily in sight of the peaks who keep the fires burning, and who keep a globalised Ngāi Tahu connected to their land. Auntie Jane Davis, Tā Tipene O'Regan, Matapura Ellison, David Higgins, James Russell, Kelly Davis, Trevor Howse, Takerei Norton and many others have driven initiatives like Kā Huru Manu, the Ngāi Tahu online atlas, and Kareao, the tribe's digital archive of maps, photos and manuscripts. But such knowledge was never intended to begin and end online.

I remembered that David Higgins once told me, 'I've always been determined to ensure that these stories and traditions are passed on, but only on the basis that if you're going to talk about a place, you go there. You visit that place, you feel it, and you come home and talk about it. Our stories are indelibly linked with the land.'

When I'd spoken with Lisa Tumahai, the chair of Te Rūnanga o Ngāi Tahu, she'd stressed how essential it was to help our people get out into the bush and the hills. 'We have to protect and preserve the high country and the mountains, and maintain our knowledge and our presence on the landscape for future generations,' she said. When you're out there, 'there's this absolute sense of knowing who you are, of *being-in-place*.'

•

I put my headphones on and closed my eyes. I felt the vibration of the plane beneath me like the purr of a huge animal, and the weight of the pounamu around my neck. I had a handful of pebbles in my bag that I'd found along the way, including takiwai from Piopiotahi, and the bird's-egg pebble from Nōti Raureka: little pieces of Te Waipounamu.

The whole project had been harder than I'd imagined, and I had only just begun. The more I spent time with the real tohuka, the more I realised I had to learn. Bridging the gap between knowing and truly understanding would take the rest of my life.

But there was one moment I treasured, and sometimes turned over in my mind on the cusp of sleep. It wasn't really knowledge as I recognised it, but something else.

While resting up in Arthur's Pass between trips, I'd dreamed of walking through tussock lands beside the Hurunui River. The day was warm and gusty, with an electric charge in the air. My companions and I paused to survey the route ahead. Looking up through a fringe of golden-brown tussock, I saw the shaley dry foothills, the stubborn midlands peaks, and the higher mountains behind, rising into a dark nor'-west sky. Cloud swarmed their faces.

For the first and only time in my life, I saw that the mountains were alive. Not as a metaphor or a symbol, but as living, breathing creatures, seething with life, related through whakapapa, in conversation with each other and the winds. They crackled with life-force. They were the source of the weather, to be placated, spoken to, mediated with. The thought of walking towards them filled me with awe, and fear.

I'd woken up before I could take my first step.

Notes

INTRODUCTION

'**How then are we Ngāi Tahu going to walk through this ancient landscape in the new century…**' Tā Tipene O'Regan, 'Māori Identity in the Aotearoa Landscape: An Old Culture in the New Century' in *Visions of Future Landscapes* (1999), p. 232.

…the gleaming glacier spilling from the southern flank of Kaimatau (Mt Rolleston)… The name Kaimatau comes from the Department of Conservation's *Arthur's Pass National Park Management Plan* (2007), p. 20. James Russell at Arahura gives Tarahaka as another name for Mt Rolleston (personal communication, 6 March 2021).

'**It will all be residue with no meaning, laws without substance…**' O'Regan, 'Māori Identity in the Aotearoa Landscape', p. 233.

1. NŌTI RAUREKA

…a woman named Raureka, who set off into the mountains from near here, in around 1700. Raureka is pronounced 'row', as in 'row your boat', and 'recka'; only the 'r's are a little Spanish, pronounced on the tip of the tongue—almost a 'd'. Numerous oral histories of Raureka's journey still circulate today, while published sources include John White's *The Ancient History of the Maori* (1887), Volume III, pp. 106–08 & 177, Volume IX, pp. 7–8; the manuscript of mountain lore collected from Makaawhio kaumātua by G. J. Roberts, *Nomenclature, Legends &c. as Supplied by the Maoris in South Westland* (1897), p. 149; Canon James Stack's *Traditional History of the South Island Maoris* (1877), pp. 86–87; and James Cowan's *Hero Stories of New Zealand* (1935), pp. 252–57.

Soon after Ngāi Tahu arrived, we sent delegations over to learn from their priests... See Atholl Anderson and Te Maire Tau's *Ngāi Tahu: A Migration History* (2008), p. 116. Many Ngāi Tahu today suggest that there were multiple trips back and forth to learn 'the kawa of the land', which have been condensed into a single incident in oral history (David Higgins, personal communication, 29 July 2019; Ben Te Aika, personal communication, 27 July 2019).

...he and his party encountered a Kāti Wairaki force led by the famous chief Uekanuku. See Paul Madgwick's *Aotea* (1992), p. 23.

Toitū te whenua...The better sentiment is 'cleave to the land'. Tā Tipene O'Regan, personal communication, 15 March 2021.

The chief Pūhou, who was perhaps the man Raureka married, led an expedition back west. See *Nomenclature, Legends &c.* (1897), p. 149; James Herries Beattie's *Maori Lore of Lake, Alp and Fiord* (1945), p. 64; and Teone Taare Tikao and James Herries Beattie's *Tikao Talks* (1939), pp. 121–22, which has a possible variation of the story involving Te Rakitāmau and Tānetiki.

It only took the first Polynesian explorers a few decades to track down all the sources of useful stone in the entire country, including some well above the bush line. Pounamu expert Russell Beck, personal communication, March 2016; see also Atholl Anderson, Judith Binney and Aroha Harris's *Tangata Whenua: An Illustrated History* (2014), p. 76.

Poutini was the guardian taniwha of pounamu... Again, there are many variations of Poutini and Waitaiki's tale; here, I've paraphrased Tā Tipene O'Regan's retelling in *Place Names of the Ancestors: He Kōrero Pūrākau Mo Ngā Taunahanahatanga a Ngā Tūpuna* (1990), pp. 83–84. For a vivid version from Te Tai-o-Poutini see James Russell's evidence to the Waitangi Tribunal in *Ngāi Tahu Māori Trust Board Claim Before the Waitangi Tribunal Wai-27* (1989–90), Vol. 18, H8, pp. 45–49.

'...the mountains are peopled with mysterious and misshapen animals...' Ernst Dieffenbach's *Travels in New Zealand* (1843), Vol. I, pp. 155–56, quoted in Margaret Orbell and Geoff Moon's *The Natural World of the Māori* (1985), p. 89.

The story goes that a scout named Ngātororangi intercepted them near the pass. Ngātororangi's story is recorded in W. A. Taylor's *Lore and History of the South Island Maori* (1950), p. 189, and quoted in Barry Brailsford's *Greenstone Trails* (1984), p. 130. I'm curious about the provenance of the story because Ngātoro*i*rangi is a famous ancestor from the North Island.

Tell them who I was, and sink my pounamu axe into their wood. When asked in 1897, Kāti Māhaki kaumātua knew the name of the piece of pounamu that Raureka gave to the chief Pūhou when she arrived in Ngāi Tahu territory. Sadly, the scribe, George Roberts, didn't record the name: 'I have mislaid my notes.' (*Nomenclature, Legends &c.*, p. 149.)

In a footnote by the leading Ngāi Tahu scholars Atholl Anderson and Te Maire Tau… Anderson and Tau's *Ngāi Tahu* (2008), p. 120, n. 10. Tā Tipene O'Regan suggests the confusion may also stem from a pun on Raureka's tribal roots: Wairaki can mean foolish, irrational, or crazed (personal communication, 20 March 2021). See also White's *Ancient History* (1887), Volume IX, pp. 7–8, for an 1857 version from Assistant Native Commissioner James McKay, based on conversations with Poutini Ngāi Tahu. He says Raureka was simply part of a party from Arahura who visited Kaiapoi. She showed them a beautiful adze of 'Taranga' greenstone, and it was agreed that some Ngāi Tahu would accompany her and the Kāti Wairaki people back to the source.

Tensions came to a head when they ambushed a major Ngāi Tahu party at Lake Māhinapua, south of Kaniere. There are many versions of this history. Here, I'm drawing on Atholl Anderson's *The Welcome of Strangers: An Ethnohistory of Southern Maori AD 1650–1850* (1998) and Tikao's *Tikao Talks* (1939).

The bones came from moa, the huge flightless birds that kept our earliest ancestors in abundance. See Rosemary Britten's *Lake Coleridge: The People, The Power, The Land* (2000), pp. 60–62, quoted in Takerei Norton's report *Rakaia ki Whakamatau: Ngāi Tahu Cultural Association with the Rakaia River and Whakamatau (Lake Coleridge)* (2012), p. 26.

[Brailsford] claimed Raureka's story wasn't found in local traditions: 'its source is a mystery and its authenticity questionable'. *Greenstone Trails*, p. 125.

2. NŌTI HURUNUI (HARPER PASS)

Nōti Hurunui This pass is also sometimes referred to as Nōti Taramakau, or Nōti Hurunui Taramakau (James Russell, personal communication, 6 March 2021).

…**Werita Tainui and his son Ihaia received a visit from Bishop Henry Harper and his son Leonard.** For an account of this meeting, and Leonard Harper's version of the journey, see Arthur P. Harper's *Memories of Mountains and Men* (1946), Appendix III, 'Leonard Harper's Narrative of the first Crossing of the Southern Alps in 1857', pp. 201–08.

…**Te Rauparaha, leader of the North Island Ngāti Toa tribe, embarked on an extended vendetta against Ngāi Tahu.** There are multiple overlapping versions of the fall of Kaiapoi Pā. This account is based on chapter five of Anderson's *The Welcome of Strangers* (1998), pp. 78–90.

Many defenders were killed, some captured and bled to death, and hundreds enslaved, while hundreds more escaped. Nineteenth-century accounts of thousands killed are wildly exaggerated—see *The Welcome of Strangers*, pp. 89–90—but the effect was still severe: a loss of leadership at a time of great upheaval, with the arrival of Pākehā; confusion over land rights, with refugees spilling south; and subsequent disputes over land sales, with Ngāti Toa mischievously trying to sell to the government Ngāi Tahu land they'd briefly occupied but did not own.

In 1863 [Ihaia] told Pākehā goldminer William Smart that he'd been brought through the mountains to safety as a refugee from Kaiapoi Pā. Ihaia Tainui and three companions met Smart along the Taramakau in 1863. Smart recorded in his diary: 'All these Maories had been over here from Kaiapoi several times and lived at the Grey when they were children; their fathers or friends took them over when the Kaiapoi pah was being besieged by Te Rauparaha and other North Islanders.' See Hilary Low's *Pay Dirt: The Westland Goldfields, from the Diary of William Smart* (2016), p. 63.

For centuries travellers on alpine crossings stopped here and at nearby Hokakura (Lake Sumner) to stock up on tuna (eels) and waterfowl. Ngāi Tahu Cultural Map Heritage Viewer, 'Hokakura'; Department of Conservation, *Lake Sumner and Lewis Pass* (2010), p. 44.

…**I can imagine [Ihaia] sat across a campfire from Leonard Harper,**

pointing out the same features, bringing a newcomer face to face with his home. Ngāi Tahu history is full of accounts of our people giving early Pākehā travellers detailed introductions to the landscapes they were passing through. Examples include Ihaia's uncle Tarapuhi outlining various alpine passes, including what is now Arthur's Pass, to surveyor Arthur Dobson; or Kāti Huirapa rakatira Tarawhata detailing the headwaters of the Rakaia to the Protector of Aborigines Edward Shortland. Ihaia and his friends later passed on place-name information about the western side of the pass to William Smart.

... Ema Turumeke gave a chilling eye-witness account of being stalked by Te Rauparaha's warriors... 'Narrative of the Battle of Omihi, As related by Ema Turumeke to her Daughter, Mrs. C. J. Harden, and translated by the latter' in *Journal of the Polynesian Society*, 3(2), 1894, pp. 107–09.

...the one hill on the far ridge with a European name—Niggerhead, until recently... At the end of 2016, Niggerhead was officially renamed Tawhai Hill.

His grandfather had participated in the famed Ngāi Tahu war party that crossed Nōti Hurunui to defeat Raureka's people and ultimately settle the West Coast. Kaumātua from Makaawhio noted that this was the route taken in *Nomenclature, Legends &c.* (1897), p. 106.

...'the headwaters of the Hurunui were reached for the first time.' Christchurch *Press*, 21 April 1908, p. 9.

[Ihaia's] party found several 'fine specimens' on the western side of the pass; later accounts suggest it was the Māori members who discovered the gold. See Mark Pickering's *The Colours* (2010), p. 35.

The Canterbury Provincial Government had offered a thousand-pound reward for the discovery of a payable goldfield. Not wishing to alert Ngāi Tahu to the true value of their land, the government suppressed previous reports of gold on the West Coast until the purchase of the Coast was complete. See Pickering's *The Colours*, p. 36.

It took Ihaia four days to cross the Hurunui Saddle and walk to Christchurch. This account comes from William Martin's *A Pioneer's Reminiscences* (1863), MS-0205 in the Hocken Library, University of Otago, quoted in Pickering's *The Colours*, p. 77. Martin's own sources aren't given, but he knew many of the players from that era. Ihaia's astonishment at Dixon's package containing gold comes from the *Lyttelton Times*,

20 December 1862.

In the end, both claims were denied on technicalities. Neither man was ruled to have demonstrated the goldfield was viable, and in any case, the reward was deemed to have been withdrawn. The government also considered Māwhera too far from Christchurch to profit the colony, though it was only four days' walk away for Ihaia.

... in the old days, one owl calling through the night spoke of bad weather, two or more of storms. *Tikao Talks* (1939), p. 81.

The Hurunui's full name is Huruhurunui, referencing a cloak of fur or feathers. For a fascinating discussion of the name and its various possible meanings, see Takerei Norton's *Statement of Evidence in an Application for a Water Conservation Order on the Hurunui River and Lake Sumner (Hoka Kura)* (2008), p. 7.

... 'a dismal narrative of gloomy skies, and incessant rain, of a country kept in perpetual solitude, incapable of occupation, niggardly of promise.' Christchurch *Press*, 24 March 1863, p. 1.

... Henry W. Harper called them an 'impassable barrier' to what Leonard described as an 'uninhabitable' place. Henry W. Harper's *Letters from New Zealand 1857–1911* (1914), pp. 50, 58.

'Mr Harper has discovered no country of value.' *Lyttelton Times*, 20 January 1858, p. 4.

... 'covered with rags, and whose hollow features showed only too plainly traces of the unaccustomed privations they had endured'. Julius von Haast's *Geology of the Provinces of Canterbury and Westland, New Zealand* (1879), p. 70.

... Ihaia's elders had sold most of the West Coast to the Crown, and now they were pressured to give up more of what little they'd retained. See Te Rūnanga o Ngāi Tahu's 'The Arahura Deed 1860' (2017): ngaitahu. iwi.nz/our_stories/arahura-deed-1860

Near the traditional camping place known as Whakamoemoe... W. A. Taylor's *Lore and History of the South Island Maori* (1952), p. 177.

In 1877 the committee charged with hearing such petitions simply sent their rejection letter from the previous year. Reports of the Native Affairs Committee, 1876, I.—8, p. 47.

... 'there is a large class at Home to whom New Zealand means Canterbury, and Canterbury [means] Harper and Co.' *Poverty Bay Herald*, 24 April

1893, p. 4.

...'it is impossible to acquit Messrs Harper and Co. of culpable weakness and moral cowardice.' *Poverty Bay Herald*, 24 April 1893, p. 4. Harper's personal estate was also £30,000 in debt.

Harper insisted it was pointless charging him, because the money was long gone. For details of the case see *Evening Star*, 20 May 1895, p. 2; *Daily Telegraph*, 10 July 1895, p. 2; *Timaru Herald*, 4 June 1894, p. 3.

Once Ihaia and Leonard's party crossed the Ōtira, they spent a day cutting and binding rushes to construct a mōkihi... Details of their journey down the river come from Leonard Harper's account published in the *Lyttelton Times*, 20 January 1858, p. 4.

In a letter dated 10 July 1868, Harper wrote of receiving a deputation from Arahura... Henry Harper's *Letters from New Zealand* (1914), pp. 140–43.

'Do not blame anybody for my death...' *West Coast Times*, 20 October 1885, p. 2. Further published details about Ihaia's death can be found in the *Grey River Argus*, 22 October 1885, and the *West Coast Times*, 22 October 1885, p. 2.

...'**the deceased was under a misconception, thinking that the slight irregularity that he had committed was a grave breach of the criminal law'.** *Taranaki Herald*, 23 October 1885, p. 2. Ihaia thought the twenty pounds he'd been given by Hungerford was rental for the land. In fact, Hungerford had bought the lease from another man who had already acquired the lease from the tribe. The money wasn't a rental payment, but an unspecified gratuity that Ihaia was under no obligation to pass on.

3. RURUMĀTAIKAU (WHITCOMBE PASS)

The next major valley west from where Raureka descended was Ōtūtekawa (Mathias Pass), recalling the chief Tūtekawa, who played a dramatic role in Ngāi Tahu's settlement of the South Island. For an account of Tūtekawa and his life and times, see chapters 2 and 12 of Anderson and Tau's *Ngāi Tahu* (2008).

Kehu 'appears to have an instinctive sense, beyond our comprehension which enables him to find his way...' Charles Heaphy's 'Account of an

Exploring Expedition to the S.W. of Nelson', *Nelson Examiner and New Zealand Chronicle*, 7 March 1846, p. 3; quoted in Pete McDonald's *Foot Tracks* (2011), p. 35.

Our other guide to the terrain was Lauper's own account of the ordeal, republished as *Pushing His Luck,* a new translation and commentary by my aunt Hilary Low. Unless otherwise stated, all details and quotes about Whitcombe and Lauper's journey come from Hilary Low and Jakob Lauper's *Pushing His Luck: Report of the Expedition and Death of Henry Whitcombe* (2010).

'Rain, rain, all the while, no cessation night nor day, blankets and clothes all soaked through...' Richard Sherrin's 'Journal of an Expedition to the Gold Field of the Taramakau', Christchurch *Press*, 21 March 1863, p. 2; quoted in *Pushing His Luck*, p. 43.

In 1861, while out searching for more grazing land, [Samuel Butler] became the first European to lay eyes on Rurumātaikau. He and a friend reached the saddle two years ahead of Whitcombe and Lauper... Butler's journey wasn't acknowledged at the time—they weren't official government explorers—but it seems clear that Whitcombe knew of their find, and was heading straight for it. See *Pushing His Luck*, pp. 22–24.

Kahabuka chooses to withhold knowledge: 'He became uneasy, and began to prevaricate and shuffle...' Samuel Butler, *Erewhon, or, Over the Range* (1872; 1906), chapter II, paragraph 1: gutenberg.org/files/1906/1906-h/1906-h.htm

...Te Whakataupuka, the famous southern chief who was described in 1827 as 'the most complete model of strength, activity, and elegance I had seen combined in any man'. John Boultbee, quoted in Atholl Anderson's 'Te Whakataupuka' in the *Dictionary of New Zealand Biography* (1990), online in *Te Ara: The Encyclopedia of New Zealand*. See also Harry Evison's *New Zealand Racism in the Making: The Life and Times of Walter Mantell* (2010) for analysis of early race relations in the south.

Newspapers denounced 'brutal and unprovoked murder' by the 'ruthless savage'. *Daily Southern Cross*, 16 July 1863, p. 3.

Panic swept through Auckland that whites would be massacred in their beds. The rumours were false, but they enabled Governor Grey finally to convince London to send Imperial troops. See 'Invasion Plans' from the History Group of the New Zealand Ministry for Culture and Heritage's

War in Waikato resource (2014): nzhistory.net.nz/war/war-in-waikato/invasion-plans

The real prize a guide would have searched for was aruhe (bracken fern root), 'te tūtanga tē unuhia', the staple that never fails. Te Rangi Hiroa's *The Coming of the Maori* (1950), p. 93; quoted in Mere Roberts et al.'s 'Whakapapa as a Māori Mental Construct', in *The Contemporary Pacific*, 16(1), 2004, p. 17. Aruhe was particularly important in the south, where it was too cold in many places to grow tropical crops like kūmara.

As Joseph Banks, the botanist on Captain Cook's Endeavour, said: it was 'to them what bread is to us'. *The Endeavour Journal of Sir Joseph Banks, 1768–1771* (1962), 'Account of New Zealand', paragraph 29: gutenberg.net.au/ebooks05/0501141h.html#nz

When there wasn't much in the way of birds or eels, explorers like Charles Heaphy subsisted on mamaku harvested by their Māori guides. See James Cowan's 'Three West Coast Explorers: Thomas Brunner, Charles Heaphy, James Mackay' in the *New Zealand Railways Magazine*, 8(5), 1930, pp. 26–27.

4. TARAHAKA (ARTHUR'S PASS)

Tarahaka The name Tarahaka for Arthur's Pass, short for Te Tarahaka-o-Kaimatau, is referenced in the *Arthurs Pass National Park Management Plan* (2007), p. 20, though no source is given. The source may have been Kāti Waewae rakatira Tarapuhi, who described the pass to European surveyor Arthur Dobson in the 1860s (Tā Tipene O'Regan, personal communication, 15 March 2021).

'Ko Kuratawhiti te mauka kākāpō. Ko au te takata.' Tahu Pōtiki's 'Nā Wai Te Kī?' in *Te Kāraka*, 8, 1998, p. 9. Another version has Tānetiki winning the taunaha; Joseph Hullen suggests this version may have arisen after Tanetiki's death at Māhinapua, to validate Tūrakautahi's claim. Also, note that there is no consensus on how the traditional names in this area map to the common names today. W. A. Taylor writes: 'The Torlesse Range... is Whatarama—its highest peak Tawera is 6,442 feet...The Otarama Peak is Kura tawhiti, a name imported from Polynesia.' (*Lore and History of the Southern Maori*, 1950, p. 31.)

The esteemed Ngāi Tahu archaeologist Atholl Anderson... says the preferred site was a 'stretch of flax-bordered stream where eels and other fish were procured, ducks caught, and fern root or tī kōuka [cabbage-tree pith] obtained'. *The Welcome of Strangers* (1998), pp. 131–33.

The pouākai, or Pou-a-Hawaiki, was a giant eagle that nested on the side of Kura Tawhiti and preyed on travellers passing into the Waimakariri Basin via Ōtāneuru. This version comes from conversations with Joseph Hullen. See also Christine Tremewan's analysis of the many variations of this story from across the Pacific in chapter 11 of *Traditional Stories from Southern New Zealand* (2002); and Canon Stack's record of a specific account of a pair of pouākai nesting on a spur of Tāwera in *Traditional History of the South Island Maoris*, pp. 63–64.

Kennedy Warne's description of the kārearea (New Zealand falcon), a modern bird of prey evolved to hunt in the same terrain, suggests what pouākai were capable of... This comes from 'Masters of the Sky' in *New Zealand Geographic*, 4, October–December 1989. The image of being hit with a block of concrete comes from his 'Hotspot: New Zealand' in *National Geographic Magazine*, October 2002.

...there's a good chance pouākai may have prey-switched to humans; we have four separate oral traditions on this point. Jim Williams mentions some of these traditions in *'E Pākihi Hakinga a Kai*: An Examination of Pre-contact Resource Management Practice in Southern Te Wai Pounamu (doctoral thesis, 2004), p. 207, n. 203.

The chiefs still drove a hard bargain: the sale would only proceed if the tribe could keep land amounting to approximately one acre in every ten... Of the tribe's total land dealings in the colonial era, Ngāi Tahu wanted to reserve 3.4 million acres out of a total of 34.5 million acres sold. ngaitahu.iwi.nz/ngai-tahu/the-settlement/claim-history

Henry Tacy Kemp, who negotiated the purchase for the government, had official instructions to reserve 'ample portions for [the tribe's] present and future wants'. See *The Ngai Tahu Report* (Wai 27, 1991), from the Waitangi Tribunal, for details. Kemp later justified his failure to mark the reserves on the grounds it would have been too hazardous for him to walk the length of Te Waipounamu in winter. 'In the result he did not actually set foot on a single piece of the vast territory he had acquired' (p. 465).

But [Kemp] had private instructions as well: to agree to large reserves, but insist they be marked out to Ngāi Tahu's satisfaction *after* the sale. See the letter from Governor Grey to Earl Grey, 15 May 1848, in *British Parliamentary Papers: New Zealand 1847–1849*, Vol. 7, 22 ff., quoted in Evison's *New Zealand Racism in the Making*, p. 113.

Mantell demanded whole populations move, and blackballed anyone who dared argue, reporting them to the government as 'sullen and evilly disposed'. Wai 27, p. 84. Those who argued were also granted miserably small reserves. Chief Matiaha Tiramōrehu and his two hundred people at Moeraki refused Mantell's request to relocate two hundred kilometres north to the Tuahiwi reserve, so Mantell allocated them 2.5 acres per head.

The English version was enforced, and it translated mahika kai as merely plantations. Wai 27, p. 84. For a long time this view was also affirmed in the New Zealand courts: Chief Justice Fenton defined mahinga kai as 'local and fixed works and operations'.

'I have come to think that addressing the land is an essential task if the relationship between people and the natural world is to be restored.' Kennedy Warne's 'The Enchantment of NZ's West Coast', *Stuff Travel*, 9 November 2014.

'The land will naturalise us if we will let it. The land will make us "native"—a nativeness of soul.' Kennedy Warne, 'Listening to the People of the Land' in *E-Tangata*, 24 March 2019. The literary critic Terry Goldie's *Fear and Temptation* (1989) argues that this tendency to adopt native spirituality to atone for the historic appropriation of native land is common across Canada, Australia and New Zealand. 'The indigenized white is sanctified by indigenous mysticism and is able to enter the formerly forbidden regions of the alien land' (p. 146). And 'through the indigene, the white character gains soul and the potential to become of the land' (p. 16).

… in the nineteenth century, the Reverend Charles Clarke thought the stones looked like 'the circling seats of a vast amphitheatre; and… the gigantic monoliths of Stonehenge'. Quoted in Carl Walrond's 'The Rocks of Castle Hill', *New Zealand Geographic*, 44, October–December 1999.

What's more, their advanced civilisation was a nation of many peoples from the Pacific, Europe, Asia, the Americas and Africa. Since publishing *Song of Waitaha* in 1994, Barry Brailsford has moved away from the idea that Waitaha was a rainbow tribe from all over the world. He told me they were Polynesian, with just a few colourful strands of DNA from elsewhere in the world.

'Ko Rākaihautū te takata nāna i tīmata te ahi ki ruka ki tēnei motu': Rākai-hautū was the man who lit the fires of occupation in this island. Wī Pōkuku and Herewini Eli's 'Ko Te Pukapuka Whakaako ko te Korero Tipuna' (1887), unpaginated, quoted in Eruera Tarena's *He Atua, He Tipua, He Takata Rānei: The Dynamics of Change in South Island Māori Oral Traditions* (master's thesis, University of Canterbury, 2008), p. 240.

Leading Ngāi Tahu scholars denounced the book as fantasy. For an over-view of critiques of Brailsford's work, see Tarena's *He Atua, He Tipua, He Takata Rānei*. See also Te Maire Tau's 'Song of Waitaha: A Descendant's View' in *Te Kāraka*, 2, 1995, pp. 6, 20; and Tīpene O'Regan's 'Old Myths and New Politics: Some Contemporary Uses of Traditional History' in the *New Zealand Journal of History*, 26(1), 1992, pp. 5–27.

Other respected Pākehā historians and archaeologists, including Michael King and Michael Goldsmith, weighed in. See Michael Goldsmith's 'Strange Whakapapa: Colliding and Colluding Claims to Ancestry and Indigeneity in Aotearoa', *Sites: new series*, 10(1), 2013, pp. 73–92; Michael King's 'A Fraction Too Much Fiction?' in *Tread Softly for You Tread on My Life* (2001), pp. 129–30. See also Geoffrey Clark's 'Identity and Alterna-tive Versions of the Past in New Zealand', in *Terra Australis*, 35, 2011, pp. 5–16, which details the complex politics of *Song of Waitaha*, including the overlap between Pākehā new-age spiritual circles and a group of genuine Waitaha descendants who opposed the main Ngāi Tahu leadership at the time of the Treaty settlement.

Brailsford's collaborator, Peter Ruka, who turned out to have fabricated his Ngāi Tahu whakapapa... Tau's 'Song of Waitaha: A Descendant's View', p. 6.

'And our tūpuna [ancestors] looked behind the rising waves of pain and out to the stars, and in words of binding prophecy proclaimed...' Barry Brailsford, *Song of Waitaha* (1994), p. 11.

Walter Mantell ignored their instructions because the proposed reserve included significant grazing land. The grazing land that would have supported the whole of Ngāi Tūāhuriri was instead later divided between thirteen European runholders. See Wai 27, p. 474.

5. NŌTI HINETAMATEA (COPLAND PASS)

'Hinetamatea and her two sons Tatawhaka and Kōmarupeka were up the Karangarua when they saw a tūī fly down from the mountains…' Hinetamatea's story is a taoka of the Kāti Māhaki hapū, and is recorded in the Makaawhio kaumātua manuscript *Nomenclature, Legends &c.* (1897), p. 150. They say Hinetamatea crossed over into Canterbury on p. 149.

'The kiwis were of larger size than usual, and very light in colour, some being completely white on the belly…' Charlie Douglas's *Report by Mr. Douglas of Explorations made along the Copland River* (1892), p. 45.

'Ki te taha wahine a Aroarokaehe' (And to the female side and the Hooker Valley)… This whakapapa is a taoka of the Moeraki, Arowhenua and Waihao rūnaka of Ngāi Tahu. The full version is published in the Department of Conservation's *Draft Aoraki / Mt Cook National Park Management Plan* (2018), p. 6.

But Arai-te-uru was the waka (conveyance) by which people arrived here: a navigational star path… Tā Tipene O'Regan, personal communication, 20 March 2021.

Could I picture Hinetamatea, her sons and their wives standing here, wrapped in dog-skin cloaks, contemplating the new land laid out at their feet? Arthur P. Harper surmised that Hinetamatea and her whānau may have crossed a minor coastal range *into* the Copland Valley, rather than crossing the Main Divide; to support the idea he cites a coastal creek bearing Hinetamatea's name north of the Copland. See his *Pioneer Work in the Alps of New Zealand* (1896), p. 273.

Would an early Māori travelling party have had the gear needed to cross the pass? For a detailed look at travelling gear and techniques, see the first edition of Barry Brailsford's *The Greenstone Trails* (1984). Manaia Rehu's *Te Wai Pounamu Ara Tawhito* (n.d.), an internal Ngāi Tahu Archives overview of historic trails, also has excellent information.

Travellers also carried adzes, and there are accounts of steps being cut in steep earth banks… Brailsford's *Greenstone Trails* (1984) pp. 35–36.

'…mid-nineteenth-century Pākehā travellers left many…descriptions of routes up or across steep and exposed ground…' Pete McDonald's *Foot Tracks* (2011) p. 28.

One describes the death of the warrior Takawa in a blizzard while crossing

Nōti Raureka; another details an avalanche that killed twenty men. *Tikao Talks*, pp. 120–21.

There's the story of the chief Te Kaumira, who died in a snowstorm on the range known as Te Tari-a-Te-Kaumira... Beattie's *Māori Lore of Lake, Alp and Fiord* (1945), pp. 53–54.

Bob McKerrow's 1993 essay 'Māori Mountaineers of South Westland' shows how they and their descendants were living proof of Ngāi Tahu's connection to the Alps, forming a small but important dynasty of Māori guides and mountaineers. See the *New Zealand Alpine Journal* (1993), and reproduced in Lawrence Fearnley and Paul Hersey's anthology *To the Mountains: A Collection of New Zealand Alpine Writing* (2018).

One was Ruera Te Naihi. For more on Ruera's life and times, see Paul Madgwick's 'Ruera Te Naihi: Porter and Guide to Douglas', presented by Susan Wallace at the 2017 Charlie Douglas Centennial Commemorations held in Hokitika: vimeo.com/171182688

Rakatira (chief) Kerei Tūtoko was another of the figures sitting at the fire telling Hinetamatea's story in 1897. See A. A. Pullar's notes on Kerei Tūtoko in *Wilderness Days in Bruce Bay* (1990), pp. 32–36.

'Certainly, if his physique is a typical instance of that of the Maori race,' [FitzGerald] wrote later, 'a fine race of alpine guides might be cultivated from them'. Edward FitzGerald's *Climbs in the New Zealand Alps: Being an Account of Travel and Discovery* (1896), p. 292; quoted in McKerrow, 'Māori Mountaineers'.

But as they travelled they saw a rainbow, sent by the taipō (an evil spirit). 'Taipō' is a relatively recent word to enter the Maori language; it is often translated as demon or goblin, but is also a transliteration of 'typhoid': an invisible evil that killed Maori in numbers in the nineteenth century. See 'Taipō', *Te Aka Online Māori Dictionary* (n.d.): maoridictionary.co.nz

...But the various Māori words for rainbows all relate to atua. James Cowan's *Māori Folk-Tales of the Port Hills* (1923), pp. 7–8; *Tikao Talks* (1939), p. 41.

'Then at midnight the storm burst on us, with its peals of thunder and its vivid lightning...' Arthur P. Harper's *Pioneer Work in the New Zealand Alps* (1896), p. 248.

The changing climate had eviscerated the ice; the total volume of the Southern Alps' glaciers has reduced by more than a third in the

last thirty years. For a succinct overview of the impact of climate change on New Zealand's glaciers, see Trevor Chin, Blair Fitzharris and Jim Salinger's 'New Zealand's Southern Alps Have Lost a Third of Their Ice', *Conversation*, 29 July 2014: theconversation.com/new-zealands-southern-alps-have-lost-a-third-of-their-ice-28916

Except for the foolish like us, or the gifted like Guy and Jane, Hinetamatea's route was largely done. Since I wrote this chapter, climbers have found a slightly safer route through the moraine, accessed via Copland Gut itself. Ask at Wynn Irwin Hut for beta.

…Tim and I mused on the location of Pōpātea, where Hinetamatea's family settled. The root word, pātea, is closely linked with Raureka's Kāti Wairaki people, who originally came from a Pātea in the North Island. Hinetamatea's kōrero seems to come from Kāti Wairaki as well: the men and women who related her story in 1897 learned it from Te Kauau, the last Kāti Wairaki tohunga, who was still living with Ngāi Tahu in 1852. See *Nomenclature, Legends &c.* (1897), pp. 3, 111; and Madgwick's *Aotea* (1992), p. 25.

Donelle and Kaharoa were also on a mission to harvest the leaves of the matua tikumu (mountain daisy) for their aunties to use in weaving a cloak. Tikumu are large mountain daisies with silvery waterproof leaves, used to thatch raincapes or to make ultrafine cloaks. Travellers also used the fleshy leaves to line woven gaiters for warmth and as protection from scrub. See Sue Scheele and Peter Sweetapple's 'Tikumu—Mountain Daisy' factsheet from Manaaki Whenua / Landcare Research: landcareresearch. co.nz/tools-and-resources/collections/new-zealand-flax-collections/ weaving-plants/tikumu

6. SEALY PASS

E Ruaimoko puritia tawhia kia i ta i ta i ta e! *Tikao Talks*, p. 40.

…there had long been speculation that [Sealy Pass] was a Ngāi Tahu route. Beattie discusses the various sources for this idea in *Maori Lore of Lake, Alp and Fiord*, pp. 67–68, as does Brailsford in *Greenstone Trails*, p. 162. Of the three sources of information about Sealy Pass, only one speaks specifically of the Godley and Sealy Pass. The others may suggest a pass at the head of the Rangitata (one river system to the north: possibly Dennistoun Pass, which joins the Sealy Pass route at the confluence of Bettison Stream and Scone Creek). The version in *Tikao Talks* has 'O Ruaimoko...', but this makes little sense; North Island versions have 'E Ruaimoko...' Personal communication, Ross Calman, 1 April 2021.

...old Māori implements had been found high up the valley, right at the snout of the glacier. Johannes C. Andersen's *Jubilee History of South Canterbury* (1916), p. 39; cited in Beattie's *Maori Lore of Lake, Alp and Fiord* (1945), p. 67.

'You watched a peak and went by its signs. Fog on one side meant you could get through; fog on the other side warned you not to attempt to cross the pass.' Beattie's *Maori Lore of Lake, Alp and Fiord* (1945), p. 68.

Takapō means 'to roll up bundles at night'. Beattie's *Maori Lore of Lake, Alp and Fiord* (1945), p. 13. The other sense, 'a fall in the night', comes from T. D. Burnett's 'Mackenzie Country', Christchurch *Press*, 26 June 1925. Burnett gives Hare Kokoro of Temuka as his source.

Except that I was going straight into Te Mauru, the howling, gritty nor'-west wind. It's also called 'te hau kai takata' (the wind that devours people). Te Maire Tau's 'Ngāi Tahu and the Canterbury Landscape—A Broad Context', in John Cookson and Graeme Dunstall's *Southern Capital, Christchurch: Towards a City Biography, 1850–2000* (2000), p. 42.

When you see lightning, and hear thunder crack and roll across the peaks, that's Tāwhaki and Whaitiri. This version of Whaitiri and Tāwhaki's story comes from Christine Tremewan's *Traditional Stories from Southern New Zealand = He kōrero nō Te Wai Pounamu* (2002), chapter 9, pp. 163–92.

What [Tikao] did remember about lightning was that there were three types... See *Tikao Talks*, p. 90, for discussion of lightning and omens.

Wānaka, south of the Godley, got its name from its whare wānaka, and there was another at Manuhaea, at the head of Lake Hāwea. There are various names for these schools: whare pūrākau, whare maire, whare wānanga, or whare wānaka in the southern dialect.

7. TIORIPĀTEA (HAAST PASS)

In 1836, [Kawiti] was captured from Ōkahu (Jackson Bay) on the West Coast by a band of a hundred Ngāti Tama guerrilla fighters. We know of Kawiti's journey from our family oral history, come down from Kawiti's granddaughter Auntie Jane Davis. Written accounts only mention Ruta and Pāpako, two Ngāi Tahu women from Arahura who were taken as guides.

Having already walked most of the West Coast, they marched her across the Alps at Tioripātea, then down into Murihiku (Southland), intent on launching a surprise attack on the main settlements along the coast. The most comprehensive account of Te Pūoho's journey is in Atholl Anderson's meticulously researched *Te Puoho's Last Raid: The March from Golden Bay to Southland in 1836 and Defeat at Tuturau* (1986). Most other accounts are sensationalised.

After six months on the trail, having walked more than a thousand kilometres, the raiders surrendered without a fight. Nineteenth-century accounts fabricated a heroic last stand, the raiders fighting till dawn and selling their lives dear—but in truth only Te Pūoho and a slave named Toea died, and the others were taken prisoner.

8. AORAKI

Whakaatu rā e tāku toki... Raureka passed on 'Song of the Axe' to Ngāi Tahu, and it was written down by Māui Pōmare and James Cowan and in *Legends of the Maori* (1930; reprinted 1987), p. 299.

'If you haven't seen your tupuna maunga [ancestor mountain], then who are you? How can you stand up and do your pepeha?' Te Rūnanga o Ngāi Tahu's *Ko Au Ko Aoraki, Ko Aoraki Ko Au: Aoraki Bound Documentary* (2017).

The partnership with Outward Bound was born. It was only natural that Aoraki became the focus for a new push to get Ngāi Tahu people back out into the hills. For the full story of how Aoraki Bound began, see Anna Brankin's 'Hokia ki tō Mauka', *Te Karaka*, 70, 2016, pp. 27–30.

A year after Ngāi Tahu sold twenty million acres under Kemp's Deed in 1848, Tiramōrehu picked up a pen and laid out his case to Lieutenant-Governor Edward Eyre... Matiaha Tiramōrehu's words are in the

'Letter to Colonial Secretary from Matiaha Tiramōrehu', Appendix to the Journals of the House of Representatives, Session I, C-03, 9–10 (1858). For a full account of the Ngāi Tahu claim, including Matiaha Tiramōrehu, see Harry Evison's *The Long Dispute: Māori Land Rights and European Colonisation in Southern New Zealand* (1997), and the Waitangi Tribunal's *The Ngai Tahu Report* (Wai 27, 1991).

In his second report, Mackay noted the irony that by welcoming and facilitating European settlement, Ngāi Tahu were now kept 'in a chronic state of poverty'. Alexander Mackay's *Middle Island Native Claims (Further Reports by Mr Commissioner Mackay Relating to)* (1891), p. 5.

My English great-great-grandparents Benjamin and Sabine Low were allocated rich alluvial farmland at Willowbridge, just down the road from where we now sat at Arowhenua. Their farm was at the mouth of the Waihao River, directly across from where Rākaihautū was reunited with his son Rakihouia, and near the present-day site of Waihao marae.

But the [farmland allocation and loan] scheme was closed to Māori. Evison's *The Long Dispute* (1997), p. 373. The same year this scheme began, 1893, the government also introduced the Native Land Purchase and Acquisition Act, which gave it the power to commandeer uncultivated Māori land. European owners of large estates who had land compulsorily 'resumed' were paid twelve pounds, seven shillings per hectare. Compulsorily acquired Māori land was compensated at twelve *shillings* per hectare: one-twentieth of that amount, and well below market value.

The Waitangi Tribunal later called [the SILNA scheme] 'a cruel hoax'. Wai 27, p. 178. Not only was the land useless and inaccessible, four blocks were never even allocated to beneficiaries, and remain in Crown hands today.

'He mahi kai takata, he mahi kai hōaka'… This saying is sometimes attributed to Hastings Tipa, and sometimes to Matiaha Tiramōrehu.

'The Tribunal cannot avoid the conclusion that in acquiring from Ngāi Tahu 34.5 million acres, more than half the land mass of New Zealand, for £14,850, and leaving them with only 35,757 acres, the Crown acted unconscionably and in repeated breach of the Treaty of Waitangi.' Wai 27, p. 1066.

Ngāi Tahu is now the largest landowner in the South Island, after the Crown. Kate Newton's 'New Zealand's Biggest Fifty Landowners Revealed', *Stuff*.

co.nz, 17 October 2019.

The Crown agreed to return the mountain to Ngāi Tahu. In turn, Ngāi Tahu would gift the mountain to the nation. This has yet to take place, more than twenty-five years on. According to Lisa Tumahai, Chair of Te Rūnanga o Ngāi Tahu, 'the position at Te Rūnanga is that until the Crown has adequately dealt with the breaches of our settlement, formally Aoraki will not be returned. A lot of the breaches have got to do with the environment, including non-engagement with Te Rūnanga in key decisions like resource consenting, or being locked out or ignored over decisions the Crown has made. It'll be an ongoing journey.' (Personal communication, 12 September 2019.)

'Loving is above all a matter of knowing,' says Tā Tipene O'Regan. *Ko Au Ko Aoraki, Ko Aoraki Ko Au: Aoraki Bound Documentary* (2017).

Nā te ao / Ko te ao tūroa / Tāna ko te ao mārama... There are many variations of this tauparapara (karakia or prayer to start a speech), as is normal in the evolution of oral traditions. The version given here is enshrined in the *Ngāi Tahu Deed of Settlement Introduction* (1997), p. 3.

...'masses of ice were almost continuously falling, and the smaller pieces were rushing down the steep mountain sides with a whiz like a bullet...' Christchurch *Star*, 13 March 1882, p. 3.

'It was a glorious day and a more glorious view. It pleased Bannister so much that he could not attempt a description...' Samuel Turner, quoted in McKerrow's 'Māori Mountaineers' (1993).

9. TE RUA-O-TE-MOKO KI MURIHIKU
(FIORDLAND TO SOUTHLAND)

Short accounts of this journey were published in *Wilderness* magazine, October 2016, and *Te Karaka*, 70, June 2016.

Auntie Jane Davis, or Auntie Janie to us, is perhaps the most senior Ngāi Tahu woman alive today. Auntie Janie has since died, and is greatly missed. Moe mai rā e tō tātou rakatira, moe mai rā.

In the 1820s, a party under chief Hupokeka had been gathering takiwai here when European sealers rowed into the bay. Beattie's *Maori Lore of*

Lake, Alp and Fiord (1945), p. 109. The events are also alluded to in his *The Maoris and Fiordland* (reprinted 2002), p. 43.

Yet another place name in that bay is Te Tara-o-te-puhi-tuia, commemorating a high-born woman whom sealers attempted to rape. Place-name details come from Beattie's *The Maoris and Fiordland*, p. 48.

Some of the oldest adornments found in New Zealand were made from this stone, including rei niho pendants in an East Polynesian style, shaped like sperm whale teeth. See Russell Beck, Maika Mason and Andris Apse's *Pounamu Treasures: Ngā taonga pounamu* (2012), pp. 40–42.

One of our creation stories relates how the wives of Tama-āhua left him in Hawaiki ... and fled to Aotearoa aboard the Tairea canoe. For the different versions of this story, see chapter 5 in Eruera Tarena's *He Atua, He Tipua, He Takata Rānei* (2008). See also Beattie's *Maori Lore of Alp, Lake and Fiord*, p. 99.

Sailing down Te Tai-o-Poutini, Aoraki's nephew Tū-te-raki-whānoa and his people saw the mountains, and figured out what had happened. They grieved for Aoraki and his brothers. The version given here is drawn from Beattie's *The Maoris and Fiordland*, chapter II.

[Tū] strained so hard that the place where he stood split in two, forming Kā Tū-waewae-o-Tū (Resolution Island) and Mauīkatau (Secretary Island). In the later nineteenth century, some younger Ngāi Tahu disputed the truth of this story while sitting around a fire outside. As they did, a comet, the heavenly manifestation of Tū-te-raki-whānoa, blazed across the night sky.

I pointed to the mountain above. That was Te Nohoaka-a-Tū. Tū was sitting there resting when Papatūānuku came to ask if he could create somewhere a bit less steep. Beattie's *The Māoris and Fiordland*, pp. 9–10. I'm slightly sceptical about the authenticity of the namunamu and Nohoaka-a-Tū parts of the story. They're a little too convenient as a tourist narrative, and map neatly to the English names (Sandfly Point, Devil's Armchair).

'Anglers from other parts of the Dominion or from abroad never refer to their Waiau experiences without mentioning Hunter's name ...' *Southland Times*, 30 July 1910.

When they stopped overnight at Invercargill Hospital, John was calm. *Southland Times*, 5 August 1910.

Glossary

OF MĀORI WORDS, REGIONAL USAGES
AND MOUNTAINEERING TERMS

Books by Māori writers don't generally have a glossary of Māori words: dictionaries are readily available (such as John C. Moorfield's maoridictionary. co.nz), Māori is an official language and many of these terms are commonly used in New Zealand English. I've included a guide to the Māori words here for international readers. Most have multiple nuances; I've only included the explanation for the sense in which they're used in the text. For help with definitions I drew on Moorfield's *Māori Dictionary*.

Ahikāroa refers to the long-burning fires of occupation, and the authority that comes from living upon the land for generations. Māori hold ahikāroa in—

Aotearoa, or New Zealand, which is sometimes translated as 'the land of the long white cloud', a nation rich in—

Atua, the supernatural beings, ancestors, gods and spirits who influence various domains of our lives, including the—

Belay, a climbing technique whereby you control the rope to your partner so they can ascend freely, yet you can quickly arrest a fall. If caught out on a route overnight, you'll need to karakia to your atua and—

Bivvy, short for bivouac, meaning to sleep in a basic, often impromptu shelter, which, if it happens to be on the side of a cliff, may require—

Cams, spring-loaded devices placed into cracks, to which the rope is clipped so you're attached to the mountain if you fall. They work brilliantly, unless you're climbing on—

Choss, the fractured, rotten rock that's all too common in Kā Tiritiri-o-te-moana, in which case you're screwed.

Hapū is traditionally the main unit of Māori political organisation, being a large group of families descended from a common ancestor, while—

Iwi, or tribe, is a confederation of related hapū living on adjacent land. Whenever these groups meet on the marae, before people make speeches or sit down to have—

Kai, food, you'll hear the—

Karaka, the complex calls of welcome between senior women to negotiate the visiting party's entry. You'll also hear—

Karakia, ritual incantations or chants, used to align your actions with the ancestors and the atua, spoken rapidly, with great importance placed on getting the words right. Some of our karakia come from—

Kāti Māmoe, a historic southern iwi who were subsumed into Ngāi Tahu through warfare and intermarriage, though plenty of us still identify as Kāti Māmoe, and Māmoe place names are all over—

Kā Tiritiri-o-te-moana, the Southern Alps; in fact, some of our—

Kaumātua, respected elders, have as much Kāti Māmoe as Ngāi Tahu whakapapa today, and would be offended if you said Kāti Māmoe were wiped out (as people once did). Instead, you should offer a—

Koha, a gift or offering to maintain relationships and reciprocity, often traditionally in the form of kai like tītī (muttonbirds) or tuna (eels), taken from—

Mahika kai, literally 'making food', the locations where the husbandry and harvesting of natural resources takes place. It also refers to the social, economic and cultural activity of mahika kai. The abundance of our land is part of Ngāi Tahu's—

Mana, which means standing, prestige and spiritual power, and is a property of individuals and groups. Protecting and enhancing this land for future generations is a central part of—

Mana whenua, or authority, power and responsibility over territory; the term can also refer to the people who hold those rights. If you need to speak with the mana whenua of a place, go to their—

Marae, the ceremonial courtyard and complex of buildings, including the wharenui (meeting house), where tribal business takes place. Each marae has a mauri stone, usually of pounamu; the—

Mauri is the life force or vital essence of a thing, being or entity; everything has a mauri, even—

Névé, which is hard frozen snow and a climber's dream. Climbing steep névé can sometimes feel like scaling the walls of a—

Pā, a fortified village.

Pākehā means a European New Zealander, and does not have negative connotations in Māori.

Papatūānuku is the Earth Mother, whose first husband was Takaroa, atua of the sea, and who later married Rakinui, the Sky Father.

Pitch means a steep section of a climb requiring a rope to safely ascend.

Pounamu is an indigenous nephrite jade, sometimes called greenstone, prized in the Māori and New Zealand economies then and now.

Slot is mountaineering slang for a crevasse, while a—

'Schrund, short for bergschrund, is the often serious crevasse that forms between moving glacial ice and the permanent rock or ice above. You have to be a real—

Rakatira, chief or leader, to jump a major 'schrund.

Rakinui is the Sky Father, whose eldest son, Aoraki, was born of his first wife,

Poko-hārua-te-pō.

Rūnaka is a tribal council, and also encompasses the people and the place that council represents. Ngāi Tahu has eighteen papatipu (customary) rūnaka, each with an elected representative on the central tribal rūnaka. Serving in Māori politics has been likened to a—

Scramble, meaning to climb on moderately steep ground without a rope, which is what the—

Takata whenua, or indigenous people born of this land, used to do all the time. Those steep mountains are among the—

Taoka, or treasures, of Ngāi Tahu, and many are—

Tapu, meaning sacred, restricted, in the realm of the atua, along with the rivers and lakes of—

Te Waipounamu, the South Island of New Zealand, literally the Greenstone Waters. Our—

Tīpuna, or ancestors, looked to the mountains for omens and signs, which were interpreted by—

Tohuka, or learned people, priests or healers, who could invoke or withdraw tapu and affect wairua and mauri through karakia.

Tramper means hiker, but specifically suggests the loaded gait and dishevelled appearance of someone moving across Aotearoa's rough terrain.

Upoko is short for Upoko Rūnaka, meaning the senior leader of a tribal assembly.

Wairua is the immortal non-physical spirit or soul of a person, and sometimes of a thing like a wharenui (meeting house), though I know people who've spent a whole day debating the precise meaning of the term without reaching consensus.

Waitaha were the first people to land in Te Waipounamu, under their captain, Rākaihautū, and the oldest iwi in Ngāi Tahu's ancestral grouping. Waitaha is also used as a general term for any early southern tribe. Rākaihautū's—

Waka, or canoe, was called Uruao. In—

Whakapapa, a system of thought built upon lines of genealogical descent linking us to ancestors, the natural world and the atua, any given—

Whānau, or family, can trace their relationships to each other, and to the—

Whenua, or land, beneath their boots.

Acknowledgments

Ki te huka mate, moe mai rā e kā rakatira, moe mai rā, okioki mai rā. Ko Auntie Jane Davis, Maurice Manawaroa Gray, Uncle Rik Pitama, Koro Graeme Pepper, Russell Beck, Chris Willey, Nicola Andrews, haere, haere, haere ki te pō.

Āku mihi whakawhetai ki a koutou, rau kaiāwhina mā: kā kaumātua, kā tohuka, tōku whānau, tōku hoa rakatira, e Leigh, tā māua kākau, e Ahi.

Kā mihi mutuka kore to the rakatira who spoke with me about our traditions, histories and values over the years: Tā Tipene O'Regan, David Higgins, James Russell, Jane Davis, Paul Madgwick, Susan Wallace, Joseph Hullen, Trevor Howse, Muriel Johnstone, Maurice Manawatu, Maurice Manawaroa Gray, Lisa Tumahai, Tewera King, Karuna Thurlow, Kyle Davis, Amanda Symons, Brian Allingham and many more.

Kā mihi to everyone who gave feedback on early versions of either the full manuscript or individual chapters, including Tā Tipene O'Regan, Paul Madgwick, Muriel Johnstone, James Russell, Ross Calman, Alison Carew, Leigh Hopkinson and Daniel

Tynan. Your engagement enriched the stories and helped correct my mistakes. Any issues that remain are, of course, my own.

Kā mihi to the Ngāi Tahu Wānaka Pūrākau rōpū for the love of our traditions, and the laughs, and to the mana whenua at Wairewa, Rāpaki, Moeraki and Puketeraki for hosting us. As Maurice Manawatu says: 'Pūrākau was more crucial to our evolution than opposable thumbs. Opposable thumbs let us hang on; pūrākau tells us what to hang on to.'

Kā mihi to Takerei Norton and Helen Brown at Ngāi Tahu Archives for the incredible maps I used to navigate on my walks, and for access to databases and manuscripts. Donelle Manihera, kā mihi for the opportunity to participate in Aoraki Bound and the Ball Pass hīkoi, and for your contagious enthusiasm and support. Thanks to the Kura Marotini rōpū, and Tiaki Coates, Tui Kraal, David van der Gulik and Rangimārie Mules. Mihi atu to Te Rūnanga o Arowhenua and Te Rūnanga o Ngāti Waewae for manaaki during Aoraki Bound.

Bonny Lawrence, thank you for the loan of your father's books. Kā mihi to Eruera Tarena for your invaluable master's thesis, and illuminating conversations when I was starting out. Thanks too, Mark Revington, for encouraging me to write for the iwi.

Kā mihi to my whānau for making this book a reality. In particular, Geoff, thank you for the kilometres shared, the invaluable support and logistics, and your love for the mountains. Hikatea, for your counsel, your confidence and your love for the iwi. Tim, for being such a great climber and friend. Ben, for your curiosity and encouragement; I can't wait to take Anna and Dom into the hills! Hilary Low, kā mihi for your wonderful books, and conversations about mountain history. Quentin Duthie, thank you for snowy explorations of Lewis Pass. Thank you to Gary and Ray Hopkinson for your hospitality.

Kā mihi nui to Alison Carew for your incisive editorial work, and encouragement when I needed it most.

Kā mihi to the Ōraka-Aparima Rūnaka for throwing your support behind the hīkoi from Ōhupokeka to Takutai o te Tītī, and the warm welcome at the end. Stewart Bull, Muriel Johnstone, Sandra Cook, Rangimaria Suddaby, Vera Gleeson, Betty Rickus, Lynley McKay and Riki Dallas, huge thanks. Kā mihi to Karina Davis for making the paddling journeys a dream come true. Kā mihi to Rewi and Tāne Davis, and the Ōraka-Aparima and Ngāti Kahungunu paddling crews. Dave Wilson, kā mihi for enlisting the help of the Department of Conservation, and for sharing the trail through Murihiku. To the Southland Department of Conservation, thank you for permission to stay in staff quarters along the Milford Track.

Jon Terry, thank you for the lichen sandwiches and the seventy-metre, eleven-millimetre rope. Bridget Reweti, kā mihi mahana for joyous Rua-o-te-moko explorations; I thought I would have climbed more mountains by now, too. Kā mihi to Kennedy Warne for Flock Hill adventures and being so welcoming to a fellow writing/walking obsessive.

Kā mihi to Alpine Recreation, to Anne and Elke Braun-Elwert for your generosity in providing the trip to Ball Pass, and for guiding on Aoraki, and in particular to Lewis Ainsworth for good company, great climbing, and keeping me safe. Thanks to Daniel Tynan and Eugene Peripletchikov for climbing adventures and sanity during storms. Thanks to Cam Mulvey for beta and grisly stories, Aat Vervoorn for musings on alpine history, and Russell

Beck for insights into stone resources.

Kā mihi to Rosco and the Rosco's Milford Kayaks crew, especially Abi and Adam, for taking us paddling and sneaking us onto a buffet cruise. Thanks to Real Journeys for the Te Ana-au ride.

Thank you to LandSAR and the Aoraki / Mt Cook Alpine Search and Rescue team for your speed, professionalism and good humour.

A huge thank you to my editor, David Winter, for your tremendous patience, skill and dedication. Thank you to Chong W. H., Jessica Horrocks, Madeleine Rebbechi, and everyone at Text Publishing for bringing the book to life in style. Thanks to Ross Calman for kicking my reo into shape, Simon Barnard for going above and beyond with the maps, Izzy Joy Te Aho-White for your stunning centre map, and Morgan Matthews-Hale for the beautiful cover type.

I'm grateful to Copyright Licensing New Zealand for the 2018 Writers' Award, which gave me the time and resources needed to bring the book to fruition, and to the Federated Mountain Clubs' Forest and Mountain Trust for its production support. Thank you to the Banff Centre for Arts and Creativity, and Anthony Whittome and Marni Jackson, for hosting me at the Mountain and Wilderness Writing Programme. Thanks to Chris Willey and Cathy Ostlere for ice climbing and cups of tea.

And last of all, kā mihi aroha to Leigh Hopkinson, for saying yes to coming on that walk.